More Praise for
The People's Justice

"Few if any Supreme Court justices have been more maliciously smeared than Clarence Thomas. This big, bold-hearted man has borne the attacks with a quiet dignity while steadily protecting the rights of the American people. Now, Judge Amul Thapar sets the record straight with this can't-put-down series of stories that reveal the courage, decency, and humanity of the man behind what many are calling the Thomas Court."

   —**Megyn Kelly,** journalist

"In *The People's Justice*, Judge Thapar has written a unique and fascinating book that reveals the character and judicial conduct of Justice Clarence Thomas as found in his approach to a number of U.S. Supreme Court cases that involve the lives and rights of real people for whom the law has been a last resort. Often surprising, these stories show the reality and human side of judicial decision-making in a most interesting and entertaining manner."

   —**Edwin Meese III,** 75th U.S. Attorney General

"At a time of unrelenting assaults on both the Founding and the Constitution by academics, activists, and politicians, Amul Thapar gives us hope in the pages of *The People's Justice*. In this compelling account of the judicial philosophy and pivotal opinions of Justice Clarence Thomas, readers will find a new appreciation of both the man himself and our Framers. Thomas's life's work embodies the keen understanding that the preservation of liberty requires vigilance."

   —**Laura Ingraham,** host of *The Ingraham Angle* on Fox News and
      former law clerk to Justice Thomas

"Amul Thapar's *The People's Justice* is two superb books in one—a breezy and accessible intellectual biography of Justice Clarence Thomas and a survey of some of the most important Supreme Court cases of the modern era. By the time Thapar's done carefully laying out the facts, it's impossible not to see the connection between the constitutional originalism expressed in his rigorous opinions and Thomas's deeply felt desire to rectify the injustice ordinary Americans suffer at the hands of an unfeeling government."

   —**Mollie Hemingway,** editor-in-chief of The Federalist, senior
      journalism fellow at Hillsdale College, Fox News contributor, and
      co-author of *Justice on Trial: The Kavanaugh Confirmation and
      the Future of the Supreme Court*

"Amul Thapar's *The People's Justice* is really two books. The first one is a pleasantly accessible introduction to the legal philosophy that guides Justice Thomas's approach to judging. The second one gives the reader every reason to believe that Justice Thomas will be remembered as a man of principle, courage, and compassion long after many of his detractors have been forgotten."

—**Jason L. Riley,** *Wall Street Journal* columnist and author of *Maverick: A Biography of Thomas Sowell*

"Justice Clarence Thomas is deeply committed to the rule of law and the original meaning of the Constitution. At the same time, he is intensely sympathetic to the human struggles that play out in the cases that come before the Court. Judge Amul Thapar makes all this abundantly clear in this fascinating and immensely readable book."

—**Lillian BeVier,** David and Mary Harrison Distinguished Professor of Law Emeritus

"Justice Clarence Thomas grew up in poverty and segregation in the tidelands of Georgia. Judge Amul Thapar is the son of working-class immigrants from India. It's quite a testament to the transcendent appeal of the interpretive method of originalism that they are two of its leading proponents. In this engaging account of the stories that lie behind a dozen of Justice Thomas's opinions, Judge Thapar illustrates why."

—**Edward Whelan,** Antonin Scalia Chair in Constitutional Studies at the Ethics and Public Policy Center

"Carefully researched and innovative in format, *The People's Justice* marks an important entry in the growing literature chronicling the life and career of Supreme Court Justice Clarence Thomas. For more than three decades, liberal scholars and analysts have willfully distorted the opinions of one of the Court's most ideologically consistent and intellectually rigorous jurists. Standing athwart all that is Sixth Circuit Judge Amul Thapar, a rising star on the appellate bench whose selection of twelve cases through which to examine the justice's jurisprudence offers lawyers and lay readers alike a fresh opportunity to understand the originalist approach to the law that Thomas, the Court's longest-tenured justice, has stood for all these years, and continues to champion today."

—**James Rosen,** chief White House correspondent for Newsmax and author of *Scalia: Rise to Greatness, 1936–1986*

"If you thought you knew Justice Thomas's impact on constitutional law, think again. Through exclusive interviews and original research, Judge Amul Thapar reveals the human drama behind some of Justice Thomas's most significant cases and showcases the ascent of originalism."

> —**Carrie Severino,** president of the Judicial Crisis Network, co-author of *Justice on Trial: The Kavanaugh Confirmation and the Future of the Supreme Court,* and former law clerk to Justice Thomas

"More than any other justice in the history of our Republic, Justice Thomas has—through his opinions—helped to unearth, recover, and restore the United States Constitution as it was originally understood. And for this project of excavation and restoration, he has rightfully earned a place among the greatest jurists to ever serve on the Supreme Court of the United States. But far too few know that Justice Thomas's goodness as a man matches his greatness as a justice. By telling his story through the lens of his opinions, *The People's Justice* illuminates both the mind—and even more important, the heart—of Justice Clarence Thomas."

> —**Nicole Garnett,** associate dean and professor of law, Notre Dame Law School

"*The People's Justice* is a beautifully written, meticulously researched exploration of Justice Thomas's jurisprudence. Through compelling storytelling and lucid legal analysis, the book makes a novel and persuasive case for how originalism often protects ordinary people over powerful special interests."

> —**David Lat,** journalist and author of *Supreme Ambitions*

"This ground-breaking book is a must-read for Americans seeking an honest account of our nation's most misunderstood Supreme Court justice. In a cacophony of polarizing voices shouting about Justice Thomas's legacy, Amul Thapar cuts through the noise. This riveting narrative of Justice Thomas's jurisprudence will capture readers of every racial, socioeconomic, and political background. There's only one qualification necessary to appreciate *The People's Justice*: a desire to know the truth."

> —**Jeremy Hunt,** Hudson Institute Media Fellow and U.S. Army veteran

"This book is a must-read for anyone that cares about our court system, and frankly, our country. From the very beginning, the book brings to life twelve cases that came before the Supreme Court. Unlike most accounts, this book allows the reader to live alongside the litigants and decide for themselves who is right. For many, who have only read the willful distortions of Justice Clarence Thomas's record, it will surprise. In these pages, the reader will find Justice Thomas championing Cleveland parents who are just trying to obtain a high-quality education for their children; an actress fighting to get her day in court to prove that her accused rapist, Bill Cosby, is not only a rapist but a liar; a working-class mother trying to stop a city from giving her home to a corporation; a Chicagoan battling to protect his home and family from rising crime; and many other riveting stories about inspiring Americans. The cases will highlight not only Justice Thomas's principled originalist jurisprudence but his deep humanity. Justice Thomas applies the original meaning of the Constitution to the case at hand fairly and consistently—and Amul Thapar lets you judge the outcomes for yourself. The result is a gripping, inspiring read."

—**Mark Paoletta,** co-editor of *Created Equal: Clarence Thomas in His Own Words*

"Finally, a book about a single Supreme Court justice written for every American who wants to understand the work of the whole Court and the lives of every man and woman who sit behind that raised bench and from there rule on the cases and controversies that come to define all of our lives.

"*The People's Justice* by federal Sixth Circuit Court Judge Amul Thapar is that book, and it's for everyone who has wondered from far away about our country's highest court and the Constitution's enduring direction for how a free people ought to govern themselves if they would preserve that plan and thus that freedom.

"If you want to know and really understand what the Court does and how it does it, here is the book for you. The most controversial and interesting justice since he was confirmed to his position in 1991, United States Supreme Court Justice Clarence Thomas is the central character in a remarkable telling of his three decades of service on the Court. Through the cases and controversies on which Thomas has ruled and written and, crucially, via the stories of the actual people whose lives those rulings helped define, *The People's Justice* does more to pull back the curtains on the Court and, crucially, on how the Constitution actually works—through the published opinions of its members—than any book in decades. *The People's Justice* is not a conventional biography and not a recap of the past three decades in American Constitutional law, but rather both and much, much more. This is an American story, about how we govern ourselves and trust nine justices and the scores of lower courts they supervise, to make sure that we continue to do so. It is also a deeply personal portrait of Clarence Thomas by a gifted judge and writer.

"Judge Amul Thapar's own story is quite compelling, and the record of his own rulings, opinions, and career remarkable. What Thapar has done for the average American interested in the Court is nothing short of unprecedented. In this book, Judge Thapar has made the rulings of Justice Thomas accessible, his judicial philosophy understandable and even transparent, and the work of our Court inspiring.

"Forget—or push aside for a day or two—everything you know or think you know about Justice Clarence Thomas. Even if you have read and been moved by the justice's inspiring 2008 autobiography *My Grandfather's Son* or have been one of the thousands of Americans who have found themselves parked next to the justice and Mrs. Thomas's RV somewhere in our country during the summer and found themselves deep in conversation and even sharing a meal with Justice and Mrs. Thomas on their annual summer trips crisscrossing our land in their home on wheels, set that view or memory aside and prepare to be surprised. Very surprised. Amul Thapar has done what even gifted law professors and professional 'Court watchers' often fail to do: Thapar has focused on the men and women whose lives are before the nine and on how one justice, Clarence Thomas, has carefully, consistently, and compassionately applied his understanding of the Constitution to those lives.

"Judge Thapar explains 'originalism' in *The People's Justice* by expertly and compellingly retelling the stories of the people who have brought their legal battles—their literal and figurative "trials"—all the way to the Supreme Court. 'Originalists believe that the American people, not nine unelected judges, are the source of the law that governs us—through the Constitution and statutes enacted by our elected representatives,' Judge Thapar writes. 'The judge's role is to determine what the words of those documents meant when they were enacted and to apply them to the cases in front of him or her.'

"That's 'originalism.' 'Nothing more, nothing less,' Judge Thapar concludes, and then he illustrates how that philosophy of judging and that understanding of the Supreme Court's role in our Constitutional order drives Justice Thomas's rulings, year after year and decade after decade, down through the longest tenure of any justice now serving, but always in an accessible, compelling, and fascinating retelling of the cases and controversies before the Court and Justice Thomas's rulings on them.

"Justice Thomas has sometimes written for the whole Court and sometimes he has been a lonely dissenting voice. The most surprising chapter in this book of amazing stories is perhaps chapter 5, 'Standing Alone,' where Justice Thomas strongly dissented from his colleagues' refusal to hear the case of a one-time West Point cadet raped by one her fellow soldiers yet denied the ability to have a jury weigh the facts of her case. I had never read anything that I could recall of *Doe v. United States*, and I had certainly never read Justice Thomas's dissent from his colleagues' decision. Judge Thapar's book led me to find and read the brief but powerful dissent in its whole. No other book of the dozens and dozens of books I have read on the Court and its work, on the justices and their lives, has ever prompted me to do that: put the book down and go find the whole opinion to which it refers. It is a salute to Judge Thapar's writing that this prompting happens again and again.

"Our understanding of the Supreme Court should not be limited to headlines and columns, with the opinions of its justices only read by 'experts.' The Constitution was written by brilliant men but intended to be read and understood by farmers, merchants, and tradesmen. It is not a black box surrounded by nine justices in black robes who then rule for mysterious reasons this way or that way. It is our governing document, the justices themselves explain in their opinions. Justice Thomas especially, and for the longest unbroken period of any justice now serving, has never lost sight of the Constitution's promises to the American people or the peril presented to its design by activist judges with agendas.

"Most important of all, and as Judge Thapar has made so abundantly clear in this book, 'Justice Thomas's compassion and his deep understanding of the challenges Americans have faced throughout our nation's history' have defined Thomas's record as a justice. What a deeply caring and compassionate man Thomas is—what a 'People's Justice.' When you have finished this book, your understanding of Justice Thomas's long and continuing battle to restore the Constitution's and its Amendments' original meaning to the Court's deliberations will be focused and clear. Most memorable of all, you will have put yourself in the shoes of all justices, but particularly those of Justice Thomas, and seen the people who have come before that Bench not as case names but as Americans seeking justice.

"Read this book for yourself but also give it to anyone you know who doesn't know the story of Justice Thomas or of the Constitution."

—**Hugh Hewitt,** host of *The Hugh Hewitt Show* and professor at Chapman University School of Law

"This beautifully written book is a page-turner, bringing to life Clarence Thomas the man, as well as the pivotal cases that define his jurisprudence. There are stories in the book that will surprise readers, as they did me. Thapar's skillfully woven portrait reveals Justice Thomas as a true hero dedicated to preserving our great Republic and the rule of law. For anyone concerned about the country's future, this is a must-read."

—**William P. Barr,** 77th and 85th U.S. Attorney General

The People's Justice

The People's Justice

Clarence Thomas and
the Constitutional Stories
That Define Him

Amul Thapar

REGNERY GATEWAY
Washington, D.C.

Regnery Gateway™ is a trademark of Salem Communications Holding Corporation
Regnery® is a registered trademark and its colophon is a trademark of Salem Communications Holding Corporation

Cataloging-in-Publication data on file with the Library of Congress

ISBN: 978-1-68451-452-6
eISBN: 978-1-68451-466-3
Library of Congress Control Number: 2023932932

Published in the United States by
Regnery Gateway, an Imprint of
Regnery Publishing
A Division of Salem Media Group
Washington, D.C.
www.Regnery.com

Manufactured in the United States of America

10 9 8 7 6 5 4 3 2 1

Books are available in quantity for promotional or premium use. For information on discounts and terms, please visit our website: www.Regnery.com.

To my beautiful wife and three amazing children

Contents

Author's Note

Writing this book has given me the opportunity to immerse myself in twelve cases featuring opinions by Justice Clarence Thomas. I've mostly relied on the legal records, including trial testimony, documents filed by the parties, oral arguments, and opinions of various courts. In addition, newspaper, magazine, and online articles about the cases and the surrounding circumstances were very helpful.

In several chapters, I've also relied on books written about or by central figures in these stories. These accounts allowed me to go beyond the facts found in court documents and share more about the individuals involved. I owe special debts of gratitude to Jeff Benedict, whose *The Little Pink House: A True Story of Defiance and Courage* is a deep dive into Susette Kelo's fight to keep her home; to Don Yaeger and to Warrick Dunn, the oldest son of police officer Betty Smothers, the murder victim in the *Brumfield* case, who tells his own moving life story in *Running for My Life: My Journey in the Game of Football and Beyond*; to David Brennan and Malcolm Baroway, who in *Victory for Kids: The Cleveland School Voucher Case* recount Cleveland's citizens' battle to educate the city's children; and to Frederick Jones and Sue Bowron, who wrote *An Act of Bravery: Otis W. McDonald and the Second Amendment* about the grandson of slaves who became a champion of Second Amendment rights.

Another great source of information for me has been Duke Law School's *Voices of American Law Project*, run by Professor Thomas Metzloff. The case documentaries on this website are a rich source of information.

Finally, I'm grateful to the real heroes of this book: the parties, lawyers, and witnesses, many of whom graciously agreed to interviews. Several of them even shared photographs from critical moments in their lives and legal cases.

I hope the material drawn from all these sources will bring the stories to life and help you better appreciate not only Justice Thomas, but also originalism.

Introduction

J ustice Clarence Thomas walked out of church after daily Mass on a crisp, clear morning in the fall of 1998. He descended the granite steps of St. Joseph's Church on Capitol Hill in Washington, D.C., and began his walk back to the Supreme Court when a homeless man came running toward him. "Justice, Justice, I got another petition coming to you," the man yelled.

Nicole Garnett, one of Justice Thomas's law clerks, who had joined Justice Thomas at St. Joe's, tensed. But the justice did not. Instead, he walked toward the man and soon became immersed in conversation. Nicole couldn't hear what the man was saying, but he was certainly animated. The justice listened patiently, like he always did.

After a few minutes, Justice Thomas and the man concluded their conversation, and the justice rejoined the group of Supreme Court clerks on the church steps. "You know," he said, "these are hard days for him. Last week was the anniversary of his mother's death."

Justice Thomas, it turned out, had known the homeless man for some time. When the two first met, the man had been addicted to drugs, and sadly, that addiction had driven a wedge between him and his mother. But over time, the justice had convinced the man to get clean, and in the process, he had reconciled with his mother before she passed.[1]

To Nicole, this story was more proof of what she and many others close to the justice already knew: Justice Thomas cares about people. His clerks aren't the only ones who notice this about him. One of his colleagues on the Supreme Court, Justice Sonia Sotomayor, recently described Justice Thomas this way: "Justice Thomas is the one justice in the building that literally knows every employee's name, every one of them. . . . [H]e is a man who cares deeply about the court as an institution, about the people who work there—about people."[2]

● ● ●

Today, few dispute that Justice Thomas is one of the greatest originalist jurists ever. But sadly, stories like this, which show Justice Thomas's true character, are rarely told. Nor are the stories of the people whose cases have come before him. That is the purpose of this book: to tell you what few others will; to give a face and a voice to those whose lives have been changed forever by the many cases that have come before the Supreme Court; to show how Justice Thomas champions our Constitution and the people it protects.

In the coming pages, you'll learn of the quiet dignity of people like Susette Kelo, who fought to keep her beloved house when the government and a big corporation partnered to take it from her. You'll meet the Cleveland parents who wanted their children to have access to effective education in safe schools. You'll learn about Angel Raich's valiant fight to keep big government out of her medical treatment. You'll see how the people of Chicago battled to take their neighborhoods back from violent gangs. You'll read about football star Warrick Dunn, who struggled to keep his family together after the brutal murder of his mother. And you'll learn about cross-burning

Klansman Barry Black—and David Baugh, the black lawyer who defended him. In these cases, you will also see how Justice Thomas, applying originalist principles of jurisprudence to the cases before the Court, responds to the struggles of everyday Americans.

By cherry-picking his opinions or misrepresenting them, Justice Thomas's critics claim that his originalism favors the rich over the poor, the strong over the weak, and corporations over consumers. They have called Justice Thomas "the cruelest Justice," "stupid," and even "an Uncle Tom," a traitor to his race.[3] But as you'll see in these pages, Justice Thomas's originalism more often favors the ordinary people who come before the Court—because the core idea behind originalism is honoring the will of the people.

Originalists believe that the American people, not nine unelected judges, are the source of the law that governs us—through the Constitution and statutes enacted by our elected representatives. The judge's role is to determine what the words of those documents meant when they were enacted and to apply them to the cases in front of him or her. Nothing more, nothing less.

As an originalist, Justice Thomas is committed to applying the law equally to all, come what may. Sometimes that will mean that the less sympathetic party triumphs. But more often, the opposite is true.

Reading these gripping stories, you will see for yourself what his originalist jurisprudence has to say about race, about corporations, and about the poor and downtrodden. You will see firsthand what originalism means in practice and what it has to offer the least privileged Americans. And I guarantee you, whatever you think you know about Justice Thomas and about originalism, something in the coming pages will surprise you.

You may be surprised by how often originalism counsels a result for the little guy. After all, as Justice Thomas knows and frequently reminds the Court, the Founders set up American law to protect the citizens from government—and to ensure that law-abiding citizens could protect themselves from predatory ones.

You may be surprised by how often Justice Thomas gives a voice to those forgotten. For years, he famously sat silent on the bench because he wanted to respect the advocates' limited time to present their arguments. But Justice Thomas speaks forcefully in his opinions—not only about the original meaning of the law, but also about those who suffer from its misapplication. His opinions speak for the victims of violent crimes, who are often denied justice by legal innovations. He speaks for those who suffer from federal overreach and for those who are on the losing end of seedy government partnerships with wealthy corporations. Throughout his decades on the Court, Justice Thomas has repeatedly pointed out that when we actually follow the original meaning of the Constitution, the weak and the politically powerless stand to benefit the most.

Sometimes being that voice is not easy. "Finding the right answer," Justice Thomas has observed, "is often the least difficult problem." Rather, it's "[h]aving the courage to assert that answer and stand firm in the face of the constant winds of protest and criticism [that's] often much more difficult."[4] No one knows this better than Justice Thomas, who has been singled out for attacks from the academy, the legal world, and the media. Nevertheless, he finds the right answer and then sticks to it. Justice Thomas's immense courage gives him the freedom to do what is right rather than worry about what might look right.

Courage is something he has practiced his entire life. Born in the tidelands of Georgia during the era of segregation, Justice Thomas knew what it was to be poor. People think "dirt poor" is a figure of speech. For Justice Thomas, it was a reality—the floor of the shanty he was born in was hard-packed dirt.

He was abandoned by his father as a young boy. Then, when his mother couldn't afford to keep her boys—she was making only $10 a week—she sent them to live at their grandparents' house, with not much more than the clothes on their backs.

There, Clarence Thomas's grandfather, Myers Anderson, taught him two foundational lessons. First, there is nothing you can't do if you put your mind to it. As his grandfather often said, "Old man can't is dead. I helped bury him."[5] Second, he learned to believe in himself and "assert my right to think for myself, to refuse to have my ideas assigned to me as though I was an intellectual slave because I am black, . . . to state that I'm a man, free to think for myself and do as I please [and] to assert that I am a judge and I will not be consigned to the unquestioned opinions of others."[6]

Justice Thomas's grandfather, who could barely read or write, understood the value of an education. To him, education equaled emancipation. So he saved his money to send Justice Thomas and his brother to the local all-black Catholic school run by Irish nuns (like most schools in that time and place, it was segregated). His grandfather knew that the values instilled at home had to be reinforced in the boys' education. Sister Mary Virgilius, the school principal and Justice Thomas's eighth-grade teacher, had a formative impact on the young man—helping to shape not only the most powerful originalist voice of our day, but also a voice for those, like himself, who were left behind, unseen, unheard.

The upcoming chapters tell the stories of ordinary Americans struggling for justice in some of the hardest circumstances imaginable. See for yourself a justice who always has the courage to do what he believes the law, and therefore his duty, requires. See how he addresses the plight of these Americans.

You will find a justice who cares about the people behind the cases. You will find a justice who does not fit the stereotypes. You will find a justice who always tries his best to follow the original meaning of the Constitution. And you will leave these pages knowing that Justice Clarence Thomas truly is "The People's Justice."

CHAPTER 1

"The Wolves Are at Our Door"

Kelo v. City of New London

I t was in the spring of 1997, and with the last of her five sons soon to graduate from high school and her marriage souring, Susette Kelo was looking for a new place to live. The Long Island Sound seemed a natural fit: Susette was a paramedic, and each time she responded to a call on or near the Sound, she was enraptured by the views of the water.

Eventually, Susette spotted a house on the Sound with a "For Sale" sign, and she felt she had to have it. It was beautiful—complete with an amazing view of the water and a private boat dock. She loved the home, but she could not afford it alone.

Elated by her new dream, Susette approached her husband about selling their house and moving there together. But his answer was firm: No. No discussion. No acknowledgment that what she wanted might matter at all.

To Susette, this was the final straw; it was time to move on. If they parted ways, it would be better for them both. Still, she was stuck. The $170,000 price tag was too high for her modest salary as a paramedic.

A few weeks later, she found herself on another call, this time in the Fort Trumbull neighborhood of New London, Connecticut.

Unlike most of the communities on the Sound, Fort Trumbull was a blue-collar neighborhood with more affordable housing.

Once a busy seaport, New London had lost much of its industry but kept much of its charm, so it is perhaps unsurprising that Susette fell in love with a house there. Granted, this one was not like the first one. It was a run-down, two-story Victorian. It looked abandoned—plagued by overgrown vines, ugly paint, and cracks running all over. Even the sidewalk was cracked. But the house checked one very important box for Susette: it had a view of the water. She knew she couldn't buy an already perfect house on her own; she needed a home that she could afford—even if it was 107 years old. Asking price: $59,000.

Though the realtor was almost embarrassed by the home's current state, Susette wasn't worried. She knew what she could do with the place. When the realtor asked, "Are you sure you don't want to see other places?" Susette immediately said, "NO." Zero hesitation. This was the right place. She had a vision, and she made an offer on the spot. And after some haggling, the house was hers! This was the first home she had ever owned.

As soon as she could, she started working on it. First, the house needed a new paint job, so she turned to a friend who specialized in painting historic homes. This was a special house, and so Susette gave it a special color: a subtle shade of pink called *Odessa Rose*.

Susette had more improvements in mind, but she needed money. She looked for a second job and discovered that she could become a nurse right from the comfort of her new home through correspondence classes. The university would send her the books, and she could complete the classes remotely. Resolutely, she signed up. With the extra income from nursing, she could make the house perfect. In the meantime, until she could hire professionals, she would continue working on the house herself.

She dove right in, tearing down the overgrowth and fixing anything she could. As she toiled, the house looked better and better. Through her own blood, sweat, and tears, Susette worked wonders. But the repairs were not the only monuments to her work. Susette also had a round oval sign made for the front of her house. It was white with a pale green outline, and it read, "The Kelo House." She had the sign placed right above the front door, below the center window. It was perfect.

After each hard day's work, Susette enjoyed the thing she had wanted most in her new home: a view of the water. As she sat on her porch and looked over the Thames River one night, she thought to herself, *This is true happiness.*

But unbeknownst to Susette, there was trouble in paradise. While Susette was busy polishing her diamond in the rough, politicians were trying to find an occupant for the 24-acre parcel down the street, where an old industrial mill sat vacant along the Thames River.

Governor John Rowland and the local politicians dreamed of bringing in a Fortune 500 company, but they knew they couldn't do it alone. So they turned to the New London Development Corporation (NLDC), a non-profit founded in 1978 to assist the city with economic development. In order to make it happen, the NLDC needed a dynamic project leader.

The politicians found one in Dr. Claire Gaudiani. She was the president of Connecticut College, the prestigious school that sat on the hill overlooking New London. Dr. Gaudiani was a natural leader, with the drive to make the politicians' dream a reality.

The politicians and Dr. Gaudiani agreed that getting a Fortune 500 company to take the vacant lot would do wonders for New London. The corporation could take credit for replacing a run-down eyesore with a state-of-the-art facility. In the process, it would produce jobs and tax revenue for New London and beyond.

The NLDC had a leader. It had a plan. Now it needed a Fortune 500 company.

In Pfizer, it found the perfect candidate. For starters, Pfizer already had a facility right across the Thames River in Groton, Connecticut. Second, Pfizer was in the process of getting its new wonder-drug, Viagra, approved by the Food and Drug Administration. Once approved, the drug would make hundreds of millions of dollars for Pfizer, and Pfizer would need a facility to produce it.

But Pfizer immediately expressed reservations about the 24-acre site. Not every one of these reservations was necessarily a dealbreaker, but they would all be costly to address. For example, Pfizer knew it would have to do significant environmental remediation on the industrial mill site before it was even usable. More important, Pfizer questioned whether New London's infrastructure—from the roads to the utilities—could handle the demands of a large research facility.

One problem, however, loomed larger than all the rest: the plot was simply too small. Twenty-four acres was not enough. Pfizer wanted enough land so that the facility could expand. It wanted at least a hundred acres.

As a proposed solution to this problem, Pfizer recommended that Dr. Gaudiani invite the State of Connecticut to join the venture as a partner. Dr. Gaudiani knew this was a reasonable request, so she called the governor to set up a meeting.

At the meeting, Pfizer outlined for the governor what had to happen to make the deal work: the city's sewage treatment plant in Fort Trumbull needed to be upgraded and capped to contain the smell, the state needed to clean out the scrap metal junkyard by the site, and the nearby state park needed to be restored. But Pfizer made one final demand, and it was a big one. The NLDC would need to acquire more than ninety additional acres for a future luxurious hotel, office space, high-end housing and stores, and a top-notch conference center.[1]

How would they do this? Pfizer wanted the state to acquire not only the original 24-acre site and the nearby abandoned naval base, but also everything in between, including the residential properties in Fort Trumbull. In other words, Pfizer wanted the state to displace seventy-five to one hundred people. And not just any people. With an average family income of approximately $21,250, these were close to the poorest citizens of New London.

Pfizer and the NLDC recognized that the state couldn't simply kick people out of their homes. So in light of this financial problem, they proposed a financial solution. They would send real estate agents to buy the residents out. With generous offers, how could they say no?

The governor and his staff were thrilled. Not only did they approve the proposal, with only minor modifications, but many of the politicians added their own requests. For example, the governor's chief of staff, Peter Ellef, asked that one of the high-end housing units be reserved for him. He wasn't the only one. After all, these units would be right near a new park with a great view of the Thames. Dr. Gaudiani started a list.[2]

Both the government officials and the Pfizer executives were aware that, in some ways, they were biting off more than they could chew. Pfizer wasn't in the social experiment business; it was in the finance and pharmaceutical business—and yet the proposed plan was supposed to restructure Fort Trumbull's society. The city, for its part, didn't have much money to contribute, but this large-scale development project required a sizeable war chest. It was for this reason that the partnership between the state, city, the NLDC, and Pfizer seemed like a natural fit. Pfizer and the state would pay the bills; the city and the NLDC would handle the details of clearing out the residents. Pfizer committed to paying the lion's share of the project: almost $300 million (over half a billion in 2023 dollars) while the State of Connecticut kicked in close to $80 million for the Fort Trumbull project. The NLDC promised to clear out the current Fort Trumbull residents.[3]

As all of this was taking place, Susette was finishing up her home. She worked two jobs and saved enough money to make her house truly her own. It was finally coming together.

Then she saw the news headline: "Pfizer to Expand into New London." This shocked her. Why would the corporation want to come to New London? Then she received an even greater shock. A real estate agent knocked on her door.

The agent identified herself, and Susette, curious, let her in. The agent immediately complimented the house, and Susette could tell she was impressed with the renovations. But after pleasantries, the agent got down to business: $68,000. That is what the city and the NLDC would be offering to buy the property. The offer was not much more than what the home had been worth before Susette's substantial investments.

Susette was offended. A year ago, she had unhesitatingly told another realtor that she wanted this home, not any other. Today, she even more quickly told this woman the same thing. She was not selling. This was her home, her dream.[4]

The agent persisted and warned Susette that if she did not sell her property, the city would take it through eminent domain. This upset Susette. How dare someone come into her house, undervalue the worth of her home, and then threaten to *take* it? After some discussion about the city's plans, the agent left.[5]

Susette knew what eminent domain was—it is when the government takes your property for a public use. In essence, the government takes your property through condemnation-type proceedings and gives you "fair market value" for it. In this case, that amount would not be very "fair."[6]

As the days passed and some of her neighbors were convinced to sell, Susette grew even angrier. She had just invested so much blood, sweat, and money in her house. Now that it was perfect, and truly her own as no other home had ever been, the city was threatening to take it. She was not going to give in without a fight.

A couple weeks later, Susette heard another knock on her door. The agent was back. This time, the offer was $78,000, but Susette's answer was the same: No. It would take much more to convince her to give up her dream. So once again, Susette told the agent to leave. This time, she slammed the door behind her and told her not to come back.[7]

Susette's opponents would not be deterred so easily, however. A few days later, she received a letter from the agent, telling her that real estate agents would exhaust all possibilities to purchase the house and "relocate the displaced persons." Then came another letter, this time from Dr. Gaudiani, lauding the virtues of the project while implying that Susette's home was relatively insignificant. Susette tossed the letters into a pile. She had no interest.[8]

Susette was not alone. Several families on her block also refused to sell. Some were so poor that they were worried they would become homeless if they sold for such a meager price. Others didn't know how they could bring themselves to part with the houses that their families had built and maintained for more than a hundred years.[9]

Susette helped organize a group of neighbors to fight the NLDC's and Pfizer's efforts to kick them out of their homes. She even penned an opinion letter on her neighbors' behalf, noting that while other neighborhoods around the country were fighting for speed bumps and better lighting, she and her neighbors were fighting to keep their homes. They paid their bills. They beautified and improved their neighborhood. And yet the NLDC was telling them they must leave so it could gentrify New London. Susette and her fellow residents were willing to welcome Pfizer and the renovated park as neighbors. But they didn't want to lose their homes.

The politicians, meanwhile, were becoming tired of the home-owners' resistance. In their minds, the NLDC had offered the residents more than their houses were worth. If they wouldn't leave, it was time to pull out the trump card: eminent domain. They knew that not even one home could be left standing—otherwise, no developer would take on the property. But, fearing a negative reaction from their constituents, the city council authorized the NLDC to use the city's eminent domain power instead of acting on its own behalf. The politicians wanted more taxpayer dollars, but they didn't want to look like bad guys before election day, so they used the NLDC as a smokescreen.

Susette met with her neighbors. Some cried. Others despaired. One even had to check into the hospital. But Susette stood strong. They couldn't give up now. They were up against some powerful opponents. They knew they were just a group of low-income residents the city saw as expendable. But they had to fight.

The residents needed a champion to stand up for them. Someone brought up a group in Washington, D.C.—the Institute for Justice. IJ, as it is known, had just made a name for itself in the eminent domain area, representing a widow in her fight with the State of New Jersey and casino magnate Donald Trump (you may have heard of him). In that case, New Jersey had planned to condemn the widow's property along with a couple of others so they could convert those properties into a limousine waiting area near the Trump Plaza Hotel and Casino. But IJ fought the condemnation plan in New Jersey state court and won.[10]

While Susette and her neighbors doubted IJ would take their case, they didn't see any harm in asking. Peter Kreckovic, a local artist and one of Susette's neighbors, penned the letter, which ended up on the desk of a young but experienced lawyer at IJ—Scott Bullock. Scott is known not only as a brilliant lawyer but as a tenacious fighter for his client's interests. His clients affectionately call him "Bull."

But IJ routinely received hundreds, if not thousands, of letters asking for help. While Scott tried to read all the letters he received, he couldn't help everyone. In fact, he wanted to help many more people than IJ's resources allowed. But the New London letter struck a chord with him. Two key components made the case attractive: (1) an interesting legal issue and (2) an outrageous government action. But before IJ took on the case, Scott needed to make sure he had the right plaintiffs. So he visited Fort Trumbull.

Scott was shocked by what he saw. While there was nothing extravagant about the houses, there was no blight, no streets full of boarded-up windows. Instead, what he found was a proud blue-collar neighborhood where people took care of their houses and looked after each other. And the view of the Thames was indeed stunning. It was not what he had been expecting.

He started interviewing the neighbors. And he looked into what the government planned to build on their block. Though there were plans—for the hotel and conference center, for example—drawn up for most of the land, there were no plans yet for the area where most of these houses were located. Scott almost fell over when he realized this. Usually, the government plans to build something before it takes someone's land. And these people were not harming anyone or adding blight to the city's environs, so knocking their houses down served no real purpose at all.

Scott really liked their homes. They reminded him of quintessential blue-collar America, just like where he grew up. He didn't want to see them taken as mere placeholders for the future parking lots of a powerful pharmaceutical company's white-collar employees—or their buddies in city hall.[11]

So IJ took the case, but Scott wanted Susette to be the face of it. He knew Susette was a fighter and that she wouldn't sell out. She was willing, and Scott and his colleagues got to work. Next, he started looking for a resident who had been there a long time.[12]

In Wilhelmina Dery, he found the perfect co-plaintiff. Wilhelmina had been born in 1918 in the very house she was still living in. She had met Charles, the love of her life, in that house. The couple had made the house their own after they got married in 1946.

As the Dery family had grown, so, too, had their stake in the community. When their son got married, they bought him the house next door as a wedding gift.[13]

Scott liked the Derys, and he enjoyed their company. But as he visited with them, he knew the shadow of the NLDC threat loomed over them. This family had such deep roots in this town. Scott had found another fighter. He thought to himself, *How could anyone want to take this all away from them?*

Now Fort Trumbull's residents had a lawyer, but what next? They didn't need to wait long to find out. On November 22, 2000, Susette returned home from working a long and hard shift in the hospital. As she walked up her front steps, she spied a condemnation notice taped to her front door. Her time had run out. It was the day before Thanksgiving.

She immediately called Scott and told him, "The wolves are at our door." While Scott had known this day was coming, he was outraged by the timing. He spoke with his partner, Dana Berliner. Knowing what their clients were facing, the two of them spent most of their Thanksgiving weekend preparing to file a lawsuit against New London and the NLDC.[14]

They knew they faced an uphill battle. The Supreme Court had long ago strayed away from the original meaning of the Takings Clause, making it easier than ever for governments to use their eminent domain power. That clause, found in the Fifth Amendment to the United States Constitution, provides that "private property" shall not be "taken for public use, without just compensation."

In their complaint against New London and the NLDC, Scott and Dana tried to bring the Supreme Court back to the original meaning of the Takings Clause by pointing out that their clients' property was not being taken for a "public use," but rather for private redevelopment. The property was destined for Pfizer's and the other developers' "use," not the city's. To make matters worse, the city did not even know to what use the plaintiffs' property would be put; the politicians just wanted the properties so they could offer them to a developer as part of a potential package. For both these reasons, IJ argued that the Constitution did not permit the city to take its residents' homes in this case.

They knew well, however, that Supreme Court precedent stood in their way. In the early 1950s, Congress had authorized the Redevelopment Land Agency (RLA) to hand over "blighted" areas or those with "substandard housing" in the District of Columbia to private developers.

What is "substandard housing" or "blighted housing"? According to Congress, any facilities lacking sanitation, ventilation, or light; dwellings that are overcrowded with "faulty interior arrangements"; or housing arrangements that negatively impact public safety, health, morals, or welfare. In other words, wherever the government might see potential for gentrification by taking over the homes of the poor and the underprivileged.

One of the D.C. residents affected by the legislation objected and filed a lawsuit that ultimately reached the Supreme Court. In that case, *Berman v. Parker*, the Court did not adhere to the original meaning of the Fifth Amendment. Instead of applying the "public use" language in the Constitution, the Court in *Berman* authorized the District of Columbia to take residents' property for a "public purpose"—a term the justices did not define. The Court simply deferred to the legislature's definition.

Berman v. Parker greatly expanded the power of the government to condemn property. After all, the government can conceive of a "public purpose" for almost anything politicians would like to do with someone's property (like obtain higher tax revenues). That is a much lower standard than a true "public use" for the property, such as a street or a sidewalk. Many believed *Berman* gave cities and states free rein to do whatever they wanted.

With this green light from the Court, the RLA had taken almost 560 acres from D.C.'s poorest residents and given the properties to private developers. All told, the RLA displaced around 23,500 people in America's capital, demolishing approximately 4,800 buildings in the process.

But Scott and Dana were undeterred by *Berman* and its progeny. They felt the time had come to minimize the damage *Berman* continued to inflict on poor and politically weak Americans.

While Scott and Dana were drafting the complaint, new problems surfaced for Susette and her neighbors. They each received a second notice—this one telling them they had no more than ninety days to get out of their homes. To make matters worse, since the homes had been condemned, the city and the NLDC were now the homes' legal owners—and they wanted to charge the residents rent until they left. In Susette's case, that was $450 per month, on top of the mortgage she was already paying.

This second notice kicked Dana and Scott into high gear. They polished the complaint, and five days before Christmas they filed

Kelo v. City of New London in local court. Susette and her fellow plaintiffs did not ask for any money; they only wanted to stop the city from taking away the places they loved: their houses, their neighborhood, their home.

After the people of Fort Trumbull filed their complaint, the city's tactics changed. Billy Von Winkle, one of Susette's fellow plaintiffs, owned several rental properties in Fort Trumbull. These were his source of income, and city officials must have known it. The city entered one of his apartment buildings and evicted the tenants. Then the city padlocked the doors of each of the apartments—even with one tenant still inside. Rubbing salt in the wound, the city promised to demolish Von Winkle's properties first. Billy was furious. How was he going to live without his income?

Scott called the city's lawyer and asked that it delay demolishing the properties until the lawsuit could be resolved. The city's answer: we will bring up your request at our board meeting next month. In other words, the city refused to discuss Scott's request until after the waiting period for demolishing the properties had expired. Scott asked the city to reconsider. He received a firm no.[15]

Given that answer, time was of the essence. Scott and Dana raced to prepare a motion for a temporary restraining order and to file it with the court. Upon receiving the motion, the court set up a conference date at noon—twelve hours *after* the waiting period would end.

Scott and Dana worried that the city could begin demolition in that 12-hour window. But Scott knew that Von Winkle's vacant apartment building still had furniture and belongings in it and was a solid brick structure that would take preparation to demolish. So he turned his focus to the homes, all but one of which were occupied. Another co-plaintiff, Rich Beyer, was renovating one of his rental homes. It had been stripped down to the studs, which made it an easy target. Scott feared that if the city bulldozed the Beyer property before the hearing, this would hurt the morale of his clients. Once one fell, they might understandably begin to feel like they had already lost.[16]

Scott scrambled to figure out a plan. His public relations person, John Kramer, volunteered to stay in the empty house overnight. Scott pointed out that there was no power and that the Connecticut coast was freezing in February. Kramer replied that he would brave the cold in a sleeping bag with his winter coat, gloves, and hat.

The plaintiffs, for their part, volunteered to man the house as well. After all, this was their neighborhood—they wouldn't let someone else guard it alone.

But on the day of the conference, just after the demolition waiting period had expired, the city changed its tune. Before the judge, the NLDC and the city agreed to delay demolitions until he ruled on the injunction. In exchange, the city requested a speedy trial, which it received—the trial would be in three months. There was no trace of the aggressive tone they had taken with Scott.

In the lead-up to trial, the lawyers began the process of "discovery"—in which the lawyers on each side can obtain information from the other. Scott and Dana requested the correspondence between Pfizer and the city. Once they read the correspondence, it became clear to them: Pfizer, not the city, was driving this train. The letters described Pfizer's plans to build its research facility, to demolish the Fort Trumbull neighborhood, and to replace blue-collar homes with an upscale conference center, hotel, health club, and a condominium complex.

Scott and Dana had found their smoking gun. The project had no public purpose, much less a public use. Pfizer's letters spoke for themselves.[17]

By the time the trial began in the summer of 2000, Scott and Dana were prepared. The property owners testified the first day, and they did well. They pled to keep their homes and the neighborhood they loved so much. Pfizer was welcome to join their community, they said, but not at the expense of their homes.[18]

Then city officials and other witnesses testified about the benefits of the project. No one denied it was for private economic development.

At the end of the trial, the judge said he would issue a written decision. He had to decide whether the taking of the Fort Trumbull neighborhood for economic development qualified as a "public use."

About seven months later, the judge issued a 249-page decision that surprised everyone. The judge had split the case. First, he found that the economic development did qualify as a "public use." However, since the NLDC had no planned "use" for portions of the Fort Trumbull neighborhood, the city could not take the residences in those portions.

Unfortunately, he ruled that they *could* take the other plaintiffs' properties since the city had a planned use for those areas. The judge then ordered a halt to any demolitions while appeals were ongoing.

Both sides agreed to bypass the intermediate court and appeal to the Connecticut Supreme Court, which agreed to hear the case. Approximately one year later, the Connecticut Supreme Court ruled, 4–3, that *all* the takings were proper. The city had won. The plaintiffs were devastated. Scott and Dana, however, promised to make one final appeal—to the United States Supreme Court.

The Supreme Court picks and chooses the cases it hears. In fact, it typically receives seven to eight thousand petitions per year and denies all but about eighty. So getting the Court to take this case would not be easy. Plus, the *Berman* precedent stood in the way. The Fort Trumbull team worked hard to prepare a petition pointing out that, in spite of *Berman*, the justices could rule for Susette Kelo and her neighbors. They knew it was a long shot, but it was worth a try.

When Scott received the news that the Court had accepted the case, they were all elated. Susette was surprised by all the support the case had received from the public, and now in the Supreme Court. It seemed to her that there were not many people on the city's side. She felt confident that the Supreme Court would see what was really going on and let the people of Fort Trumbull keep their homes.

Several amicus or "friend-of-the-court" briefs were filed in support of Susette, but perhaps none was as compelling as that filed by the National Association for the Advancement of Colored People (NAACP). The NAACP's brief highlighted the disproportionate impact eminent domain had on black Americans and provided a litany of statistics supporting its argument. But perhaps no evidence in the brief spoke louder of the abuses of the takings power than a quote from the attorney general of Minnesota in the 1950s: "We went through the black section between Minneapolis and St. Paul about four blocks wide and we took out the home of every black man in that city. And woman and child. In both those cities, practically. It ain't there anymore, is it? Nice neat black neighborhood, you know, with their churches and all and we gave them about $6,000 a house and turned them loose on society."[19]

The NAACP's proposed solution to protect Americans from this kind of behavior? Return to the original meaning of "public use," and maintain a higher standard for the government's taking of private property.

With all this support, IJ's lawyers felt good about their chances. Yet Scott and Dana didn't take victory for granted. They prepped for argument, knowing they were still the legal underdogs at the Supreme Court. The goal was to convince the Court that if it allowed this land to be taken for private economic development, then homes everywhere would be at risk—especially the homes of poor and vulnerable Americans.

Argument day finally arrived on February 22, 2005. When the justices entered the courtroom, Scott felt like he was ready. Showtime. The questions were not easy. Justice Breyer asked why the Court should not say that "virtually every taking is all right, as long as there is some public benefit." Scott pointed out that if this power were so unrestricted, no one's home was safe. But Justice Breyer seemed unfazed. In response, he commented that private property "could only be taken if there is a public use, and there almost always is."

This line of questioning continued throughout Scott's arguments. Scott had his work cut out for him.

But the city's lawyer, Wes Horton, did not have it much easier. Justice Scalia asked him whether the city could simply take property from the poor and give it to those who would pay more taxes? Surprisingly, Horton said yes. Stunned by his answer, Justice Scalia followed up with, "You can take from A and give to B if B pays significantly more taxes?" Horton doubled down.

In rebuttal, Scott emphasized what Horton had admitted: under the city's reasoning, governments could play reverse Robin Hood. Nothing would stop cities from kicking out their poor citizens in favor of Fortune 500 companies. Every poor neighborhood in America would be in jeopardy of gentrification.[20]

With that, argument ended. All that was left now was the waiting.

Scott knew the opinion would not be released until near the end of the Court's term, which is in June. As the time got closer, Scott grew more anxious. Finally, his receptionist informed him that a clerk from the United States Supreme Court was on the line. His hand shaking, he picked up the phone. The clerk told him the news—the Supreme Court had affirmed the Connecticut Supreme Court's ruling. He could barely get out a thank you, nor did he feel very thankful. Susette had lost her case—and her house.

When Scott's paralegal returned with a written copy of the opinion, he saw that the loss had been a very close one: a 5–4 vote. Not that that mattered to his clients. The city still got their homes.

Justice Stevens had written the opinion for the Court, joined by Justices Kennedy, Souter, Ginsburg, and Breyer. The majority had found that the takings qualified as a "public use" because the city had a "carefully considered development plan."

According to the majority, "[p]romoting economic development is a traditional and long accepted function of government." After all, economic development is a "public purpose." And who were courts to second-guess the legislature?

This was especially clear after *Berman*, Justice Stevens said. Cities know better than courts what areas are "sufficiently distressed to justify a program of economic rejuvenation." According to Stevens, it seemed, nobody was taking property from A and giving it to B. The city was just "rejuvenating" a neighborhood.

Justice O'Connor wrote the main dissent, joined by Chief Justice Rehnquist, Justice Scalia, and Justice Thomas. In her dissent, she distinguished Susette Kelo's case from *Berman*: in *Berman*, the government had removed "blight" that was "inflicting an affirmative harm to society," whereas in this case, not a single person claimed that the plaintiffs' "well-maintained homes are the source of any social harm." Thus, the majority was not simply following precedent, but expanding it. Justice O'Connor warned that "under the banner of economic development, all private property is now vulnerable to being taken and transferred to another private owner, so long as it might be upgraded."

Only Justice Thomas, in his separate dissent, revisited the original meaning of the "public use" requirement—as the NAACP had advocated. Thomas argued that to be for "public use," the new property must actually be used by the public—not only by private parties. By changing the standard from "public use" to "public purpose," he said, the Court held "against all common sense, that a costly urban renewal project whose stated purpose is a vague promise of new jobs and increased tax revenue, but which is also suspiciously agreeable to the Pfizer Corporation, is for a 'public use.'" If economic development takings are permissible, he noted, then "any taking" is permissible.

If the Court went back to the original meaning of the Takings Clause, Justice Thomas argued, legislatures wouldn't be free to take from the poor and give to the rich. Rather, cities and states would be limited to taking property for projects truly designed for "public use," such as streets or sidewalks.

And, with constitutional rights at stake, the courts should be vigilant. After all, Justice Thomas pointed out, courts don't defer to the government's determination of whether a search of a home is reasonable, or whether a suspected murderer needs to be shackled. "Something has gone seriously awry with this Court's interpretation of the Constitution," he warned, when "[t]hough citizens are safe from the government in their homes, the homes themselves are not safe."

Justice Thomas was not done. If the majority didn't care about the alteration of the Constitution that the Court had undertaken, he would at least make them aware of the painful consequences of their decision. In Justice Thomas's words, allowing the government to take private property not just for a "public use" but for a "public purpose," including economic benefits, "guarantees that these losses will fall disproportionately on poor communities" such as the people of Fort Trumbull or Washington, D.C. And because these communities are also the "least politically powerful," they will not be able to stop the "indignity" of being kicked out of their homes for the sake of some vague economic benefit to their city.

Powerful corporations, by offering the government a chance to collect more tax dollars, could now use cities to "victimize the weak." In this respect, the majority risked reintroducing the harmful urban renewal practices of the 1950s and '60s. During those years, Justice Thomas wrote, governments destroyed "predominantly minority communities" in St. Paul, Minnesota, and Baltimore, Maryland, under the guise of economic redevelopment. These were the very harms the NAACP had pointed to in its brief.

During that time, Justice Thomas pointed out, "urban renewal" became known as "Negro removal," and, in fact, "[o]ver 97 percent of the individuals forcibly removed from their homes by the 'slum-clearance' project upheld by this Court in *Berman* were black." The majority's decision in *Kelo* would only make things worse.

Susette and her neighbors were devastated by the ruling. How could these five justices take their homes? She knew nothing like this would ever happen to the justices' homes.[21]

But the people of Fort Trumbull were fighters. They intended to fight until the bitter end, and they did. Unfortunately, the city was not going to give up. Luckily, however, IJ had generated so much publicity and support for Susette and her neighbors that the city at least had to pay them a significant sum to move. Every one of them left New London.

But Susette knew this would not protect the next person. She and her friends, with IJ's help, had managed to put up a strong fight and gain the attention of the press. But other Americans might not be so lucky. And the Court's decision in *Kelo* would make it even harder to fight government takings of private property for "economic development," neighborhood "rejuvenation," higher projected tax revenues, and other nebulous examples of a "public purpose." Susette knew that the poor would often be driven from their homes and given less compensation than they would need to acquire a new home. And even when people could afford to go somewhere else, no compensation could replace what they would lose.

• • •

Things did not end well for some of the Connecticut politicians, either. In an unrelated corruption scandal, Governor John Rowland was indicted and pled guilty to a federal corruption charge. He received a little over one year in federal prison. His chief of staff never got a condominium in the new section of New London. Instead, he received thirty months' accommodation in a federal prison for his part in the scandal.[22]

Only eight years after arriving in New London, Pfizer left.[23] The place where Susette and her neighbors once lived remains barren, home only to rubble, feral cats, and weeds. The city hopes to put a community center there if it can raise the money.

One piece of good news: forty-five states have now passed eminent domain reform laws.[24] Some are more protective than others. Maybe some of them will stop future cases like *Kelo*. But as Justice Thomas noted, the Fifth Amendment was supposed to do that.

Chapter 2

"Education Means Emancipation"

Zelman v. Simmons-Harris

George Voinovich was not your typical politician. Cleveland born and bred, he was shy and avoided media attention. When he first ran for mayor of his home city in 1971, few thought he could win. And he didn't. But that loss did not lessen his love for his home city or its residents.

By 1979, Cleveland was the laughingstock of the nation. Media outlets had labeled the city the "mistake by the lake." It had defaulted on its multimillion-dollar debt—the only major city to go bankrupt at the time. Its population had declined 24 percent in the previous decade. Its river even caught fire when sparks from a passing train ignited the polluted water, causing flames towering five stories high.[1] When Voinovich decided to run for mayor again, it was not an easy decision. But his love for the city had not waned, and he felt he could help. He ran again, and this time, he won.

Voinovich's goal as mayor was to turn the city around and bring businesses back to town. His first task was to persuade the city's residents to raise taxes so he could pay off the city's debt. They agreed. Voinovich followed this success with a lobbying campaign to entice businesses to come to Cleveland. And it worked. With each success, what was once a dormant and dying city grew livelier.[2] Buildings started springing up—not just any buildings, but national attractions like the Rock and Roll Hall of Fame, a new basketball arena for the Cleveland Cavaliers, a baseball stadium for the Cleveland Indians (now the Cleveland Guardians), and a rejuvenated theater district.

The once beaten-down city had come alive. *Time* Magazine declared that Cleveland was making a comeback.[3] Sixty-five percent of the city's residents reported satisfaction with their life in the city.[4] And they were happy with Voinovich. They reelected him with overwhelming majorities in back-to-back elections.

In 1990, Voinovich decided to run for governor of Ohio. He won, but he left Cleveland with a knot in his stomach, knowing his work was not done. He had presided over a great rejuvenation of the city, but he had not accomplished all he set out to do. The city's schools were still in a state of disrepair. No matter what he tried as mayor, bureaucratic resistance and simple inertia had prevented him from improving the schools.

Voinovich knew this was not acceptable. Indeed, unlike many others in administration, he had firsthand knowledge of the schools—he had attended a Cleveland public school, as had his children. But when his oldest reached seventh grade, a teacher advised Voinovich and his wife that they should consider sending their children elsewhere, because the school was "not what it should be."[5] Voinovich was able to move his kids to a better school, but other parents could not afford to do so. He knew this did not bode well for the city. Parents with means fled the city schools, putting their children in private schools or moving to the suburbs. Poorer students, though, were trapped.

So as Voinovich gave his victory speech as governor-elect, he knew that work remained to be done in Cleveland. With the public schools in such dismal condition, he felt he could not truly celebrate his victory. After taking office, he immediately assembled a task force to study the schools throughout the state and propose reforms, with a specific eye toward the situation in Cleveland.

Voinovich tapped David Brennan to lead the task force. While Voinovich and Brennan did not always agree politically, the new governor felt sure that Brennan was the man for the job. The larger-than-life Akron native, who almost always wore a cowboy hat, had started his career in accounting, then pursued a law degree, and ultimately ended up in the steel industry. He was a hands-on business owner who interacted every day with his employees. In doing so, he observed that very few of those employees advanced within the company. It was not work ethic or talent that was holding them back, but rather their lack of education. Many were functionally illiterate. This prevented them from climbing the ladder or pursuing their dreams. This realization led Brennan to do two things: First, he started an educational program for his own employees. Second, he became a pioneer for educational reform.

When Brennan's task force began investigating the Cleveland public schools, what they found was worse than anyone could have imagined. A 1991 study concluded that "between 14 and 25" of the school district's buildings were in such a state of disrepair that they should be replaced or abandoned altogether.[6] The school board ignored that recommendation for nearly three years.[7]

As a result, in 1995, a federal district court ordered that the state superintendent take over management of the Cleveland public schools. When the state auditor began investigating, he found that the schools had failed on *every* metric the state set. The schools were also mismanaged, mired in a financial crisis so severe that it was "perhaps unprecedented in the history of American education."[8]

Of course, the students at these schools were the ones who suffered the most. Many complained that the schools lacked even the most basic necessities—like hand soap and toilet paper in the rest-rooms.[9] The students were also being passed from grade to grade without learning anything. In 1996, only 9 percent of Cleveland's public-school students passed all four sections of Ohio's ninth-grade proficiency test. More than two-thirds of Cleveland's students failed to graduate high school. Even among those who reached senior year, one in four still failed to graduate. Most of the parents could do little, if anything, about the failing schools—72 percent of the students were economically disadvantaged.

Plain Dealer columnist Dick Feagler described the situation this way: "[S]ociety has gone to hell . . . and the Cleveland schools went with it." Feagler had "heard 15 years' worth of school superintendents arrive in Cleveland to announce that a whole generation of children has been lost."[10]

Something drastic had to be done. So Voinovich asked the speaker pro tempore of the Ohio House of Representatives, Bill Batchelder, to work with Brennan to create a voucher program that would pro-vide impoverished children a way out of failing schools.

Voinovich tapped Bill Batchelder for a reason—Batchelder, who would soon become the "godfather" of Ohio's voucher program, was known as a force of nature. Elected to the Ohio House at age twenty-five, he would serve there for thirty-eight years. "As with Reagan, anyone who made the tragic mistake of underestimating Bill Batchelder inevitably would regret it."[11] Batchelder was known for building coalitions without sacrificing principle—he was never afraid to reach across the aisle to get something done if it would make Ohio a better place. Like Voinovich, Batchelder knew Cleveland had a seri-ous problem. He had heard from "numerous industrialists, business people, and bankers [that were] concerned they would have to leave Cleveland. They were saying they could not get employees within the city who had the ability to do the jobs they had available."[12]

Governor Voinovich wanted all Ohio parents to have the freedom and power he himself had exercised to direct his children's education. He believed kids should be able to pursue the American Dream regardless of their parents' income level or the property taxes in their zip code. When it came to education, many Cleveland parents and students were powerless. So Voinovich asked Batchelder and Brennan to put together a program that would allow parents to choose the best school for their children—be it a public school, religious school, or other private school.

But the new voucher program, Voinovich warned, had to be consistent with the Constitution's Establishment Clause, which prohibits government establishment of religion. Voinovich worried that if the state paid religious schools directly to subsidize poor kids' tuition, the courts might strike the program down. Batchelder, an accomplished lawyer who was in charge of drafting the bill, assured the governor that he would put together a program that could withstand the courts' scrutiny.

Before devising the exact details of the program, Batchelder went on a fact-finding mission. He started with the Cleveland City Council. There he found two critical allies and friends, Fannie Lewis and Bill Patmon. Lewis had grown up in Marion, Arkansas, and Memphis, Tennessee, where she attended public schools. She and her husband had moved to the Hough neighborhood of Cleveland in 1951. Lewis was the ideal neighbor. She would never shy away from helping someone who was in need. When a neighborhood house caught fire during riots in 1966 and the National Guard was sent to put out the fire, Lewis arrived on the scene to maintain order, both by helping to keep the crowd at bay and by keeping an eye on what the Guard was doing. Lewis was thrust into the spotlight when a picture of her talking to the National Guard appeared in the *Plain Dealer*.[13]

In her new and more prominent role, she became an outspoken critic of Cleveland politics, particularly when she felt like the politicians were putting their own interests ahead of the communities. In 1979, she won a seat on the very council she had spent years criticizing. And she didn't tone it down when she arrived at council. If a council member was not willing to do what was in the best interests of the residents, she would call that council member out. During her tenure, she made sure to get to personally know the people of her ward. As one friend said, "Fannie's probably the safest person in the ward. If some guy would try to jump her, I bet she'd know his mama's name."[14]

What made Lewis even more remarkable is that she was never interested in taking credit for her many accomplishments. While she was a champion of public schooling, she was not afraid to call the public schools out for failing the kids. And since she believed they were failing, she was not willing to sacrifice the kids while the city waited for the schools to improve. As a result of her own life experiences, she believed that the best way to empower people was to give them access to quality education. In Lewis, Batchelder found a powerful ally. She would do anything for the kids, even if it upset the powers that be.

Bill Patmon was a product of the Detroit public schools, and he had moved to Cleveland to help the poor. But no matter what he did, it didn't seem to be enough to make a real dent, so he ran for city council. As a council member, he saw firsthand the dismal condition of the schools. Patmon worried about the city's future and the future of each of its children, so he was willing to "put his political life on the line" to do something that would improve the kids' chances.[15] Thus he, too, was willing to work with Batchelder to devise a voucher program that would work—one that would truly benefit the kids.

Batchelder, Patmon, and Lewis understood that for the program to succeed, they needed the religious schools to participate. There weren't many non-religious private schools in Cleveland, and the suburban schools weren't interested in participating in the voucher program.

Luckily, during her years on council, Lewis had developed a good relationship both with Bishop Anthony M. Pilla, of the Catholic Diocese of Cleveland, and with Len Calabrese, who ran the diocese's social justice initiatives. Both men had a high regard for Lewis and Patmon because they always put people first. Thus, when Lewis and Batchelder went to Bishop Pilla and asked the diocese to get involved, the bishop was more than willing to participate even though resources were tight. Bishop Pilla saw this as an important program to assist kids in need and parents without a voice or a choice. Furthermore, he hoped that the program would spur the public schools to do better.

Once Batchelder had all of the necessary outside support in place, he put pen to paper. The initial pilot program that Batchelder devised cost $5.25 million and was funded through the state's Disadvantaged Public Impact Aid program. The vouchers would go to the parents or guardians of Cleveland public school students, with preference given to low-income families. The parents could use the vouchers at any private, religious, or public school that would accept their child.

If parents chose a private school, they would have to pay 10 percent of the cost of the $2,500 voucher. Once a private school agreed to participate, it had to agree that tuition would be capped at $2,500 for the voucher students. Fifty-six private schools agreed to participate, forty-six of which were religious.

Before the pilot voucher program, a parent could choose to apply to a magnet or other specialized public school. If they did so, the state would pay the school directly. Under the voucher program, if a student wanted to use the voucher for a public magnet or specialized school, that school would receive approximately $7,000 per student from the state. In addition, in 1997, Ohio passed legislation creating "community schools," which were public schools but could govern themselves like private schools. Community schools received $4,518 per student. After that legislation was enacted, two private schools converted to community schools so they could receive more state funding ($4,518 rather than $2,500 per student).

The Cleveland voucher program was the first in the country to allow vouchers to be used at religious schools. The program also provided money for tutoring—any child that chose to stay in the Cleveland public schools could apply for a tutoring voucher.

Batchelder and Voinovich were happy with the initial pilot. "Where else could a 33rd-degree Mason [Batchelder] and a prince of the Roman Church [Bishop Pilla] work together, for years, to make sure Baptist Black children could go to better schools?" Batchelder asked. "This is a great country."[16] Voinovich believed this "would be the most genuine school-choice program of any in the country."[17]

The program earned bipartisan support. The ranking Democrat in the Ohio legislature, Patrick Sweeney, who was from Cleveland, teamed up with Speaker Batchelder, a Republican, to get the bill passed. Sweeney had harsh words for those who opposed the program, who, he said, "never send their children to public schools but come out foursquare against vouchers. People who have an opportunity to write a check have a voucher in their pocket. What they don't want are children . . . who are in this neighborhood, and in this inner city . . . to have a checkbook."[18]

When the legislature passed the bill, the Cleveland *Plain Dealer* said that it was a "reason to rejoice." Finally, after years of failed attempts to improve the schools, many disadvantaged children would "have a chance for a better education."[19] Those who had doubted the public's desire for such a program were quickly proven wrong: even though low-income families receiving vouchers would still have to pay a small percentage of tuition at the private schools, applications flooded in. In the first year of the program, seven thousand students applied.

Even so, the program was not without opposition. The teachers' union and a few citizens filed suit as soon as the program was open for business. State courts halted the program temporarily. But on August 12, 1996, those barriers were lifted, and the program began. Unfortunately, that was too late for most of the schools to add space. Three hundred and fifty students who had received vouchers were left without a school to attend.

Brennan stepped up. With the help of parents, friends, and volunteers, he opened the HOPE Academies to accommodate those 350 stranded students. HOPE stood for "Help Our People's Education," and it was aptly named. In 1996, every child with a voucher found a school.

Parents of voucher students uniformly loved the program. They raved about their kids' new schools, reporting that their children received individualized help from their teachers, and, for the first time, expressed joy and excitement about going to school. The parents emphasized the school officials' "pleasantness, sincerity, understanding, dedication and commitment." They praised the "multi-racial" environment, with a "good cultural mix of students." They were grateful that their children could finally feel safe at school, thanks to better structure and discipline. And they noted that their children were performing much better in every academic subject.

These parents' beliefs were reflected in the students' test scores. In 1999, the Catholic Diocese of Cleveland's schools had a 95 percent proficiency rate in writing, while the Cleveland public schools had a 57 percent proficiency rate. The results in math were even more stark: the diocesan schools had a 75 percent proficiency rate, compared with 22 percent in Cleveland public schools. What's more, 99 percent of students attending diocesan schools graduated.

Despite the program's success and popularity with parents and students, the court challenges continued. On May 27, 1999, the Ohio Supreme Court announced its decision. While it found that most of the program was lawful, it concluded that one aspect of the program violated the Establishment Clause: the provision that gave priority to students whose parents belonged to the same religious group as the school they sought to attend. According to the court, this provision would encourage parents "to modify their religious practices in order to enhance their opportunity to receive a School Voucher Program scholarship." In doing so, it favored religious parents over non-religious parents. The court also concluded that the program as enacted violated a procedural rule in the Ohio Constitution.[20]

Instead of fighting the Ohio Supreme Court's conclusions, the state sprang into action to amend the voucher program. Barely one month after the Ohio Supreme Court decision, the Ohio legislature reenacted the voucher program without the preference clause. That fall, 3,761 students received vouchers, and a comparable number of public-school students became entitled to tutorial assistance grants.

But the challengers weren't satisfied with the changes to the program. Within twenty-one days of the new program's enactment, they were back in court. This time, they went to the federal trial court in Cleveland, Ohio. In the federal system, trial courts are called district courts. The challengers asked the district court to stop the children from using the vouchers that fall. They wanted all the kids back in the public schools.

The district court recognized that putting the program on hold could inflict harm on the students. It noted that a panel of psychiatrists had interviewed "selected school children" and found that removing the kids from their new schools could cause them to "lose friendships and sometimes a sense of community and purpose . . . [and to] suffer a sense of loss of security and stability." What's more, "their emotional, social, and personal development could be severely disrupted." The district court also recognized that "the parents, principals and administrators, teachers and students" had indicated what a "positive role . . . the alternative schools have played in their lives."

Nevertheless, hours before the school year was to begin, the district court stopped the program in its tracks. Why? Most of the schools that accepted the vouchers happened to be sectarian—they were mostly Catholic schools. That meant most parents who used vouchers had only sectarian options available to them. According to the district court, the lack of non-sectarian options meant the program violated the Establishment Clause. So, despite recognizing the harm that shutting down the program would cause to the children, the court shut down the entire program.[21]

Parents were stunned, administrators bewildered. What were the kids to do? Almost four thousand kids did not have a school to attend. Fortunately, the schools stepped forward and said they would take the kids without the payments from the state while the court battles ran their course. The *Baltimore Sun* described it this way: "The school year opened in a state of confusion yesterday, a day after a federal judge blocked a school voucher program that lets Cleveland students attend private or religious schools. . . . Nervous parents tied up phone lines as private school officials said they'd continue to accept vouchers [without funding from the state] pending appeals."[22]

Ohio went back to court and asked the district court to temporarily "stay" its decision so the voucher program could continue while the state sought review in the court of appeals. Two days after its initial order shutting the program down, the district court granted Ohio's request—but only for those students already enrolled in the program. The "timing" of the initial order, the court admitted, had "caused disruption to the children previously enrolled in the program beyond that normally associated with a student's transferring from one school to another."[23] Even so, any other children who were planning to start in the program that year were left in limbo.

Not satisfied with this result, Ohio asked the federal court of appeals for an emergency stay that, if granted, would allow the voucher program to operate in full while litigation continued. While the participating schools had volunteered to take the unfunded vouchers temporarily, they could not afford to do so indefinitely. Typically, such motions for emergency stays are handled quickly. But two months passed without action by the court of appeals, at which point Ohio took the highly unusual step of going straight to the United States Supreme Court. On November 5, 1999, the Supreme Court, by a vote of 5–4, granted the state's motion for a full stay.[24] Now the state could continue to fund the program while the litigation played out.

Back at the federal district court in Cleveland, the state hoped it could convince the district court that the program didn't violate the Establishment Clause. It failed. On December 20, 1999, the district court ruled in favor of the challengers. As before, the court found that the program improperly promoted religion. It said that "because the vast majority of participating schools are sectarian in nature," the students who participated had little choice but to go to a sectarian school. "A program that is so skewed toward religion necessarily results in indoctrination attributable to the government and provides financial incentives to attend religious schools." For those reasons, the district court concluded that the program violated the Establishment Clause.[25]

On January 12, 2000, Ohio filed a notice of appeal. Twelve months later, the court of appeals affirmed the district court's decision in a 2–1 ruling largely tracking the district court's reasoning. Once again, Ohio decided to take the fight all the way up to the United States Supreme Court. When the Supreme Court accepted the case, Batchelder said, "I keep having this recurring nightmare of Justice Scalia looking down from the bench and saying that the idea here is pretty good, but who wrote this stuff?"[26]

The first question for Ohio was who would argue this important case at the United States' highest court. Ohio attorney general Betty Montgomery believed that Judith French was the right choice. While French was only thirty-nine years old and had only argued her first Supreme Court case the year before, Montgomery had recently selected French as her chief counsel, and she trusted her. Others pushed back, believing the case was too important to leave to "a rookie." But Montgomery—the first woman to serve as Ohio's attorney general—did not back down. French was her advocate, end of story.

French had grown up in Northeast Ohio, outside of Youngstown. She had attended public schools, and her mother was a public school teacher. At the time Attorney General Montgomery selected her to argue the case, French was a single mother living in Columbus and sending her young daughter to the public schools there. After she was tapped to argue for Ohio, she decided to go to Cleveland to meet with the parents and children who were participating in the voucher program.

The parents' passion for the program was immediately apparent. To them, a voucher was more than an opportunity to attend a school with better statistical outcomes. It was the chance for their children to learn in a safe and nurturing environment. Safety was key. The religious element of the schools was an afterthought for many of the parents.

After returning from Cleveland, French began preparing for her Supreme Court argument. Her soundtrack as she prepared: the Hans Zimmer score from the movie *Gladiator*. The music helped her keep calm despite the building pressure. French's daughter, then eleven years old, helped her prepare by playing the chief justice and calling the case so French could practice stepping up to the podium and delivering her opening statement. She did this hundreds of times.

Nine days before argument, French headed to Washington, D.C., to prepare with former Whitewater independent counsel, solicitor general, and Court of Appeals judge Ken Starr. Many thought Starr should be the one arguing the case. After all, he was a legend and would command the Supreme Court's attention. But Starr recognized talent when he saw it, and he believed French was the woman for the job. He would sit at counsel table to show his support, but, according to Starr, she did not need anything else from him. Not many advocates of Starr's stature would have stepped aside in such a big case.

During her preparation, French did eight to ten moot courts—practice sessions with other lawyers who were interested in the case and had agreed to help her prepare. In these moot courts, the others would impersonate the justices and interrogate French. Starr didn't think she needed quite so many practice runs. But French's success in these moot courts proved to many of the people who doubted her that she could handle the argument.

Thanks to Starr's efforts, the United States government had announced its support for Ohio's position. This was critical in getting the Supreme Court to take the case in the first place. It also meant that Solicitor General Theodore Olson would be given time to argue for the voucher program. The solicitor general supervises all Supreme Court litigation on behalf of the United States and is often referred to as "the Tenth Justice." In addition, Olson is widely regarded as one of the nation's best advocates. The Court also gave some argument time to David Young, who represented one of the non-sectarian private schools that accepted voucher students. French, Olson, and Young would all take turns at the podium, attempting to convince the Court to uphold Ohio's program.

The challengers of the voucher program selected Robert Chanin to argue on their behalf. Chanin had spent the previous thirty-three years as the general counsel for the National Education Association and had argued four cases in the Supreme Court. Also arguing for the challengers was a former federal judge, Marvin Frankel.

The Supreme Court heard the argument in the case on February 20, 2002. French was ready from the get-go. She emphasized two things for the justices. First, the program was designed to be neutral toward religion—in order to be eligible, students only had to be below a certain family income level and be in a failing school district. Second, the program involved private choice by the parents. In other words, the parents, not the state, decided which schools got the funds.

Several of the justices expressed concern about a large amount of government money ending up in religious schools. But French pointed out that this result was not of the government's doing. Instead, it resulted from parents independently choosing religious schools for their children. She emphasized that the parents could also choose to send the students to magnet and community schools, which were not religious.

Young argued next. Justice Breyer asked whether the families really had a choice, given how much better the parochial schools were than the Cleveland public schools: "I mean, if it were my children and I saw these comparisons, I'd say, send them to parochial school." After a short answer from Young, Justice Scalia noted that "Justice Breyer could send his child to one of the community schools, which is entirely nonsectarian, under this program . . . [and] would get more money." In response to both justices, Young emphasized that just because a school was successful (and enticing to parents) did not mean the government was endorsing it or forcing anyone to choose it. Like French, he pointed out that it was ultimately up to the parents' independent choices about what was best for their children's education.

Solicitor General Olson argued next. He stressed that parents had several options besides the religious schools, including magnet and community schools. Justice Souter pressed Olson on the fact that 96 percent of students taking the tuition aid were using it for parochial schools. Olson responded that the percentage was not of constitutional significance, because it was the result of private choices by the parents.

Chanin stepped to the podium to argue for the program's opponents. Justice Scalia pressed him on why it mattered if money went to religious schools since it was the result of the parents' choices. Chanin said that because most of the schools participating in the voucher program were religious, the parents were not exercising a true choice. Instead, they were merely serving a "a ritualistic role."

Justice Stevens asked whether the program would be constitutional if it included ninety-nine non-religious private schools and one religious school, and parents picked the one religious school over the ninety-nine other options. No, Chanin said. Even that would violate the Establishment Clause, he claimed, because nothing would "break the chain" of public money going from the government to the religious school. In other words, if even one penny went to a parochial school, the challengers wanted to shut the whole program down.

The argument lasted eighty minutes—twenty minutes longer than usual.[27] When it concluded, Starr remarked that French had given "one of the finest oral arguments" he had ever seen. Attorney General Montgomery was vindicated for sticking to her guns.

On June 27, 2002, the last day of the term, the Supreme Court handed down its decision. It was close, but the voucher program had survived. The Court upheld the program by a 5–4 vote. Cleveland's children could continue going to their school of choice; children without means would not remain trapped in failing public schools.

Chief Justice Rehnquist wrote the majority opinion, joined by Justices O'Connor, Scalia, Kennedy, and Thomas. The majority concluded that the program passed constitutional muster for three reasons. First, Ohio had a valid secular purpose for enacting the program—namely, helping poor children in a failing school system. Second, the program was neutral with respect to religion. And third, the program provided money to parents whose children attended religious schools as a result of their "own genuine and independent private choice."

The Court also highlighted that the voucher program actually disincentivized choosing a religious school over a secular option. If a low-income parent chose a private school as part of the voucher program, they had to pay 10 percent of the tuition, and the school had to accept a lower tuition than it would usually charge. If, however, the parent chose one of the other options available under state law, the parents would pay nothing, and Ohio would send the money directly to the school of choice. Thus, the incentives of the program were more aligned with choosing a magnet or community school, not a sectarian (or non-sectarian) private school.

The majority recognized that forty-six of the fifty-six schools that participated in the voucher program in 1999 were religious schools and that program participants overwhelmingly (96 percent) chose religiously affiliated schools. The dissenting justices and challengers placed great weight on this number, but according to the majority, the percentage of parents that independently chose religious schools did not matter for three reasons.

First, that percentage would fluctuate year to year, based on the parents' choices. It would hardly make sense that the constitutionality of the program would change from year to year depending on how many parents chose religious schools.

Second, it just so happened that Cleveland had an especially high number of religious schools. "To attribute constitutional significance to this figure . . . would lead to the absurd result that a neutral school-choice program might be permissible in some parts of Ohio, such as Columbus, where a lower percentage of private schools are religious, but not in inner-city Cleveland, where Ohio has deemed such programs most sorely needed, but where a preponderance of religious schools happens to be greater."

Finally, the children choosing magnet and community schools did not need vouchers, so the challengers had not included them in their percentage calculations. But factoring in *all* the parents who opted out of Cleveland public schools "drop[ped] the percentage enrolled in religious schools from 96% to under 20%."

The dissenters argued that parents who chose community and magnet schools should not be counted in those statistics. In response, the majority pointed out that "none of the dissenting opinions explain how there is any perceptible difference between scholarship schools, community schools, or magnet schools from the perspective of parents looking to choose the best educational option for their school-aged children." In other words, it was irrelevant to the parents whether they received a voucher they could give to a religious school or if the state sent the money directly to a government school. Either way, the parents were exercising their power of choice to provide the best education possible for their child.

Justice Thomas agreed with the majority in full. He also added a further concurring opinion, addressing the link between the Fourteenth Amendment, the Establishment Clause, and education.

Justice Thomas's concurring opinion opened by quoting famed abolitionist and former slave Frederick Douglass, who had said that "education means emancipation." As the Supreme Court had said in its famous school-desegregation case, *Brown v. Board of Education*, "it is doubtful that any child may reasonably be expected to succeed in life if he is denied the opportunity of an education." Yet, in

America, Justice Thomas wrote, "urban children have been forced into a system that continually fails them."

Beginning with first principles, Justice Thomas questioned whether the Establishment Clause placed any relevant limit on Ohio at all. He pointed out that the Establishment Clause provides that "*Congress* shall make no law respecting the Establishment of Religion." Thus, by its own terms, it does not apply to the States.

Justice Thomas acknowledged that the Fourteenth Amendment, ratified after the Civil War, had "fundamentally restructured the relationship between individuals and the States and ensured that States would not deprive citizens of liberty." After its ratification, in a process called incorporation, the Supreme Court used the Fourteenth Amendment to gradually apply several of the protections from the Bill of Rights to the states and protect individual liberty against infringement by state governments in addition to the federal government. "There would be a tragic irony in converting the Fourteenth Amendment's guarantee of individual liberty into a prohibition on the exercise of educational choice." Yet the challengers of the Ohio voucher program were trying to do just that by "handcuff[ing] the State's ability to experiment with education."

Turning to the details of the case, Justice Thomas observed that the Cleveland public schools' failures "disproportionately affect[ed] minority children most in need of educational opportunity." He surveyed how things had changed since the Fourteenth Amendment was ratified: "At the time of Reconstruction, blacks considered public education 'a matter of personal liberation and a necessary function of a free society.'" A century and a half later, "the promise of public-school education ha[d] failed poor inner-city blacks." That was why, by the time *Zelman* reached the Supreme Court, "many blacks and other minorities" supported school choice programs.

To honor its promise of providing adequate public schooling to all its citizens, the State of Ohio had tried to experiment with a school choice program, empowering lower-income parents to choose whatever type of school was best for their children. Given this new power, Justice Thomas thought it no surprise that most parents picked higher-performing alternative schools over failing public ones.

"While the romanticized ideal of universal public education resonates with the cognoscenti who oppose vouchers, poor urban families just want the best education for their children, who will certainly need it to function in our high-tech and advanced society." Low-income parents were in no position to ignore what all knew to be true: Staying in school and getting a diploma "generates real and tangible financial benefits." Failing to earn a high school diploma "relegates students to a life of poverty, and all too often, of crime." Understanding this, Cleveland parents had no interest in sacrificing their children's success for a "romanticized ideal" of public schooling.

In conclusion, Justice Thomas noted that by the time this case had reached the Supreme Court, ten other states had designed their own school choice programs. These programs, he said, successfully allowed children to escape the "failing urban public schools," where so many attempted reforms had fallen short. He gave Frederick Douglass the last word: "No greater benefit can be bestowed upon a long benighted people, than giving to them, as we are here earnestly this day endeavoring to do, the means of an education."[28]

• • •

In *Zelman*, the Supreme Court approved Ohio's voucher program, but in Cleveland and elsewhere, the fight continues. Despite the resistance, parents continue to show up in force for school choice. Take Florida, for example: a *Wall Street Journal* editorial by William

Mattox credits "100,000 African-American 'school-choice moms'" for giving Governor Ron DeSantis "his narrow margin of victory in the 2018 gubernatorial election."[29]

While the Ohio leaders who pioneered the voucher program, including George Voinovich, Bishop Pilla, Bill Batchelder, David Brennan, Fannie Lewis, and Bill Patmon, have retired or passed away, their legacy lives on in the five educational choice programs operating in Ohio today. In Cleveland in the 2020–2021 school year, 7,886 students received vouchers to attend the school of their choice (and were able to choose from 58 participating schools). All Cleveland students are eligible to participate, but low-income students continue to get priority. Statewide, the EdChoice scholarship program allows more than 50,000 children to attend schools of their choice.[30]

At the same time, opponents of school choice programs have not given up, and to this day they continue to bring challenges, constitutional and otherwise, to such programs around the country. In Ohio, approximately one hundred public school districts recently filed suit in state court, challenging the EdChoice scholarship program.

Chapter 3

"Do Nothing with Us!"

Grutter v. Bollinger

S et in the quaint and beautiful city of Ann Arbor, the University of Michigan is older than the state itself. In 1817, the Michigan territorial government founded the university and located it in Detroit. In 1837, the state of Michigan was admitted to the Union. By June of that year, the state decided to move the university to Ann Arbor, where it has been ever since. In 1841, the university admitted its first class in Ann Arbor, with seven students total: six freshman and one sophomore.

By 1858, the university was thriving and making plans to add a law department. One year later, the law department opened with ninety students and three part-time faculty. The law department graduated its first class in 1860 and opened its own building in 1863.

Breaking barriers from the start, the law department admitted Gabriel Franklin Hargo, its first African American student, in 1868. Hargo graduated in 1870, the second African American in the entire nation to earn a law degree.[1]

That same year, the law department admitted its first woman, Sarah Killgore. In 1871, Killgore became the first woman ever to both graduate from law school and be admitted to the Michigan bar.[2] Her home state of Indiana was not as forward-thinking—when she returned there in 1873, she was not allowed to practice law.[3]

In 1915, the University of Michigan Regents officially renamed the law department the "Law School."[4] By 1997, the University of Michigan Law School had become one of the top-ranked law schools in the country.

As one of the nation's elite law schools, Michigan's goal was to train leaders for the next generation. And to accomplish that goal, Law School administrators believed that it needed to have a diverse student body.

But the educational pipeline was broken. The city of Cleveland was not alone in struggling to make high-quality education available. Across the country, receiving a quality K–12 education was more of an aspiration than a reality for most poor Americans. That, in turn, meant that the pool of qualified minority applicants to both colleges and law schools was small.

Barbara Grutter hoped to bring diversity to the Law School as a member of the class of 2000. Grutter was not your typical law school applicant. She was forty-three years old, married, and a mother of two boys. In the early '70s, she had put herself through college at Michigan State University, graduating with high honors and a 3.8 grade point average. She began a career as a consultant, assisting hospitals with technology. In that role, she saw the need for lawyers with healthcare experience, so she took the Law School Admission Test (LSAT). Grutter scored a 161, putting her in the top 14 percent nationally. She figured that her numbers and diverse life experience would make her application very attractive to the University of Michigan Law School. So, in December of 1996, she applied. Though she also applied to one other in-state law school, Michigan was her first choice by far. It offered more courses in the field of healthcare law than any other law school in the area.

On April 18, 1997, Grutter went to retrieve the mail. She found a small white envelope waiting for her. When it comes to applications, small envelopes are never a good sign. For Grutter, it wasn't what she'd hoped for, but it wasn't the worst news possible—she had been waitlisted. She waited and continued to hope. But a second small envelope arrived in June. She was denied admission.

Grutter's application coincided with changes to the Law School's admissions policies. To achieve its goal of student-body diversity, the Law School sought to enroll a "critical mass" of "African-Americans, Hispanics, and Native Americans." But there was one problem: prospective students in these groups tended not to perform as well when it came to undergraduate grade point averages and the LSAT. Of course, grades and test scores were only a part of any prospective student's application. The administrators at the Law School, however, believed those numbers were good predictors of success.

The LSAT is scored on a scale that ranges from 120 at the bottom to 180 at the top. In a standard year, the top 10 percent of applicants would score 164 or better, and Michigan's Law School would choose 90 percent of its white and Asian American law students from this pool. But to admit a "critical mass" of "minority students," Law School admissions personnel had to look to a broader pool of minority applicants. For example, in 1997, the Law School received 67 total applications from African American, Hispanic, or Native American students with an LSAT score of 164 or better. In contrast, there were 1236 white and Asian American applicants in that range. In 2000, "there were only 26 African-American applicants *nationwide* with at least a 3.5 GPA and a 165 on the LSAT compared to 3173 whites and Asian Americans" with the same scores.

The Law School dean recognized that this disparity was causing a problem in admissions. So, in 1992, the dean formed a committee to study the problem and put together a plan to ensure a diverse student body. The committee crafted a policy requiring admissions officers to look beyond grades and test scores and consider race as a factor in admissions. The goal, according to the committee, was to "achieve that diversity which has the potential to enrich everyone's education and thus make a law school class stronger than the sum of its parts."[5]

The policy initially defined a "critical mass" as between "11 and 17%" of the student body. But the committee decided to remove the range from the policy in order to keep it from looking like a rigid quota. Why? To head off potential legal problems. In 1978, in *Regents of the University of California v. Allan Bakke*, the Supreme Court had ruled that the Equal Protection Clause prohibited strict racial quotas. In that case, engineer and U.S. Marine officer Allan Bakke was denied admission to the University of California–Davis Medical School—even though his test scores were well above the average admittee's. At the time, UC–Davis used a rigid quota system. In a highly splintered decision, the Supreme Court ruled that a university could consider the race of the applicant but could not use rigid quotas.[6] In crafting its new policy, the Michigan Law School committee was attempting to comply with this precedent.

Just about that same time, a philosophy professor at Michigan's undergraduate school named Carl Cohen heard that the undergraduate college, like the Law School, was also using race as a factor in admissions. He submitted a Michigan Freedom of Information request to the university to find out more. The undergraduate college, he learned, was making admissions decisions by putting applicants in grids based on their grades and test scores. But not all applicants were treated the same: the University of Michigan created one grid for underrepresented racial minorities and another for everyone else. And starting in 1997, the university began giving each student in the "underrepresented minorities" grid an extra 0.5-point boost to his or her undergraduate GPA.[7] Incensed by what he had uncovered, Professor Cohen went public with the information.

Armed with this information, rejected applicants began calling the Center for Individual Rights. The Center had made a name for itself challenging race-based programs in higher education and representing students of all races. Just the year before, the Center had won an affirmative action case against the University of Texas.[8] Around the same time, the Center also sued historically black Alabama State University on behalf of a black graduate student named Jessie Tompkins, who had lost his scholarship because of an "other-race" scholarship program—in effect, a "whites-only" program.[9] The goal of the "other-race" scholarship program was to attract a "critical mass" of white students to the predominantly black institution.

While the Tompkins suit was ongoing, the Center started gathering information about the University of Michigan's admission practices and interviewing rejected applicants. Since the University of Michigan was a public university, it had to comply with the Fourteenth Amendment's Equal Protection Clause. The Center's research indicated that the affirmative action programs at both the university and the Law School were discriminating based on race.[10] But before it could bring a lawsuit, the Center needed to find a plaintiff who would become the face of the litigation—someone who would undoubtedly have been admitted if he or she had been one of the minorities selected for special treatment. For the Law School case, they found Barbara Grutter.

Grutter had many qualities that made her an appealing plaintiff. She was friendly, intelligent, and not someone looking for a fight. Indeed, she was an extremely private person who was happy raising her two young boys in anonymity. But Grutter believed she had been denied admission because of the Law School's racial discrimination policies—and that discrimination based on race was wrong. She had experienced discrimination based on sex firsthand and seen her "generation make significant strides against" such discrimination. Now, years later, she could not believe that she was "being discriminated against on yet another basis. This time, race." And by whom? Grutter pulled no punches describing university administrators: "By people who not only admit it but are also arrogant and elitist enough to tell me and others that it is somehow good for us. My answer to them is one word: No. Discrimination is wrong, it is personal, and it hurts everyone."[11]

The Center had found a plaintiff; next it needed to find her a lawyer. That wasn't an easy task. Most of the Michigan law firms the Center reached out to were not allowed to represent Grutter because they did other legal work for the University of Michigan. Others did not want to tangle with their state's university.

Michael McDonald, then a lawyer at the Center, contacted his law school classmate and friend Kirk Kolbo. Kolbo practiced general civil law in Minnesota and knew very little about affirmative action. He didn't have strong views on the issue, but the case sounded interesting, so he flew to Michigan with McDonald to interview Grutter. As soon as he met Grutter, he was in.

On December 3, 1997, Kolbo filed a complaint on Grutter's behalf in federal court in the Eastern District of Michigan. In early 2001, the court held a fifteen-day bench trial. Three witnesses who had served as directors of admissions at the Law School testified: Allan Stillwagon, Dennis Shields, and Erica Munzel.

Stillwagon had served as admissions director of the University of Michigan Law School from 1979 to 1990. During his tenure, promising applicants had been divided into three groups. Applicants in the first group were selected based on their GPA and LSAT scores. There was a second group that had lower scores but "interesting qualities." The third group he called a "special admissions" group for "minority candidates who did not fall within the other two groups." Stillwagon testified that half the minority applicants who were admitted came from this third group. He believed the "special admissions" group was necessary in order to keep minority enrollment at the requisite levels.[12]

According to Stillwagon, even though the admissions office imposed no explicit quota, in practice 10–12 percent of each class needed to be "Black, Chicano, Native American, and mainland Puerto Rican." Those making the admissions decisions had no discretion regarding this policy, and the number of minority students admitted could deviate by only a few students on either side of the range. He further testified that the Law School had to use the "special admissions" pool to obtain these numbers because of "'considerable differences' in academic credentials between the minority and non-minority applicants."[13]

Dennis Shields had taken over as admissions director in 1990 and served in that role until 1998. He said he didn't think that race was a primary consideration in admissions. But he acknowledged that during his years as director, at least 11 percent of each entering class included the preferred minorities. And during each admissions cycle, he kept track both of how many preferred minorities and of how many Michigan residents had been admitted.[14]

Erica Munzel had become the director of admissions in 1998. She, too, felt bound to make sure that each class had a "critical mass" of minority students. While she would not give a specific percentage, she agreed it had to be more than a "token" number. She further admitted that she had to consider race because if just LSAT scores and GPAs were considered, she could not achieve that "critical mass."[15]

Each party presented an expert. Kolbo called Kinley Larntz, who was a professor in the Department of Applied Statistics at the

University of Minnesota. Dr. Larntz testified that membership "in certain ethnic groups" was "an extremely strong factor in the decision for acceptance" to the Law School. He used grids to compare odds of acceptance between racial groups. Preferred minorities who were plotted in the same LSAT/GPA grid had odds of acceptance "tens to hundreds times that of a similarly situated Caucasian American applicant." According to Dr. Larntz, this was a "tremendous advantage" for the minority applicants.[16]

The Law School called Stephen Raudenbush, a professor of education at the University of Michigan. He said the Larntz study was flawed because it failed to consider "unquantifiable factors." Dr. Raudenbush further testified that eliminating the consideration of race would have a "'very dramatic' negative effect on minority admissions."[17]

After the trial, the district court issued its ruling. The court ruled that the Law School's admission policy violated the constitutional guarantee of Equal Protection. It found that "the evidence shows that race is not, as defendants have argued, merely one factor which is considered among many others in the admissions process. Rather, the evidence indisputably demonstrates that the law school places a very heavy emphasis on an applicant's race in deciding whether to accept or reject." The court specifically adopted Larntz's analysis and conclusion that "membership in certain ethnic groups is an extremely strong factor in the decision for acceptance."

In reaching its decision, the district court noted that the median undergraduate grade point average for preferred minorities was one-tenth to three-tenths less than the median grade point average for Caucasian applicants. The federal trial court admitted that the reasons for GPA disparities were complex, and that it was no surprise students who attended struggling K–12 schools were at a "competitive disadvantage" in college. "An educational deficit in the K–12 years will, for most students, have a negative ripple effect on academic performance in college," noted the court.

Next, it took note of the fact that the median LSAT score was seven to nine points lower for the preferred minorities. Intervenors in the lawsuit had argued that the test included a cultural bias and that minority test-takers suffered from a "stereotype threat," but the court was "unable to find anything in the content or design of the LSAT [that] biases the test for or against any racial group. If such a bias exists, it was not proved at trial." In creating a lower LSAT threshold for certain minority applicants, the trial court noted, Michigan was assuming that every member of a preferred minority group had suffered adversity justifying "some degree of upward adjustment," and that "no members of non-minority groups have suffered any adversity."

The district court sharply rebuffed the Law School's seemingly random and unjustified selection of the privileged racial groups. It noted that there was "no logical basis for the law school to have chosen the particular racial groups which receive special attention under the current admissions policy." Several years of admissions were at issue in the lawsuit. In some of those years, the court noted, "the law school bulletin indicated that special attention has been given to 'students who are African American, Mexican American, Native American, or Puerto Rican and raised on the U.S. mainland.'" But, the court pointed out, the Law School never offered "a principled explanation as to why it has singled out these particular groups for special attention."

The court further noted that other groups had suffered discrimination in America, including "Arabs and southern and eastern Europeans to name but a few." Yet the Law School did not consider whether sufficient numbers of these students were admitted. The exclusion of such groups from any preference, the court found, was cause for concern. The court had "heard nothing to suggest that the law school has concerned itself as to whether members of these groups are represented 'in meaningful numbers.'" Nor had the Law School attempted to justify other aspects of the program:

> No satisfactory explanation was offered for distinguishing between Puerto Ricans who were raised on the U.S. mainland from Puerto Ricans who were raised in Puerto Rico or elsewhere. No satisfactory explanation was offered for singling out Mexican Americans but, by implication, excluding from special consideration Hispanics who originate from countries other than Mexico. A special "commitment" is made to African Americans, but apparently none is made to blacks from other parts of the world.

The court concluded, "This haphazard selection of certain races is a far cry from the 'close fit' between the means and the ends that the Constitution demands in order for a racial classification to pass muster." Furthermore, looking ahead, the court highlighted the consequences if such a program were approved: "If the law school may single out these racial groups for a special commitment today, there is nothing to prevent it from enlarging, reducing, or shifting its list of preferred groups tomorrow without any reasoned basis or logical stopping point."

The district court didn't deny that the admissions statistics demonstrated a real obstacle to achieving diversity in higher education. But the only lawful solution, the court concluded, was to use constitutional methods to fix the system—such as investment in or reformation of "under-performing primary and secondary school systems." The district court acknowledged that this was a "social and political matter, which calls for social and political solutions." But what the Law School couldn't do was "prefer some applicants over others because of race." The Constitution did not permit it.[18]

The Law School appealed to the United States Court of Appeals for the Sixth Circuit, which sits in Cincinnati, Ohio. Most appeals are heard before a panel of three circuit judges. But the Sixth Circuit decided to hear the case before the full court of its then nine active judges—a rarely-employed tool known as an "en banc hearing." The full court heard argument on December 1, 2001. An exchange during that argument made clear what was at stake. One judge asked Michigan's counsel whether Barbara Grutter would have been admitted if she were black. Counsel admitted that she almost certainly would have been—but argued that "a black woman who had otherwise an application that looked like Barbara Grutter, that would be a different person."[19]

On May 14, 2002, the Sixth Circuit, by a vote of 5–4, reversed the district court's decision. This federal appeals court held that since the Law School was not using rigid quotas but rather a "plus" system to achieve a diverse student body, its plan was permissible. While the district court had been concerned about Michigan's apparent ad hoc selection of preferred races, the Sixth Circuit majority pointed out that "without such consideration, [those races] would probably not be represented in the Law School's student body in 'meaningful numbers.'"[20]

In dissent, Judge Danny Boggs stated that picking races, as the Law School did, has "a long and sordid history." While the Law School claimed that it gave meaningful consideration to everyone regardless of their race, Judge Boggs pointed out that a middle-range Asian applicant with an LSAT score of 164–66 and a GPA of 3.25–3.49 would have a 22 percent chance of admission, whereas the "under-represented minority applicant" with a score and grades in the same range would have "a guarantee of admission."[21]

Barbara Grutter sought Supreme Court review, and the Supreme Court granted her request, as well as granting review in the parallel undergraduate affirmative action case known as *Gratz v. Bollinger*. Both cases would be argued on the same day.

Immediately after the Supreme Court took up the case, the Center for Individual Rights approached the United States solicitor general's office about weighing in on its side. The Center's request touched off a month-long debate within the White House. The president's advisors fell into two groups. One group felt strongly that President George W. Bush should come out against "race-conscious admissions policies." Another group advised the president not to take a hard line, believing it would hurt the administration with minority voters.[22]

While the internal debate was taking place, outside groups were putting pressure on the administration to pick a side. Several conservative organizations asked the administration to side with Grutter. On the other hand, several prominent Hispanic organizations said that the percentage of Hispanic youth graduating from higher education would drop substantially if the Michigan plan was struck down.[23]

A bitter debate ensued in the halls of Congress about what stance the administration should take. Some senators warned the president that opposing affirmative action "could do significant harm to our system of higher education."[24]

After weighing his options, President Bush chose a middle ground. For him, the Michigan plans were a step too far. He believed that the undergraduate school was using a "quota system that unfairly rewards or penalizes prospective students, based solely on their race." He similarly had a problem with the Law School plan because "some minority students are admitted to meet percentage targets while other applicants with higher grades and better scores are passed over." At the same time, the president said he was a strong supporter of diversity on campus. But, he observed, diversity could be accomplished through race-neutral means and, he pointed out, California, Florida, and Texas had all found ways to do just that.[25]

On April 1, 2003, the Supreme Court heard arguments in Grutter's case. The argument was lively from the very beginning.

Kolbo went first. Justices O'Connor and Kennedy wanted to know if race could ever appropriately be considered in admissions. No, Kolbo said. The Constitution did not permit it. Rather than discriminating on the basis of race, the states needed to address the root of the problem and help students of all races succeed, he argued.

A group of retired military officers had filed a brief stating that affirmative action was necessary to ensure a diverse officer corps. Surely, Justice Ginsburg asked, having a diverse military is important? Kolbo answered that the military academies needed to try race-neutral alternatives such as targeted recruiting or considering socioeconomic status in admissions. The key, for Kolbo, was to allow applicants of all races to be able to "compete on the same footing."

Solicitor General Olson argued next. Justice Stevens immediately asked him about the retired military officers' brief. Olson agreed with Kolbo: the military academies, like everyone else, should use race-neutral means, such as recruiting, to achieve diversity. Only if that failed, he argued, could they resort to alternatives that discriminate on the basis of race. He then argued that the Law School had failed at every point and was using a "thinly disguised quota" and employing "stigmatizing and divisive racial stereotypes."

Finally, Michigan's lawyer, Maureen Mahoney, got up to argue. Mahoney was a seasoned and very well-respected Supreme Court litigator from the large law firm Latham & Watkins. She had previously clerked for Chief Justice Rehnquist and served as a deputy solicitor general during the administration of President George H. W. Bush.

Justice Scalia wanted to know why Michigan didn't just lower its admission standards across the board to accomplish its goals.

"If it's important enough to override the Constitution's prohibition of racial discrimination, it seems to me important enough to override Michigan's desire to have a super-duper law school?" Mahoney resisted the argument that Michigan had to choose between "academic excellence and racial diversity." She argued that Michigan had a compelling interest in an academically excellent law school that was racially diverse.

Justice Kennedy asked if the "critical mass" was nothing more than a disguised quota. Mahoney said there were no factual findings demonstrating that it was a quota.

Justice Ginsburg asked whether Michigan was using a plan similar to Harvard's, wherein race was one factor in more holistic evaluations. The Supreme Court had previously held up the "Harvard plan" as a model. Mahoney said yes—Harvard was achieving 8–9 percent African Americans with its plan, and Michigan was achieving 7–9 percent by employing the same strategies. At that point, Justice Scalia pointed out the antisemitic roots of Harvard's admissions policies: Harvard's "holistic plan" was originally created "to achieve diversity by reducing the number of Jewish students." In response, Mahoney said that Michigan was not using holistic admissions to exclude people, but rather "to include students of all races."

Justice Scalia then asked about the quota issue. Was 2 percent a critical mass? No. What about 4 percent? No again, Mahoney said. "Now does it stop being a quota because it's somewhere between 8 and 12, but it is a quota if it's 10?" Mahoney answered that it could not be a fixed range. That, she posited, would be a quota. Instead, the range was an "aspirational" goal, she said.

Justice O'Connor wanted to know when such racial preferences would finally not be necessary. Mahoney said she could not give a definite date but that there would come a day when they would no longer be necessary. She pointed out that progress had been slow:

"[I]n 1964, when there was a race-blind policy, there were no blacks admitted, and under a race-blind policy today, probably six blacks would be admitted." Mahoney acknowledged that only the highly selective law schools were having this problem, because of their preference for applicants with top scores and grade point averages.[26]

After the argument concluded, Barbara Grutter and her lawyers descended the Supreme Court steps and were swarmed by members of the press. One reporter asked Grutter whether affirmative action was actually beneficial to white women. Grutter said no. She explained that she had "had the privilege of working with many professional women. They are decisionmakers, they are producers, and in many cases, they are mothers. And in no case can I think of one situation where they have ever asked for preference, either for themselves, for their partners, or for their children." The women Grutter knew did not believe that "their daughters [should have] a preference over their sons. They are simply asking for the opportunity to compete, the opportunity to produce, and to be able to do that in an environment of equal treatment."[27]

On June 23, 2003, the Supreme Court announced its decision. By a 5–4 vote, the Court upheld Michigan's Law School admissions program. (In a separate decision the same day, the Supreme Court found that Michigan's undergraduate preference system was too much like a prohibited quota, so it struck it down as unconstitutional by a 6–3 vote.)

Justice O'Connor wrote the majority opinion. She was joined by Justices Stevens, Souter, Ginsburg, and Breyer.

Pointing back to Allan Bakke's case, the majority noted that the nation needs its future leaders to be exposed to a wide range of ideas, something that comes with having a diverse student body. In turn, the majority said that "student body diversity is a compelling state interest that can justify the use of race in university admissions."

At the same time, the majority recognized that when an individual is treated differently because of "her race, that person has suffered an injury that falls squarely within the language and spirit of the Constitution's guarantee of equal protection." So it was the job of the courts to review any such classifications closely to make sure they were "narrowly tailored" to achieving the goal of diversity. Context matters, said the majority: "Not every decision influenced by race is equally objectionable."

The majority held that law schools have a compelling interest in assuring a diverse student body, since it is essential to their educational mission. "Our holding today is in keeping with our tradition of giving a degree of deference to the university's academic decisions, within constitutionally prescribed limits." The Court would presume "good faith" on the university's part, "absent 'a showing to the contrary.'"

If "critical mass" were really a quota, that would be unconstitutional, said the majority. But the Court concluded the Law School's program was not a quota in disguise. Rather, the Law School defined "critical mass . . . by reference to the educational benefits the diversity is designed to produce." When the student body is diverse, the discussion and education are more lively. As a result, the students come out more prepared to work in society. Preparing the future workforce is the job of universities, and "major American businesses have made clear that the skills needed in today's increasingly global marketplace can only be developed through exposure to widely diverse people, cultures, ideas, and viewpoints." The majority highlighted the retired military officers' view that affirmative action also benefits the military.

Even when the university's interest is compelling, the school must pursue that interest by means that "fit the compelling goal so closely that there is little or no possibility that the motive for the classification was illegitimate racial prejudice or stereotype." Quota systems are unconstitutional because they mechanically require admission of a certain number of minority applicants regardless of the actual benefit to the student body or the needs of the institution. But the Court held that the university may consider race as a "plus" factor, even weighing it more than other factors, so long as it considers each application holistically. According to the majority, the Law School's plan met this requirement. The majority believed that the Law School "engage[d] in a highly individualized holistic review of each applicant's file, giving serious consideration to all the ways an applicant might contribute to a diverse educational environment."

Even so, the Court declined to embrace race-conscious admissions' programs indefinitely. The majority was "mindful" that "a core purpose of the Fourteenth Amendment was to do away with all governmentally imposed discrimination based on race." Thus, affirmative action policies "must be limited in time." Even the Law School had conceded as much. And progress had been made since Allan Bakke's case. So the Court set an expiration date on its own ruling: "We expect that 25 years from now, the use of racial preferences will no longer be necessary to further the interest approved today."[28]

All four dissenters wrote opinions. Justice Thomas wrote a dissent, which was joined by Justice Scalia. As in the Ohio voucher case, Justice Thomas began with words from Frederick Douglass: "What I ask for the negro is not benevolence, not pity, not sympathy, but simple *justice*. The American people have always been anxious to know what to do with us. I have but one answer . . . Do nothing with us! . . . And if the negro cannot stand on his own legs, let him fall also. All I ask is, give him a chance to stand on his own legs! Let him alone! . . . Your interference is doing him positive injury." Justice Thomas believed "that blacks can achieve in every avenue of American life without the meddling of university administrators."

While Justice Thomas sympathized with the university's goals, he noted, "Racial discrimination is not a permissible solution to the self-inflicted wounds of this elitist admissions policy." Just as law schools may not have *more* stringent admissions standards for black applicants, they cannot have more forgiving ones for "favored races." The Law School was well aware, Justice Thomas pointed out, that it could simply lower admissions standards across the board to achieve the racial makeup it desired. But it was not willing to do so.

"The majority upholds the Law School's racial discrimination not by interpreting the people's Constitution, but by responding to a faddish slogan of the cognoscenti." While Justice Thomas agreed with the majority that the Law School's policy would be illegal in twenty-five years, he pointed out the core originalist idea that the "Constitution means the same thing today as it will in 300 months." Thus, affirmative action was impermissible now, fads favoring "diversity" notwithstanding.

Starting with first principles, Justice Thomas noted that the equal protection principle had been "purchased at the price of immeasurable human suffering" and reflects America's hard-earned view that racial classifications "have a destructive impact on the individual and our society."

Next, Justice Thomas attacked the Law School's use of "diversity" as a justification: diversity "is a more fashionable catch-phrase than it is a useful term." The Law School simply wanted "to have a certain appearance," he claimed. In other words, he believed the Law School had pursued student body diversity for merely "aesthetic" reasons. Their policy was not aimed, he said, at helping "those too poor or uneducated to participate in elite higher education and therefore present[ed] only an illusory solution to the challenges facing our nation."

He next turned to the Law School's claim that it only had two options to achieve racial diversity: use affirmative action or sacrifice its elite status. Thomas pointed out "that other top law schools have succeeded in meeting their aesthetic demands without racial discrimination": "the sky ha[d] not fallen" at the University of California–Berkeley's law school when California banned the consideration of race. In fact, "total underrepresented minority student enrollment" at the law school actually increased after California's ban went into effect.

Justice Thomas also took issue with the majority's deference to the university's conclusion that "racial experimentation leads to educational benefits." He pointed out that studies show black students excel at historically black colleges despite those colleges' not having a significant white population to enliven conversation. Indeed, Morehouse College, "one of the most distinguished HBC's in the Nation," had a student body that is only 0.1 percent white and only 0.2 percent Hispanic. What if HBCs determined that their students actually benefit educationally from being part of a student body that is 100 percent black? Might they not argue they were entitled to similar deference, which could result in outright segregation? "Contained within today's majority opinion is the seed of a new constitutional justification for a concept I thought long and rightly rejected—racial segregation."

And why hadn't the Court applied this deference to other academic institutions of higher learning? There had not been a "word about academic freedom" when a majority of the Court accepted the Virginia Military Institute's representation that it would have to change its character and method of education if it admitted women, and yet that majority did not defer to VMI. Instead, it ruled that the school would have to admit women and deal with the resulting changes to its character. But here, the Court was deferring to the University of Michigan Law School's desire to maintain its elite character. "Apparently where the status quo being defended is that of the elite establishment—here the Law School—rather than the less fashionable Southern military institution, the Court will defer without serious inquiry and without regard to the applicable legal standard."

Justice Thomas also asked why law schools insisted on continuing to use LSAT scores if black applicants underperformed on that test, as the Law School itself had argued. Indeed, the Law School had admitted "that the test is imperfect," and its supporters could not agree on whether it was even useful. The Law School could simply scrap the LSAT and try an "infinite variety" of other admission models, he pointed out. But instead of making the Law School try other methods, the majority "prefer[red] instead to grant a 25-year license to violate the Constitution."

What's more, Justice Thomas noted, the Law School's program created perverse incentives that might entrench achievement gaps between white and minority students. White students are routinely rejected if they score between 163 and 167 on the LSAT. Thus, "whites aspiring to admission at the Law School have every incentive to improve their scores to levels above that range." But black students don't share that incentive since they may score much lower and have close-to-guaranteed admission: "[T]his racial discrimination will help fulfill the bigot's prophecy about black underperformance—just as it confirms the conspiracy theorist's belief that 'institutional racism' is at fault for every racial disparity in our society."

And what happens, Justice Thomas asked, to the students who are admitted because of affirmative action? Do they perform at the same level as the others? Do the law schools even care about the students' success, or only that their presence satisfies the schools' aesthetic goals? Justice Thomas found the Law School's "silence" on this score "deafening." "The Law School is not looking for those students who, despite a lower LSAT score or undergraduate grade point average, will succeed in the study of law. The Law School seeks only a façade—it is sufficient that the class looks right, even if it does not perform right."

Justice Thomas contended that "the aestheticists will never address the real problems facing 'underrepresented minorities,' instead continuing their social experiments on other people's children." Affirmative action programs "stamp minorities with a badge of inferiority and may cause them to develop dependencies or to adopt an attitude that they are 'entitled' to preferences." That hurts *all* black students—even those who would get in without affirmative action, Justice Thomas noted. When black students succeed, others question whether "their skin color played a part in their advancement."

Justice Thomas concluded, "It has been nearly 140 years since Frederick Douglass asked the intellectual ancestors of the Law School to 'do nothing with us!' and the Nation adopted the Fourteenth Amendment. Now we must wait another 25 years to see this principle of equality vindicated."[29]

• • •

After her case was closed, Barbara Grutter continued to endorse a view similar to Justice Thomas's: "[R]ace preferences don't fix problems; they hide them! They allow society to take the lazy route, pat itself on the back, and avoid addressing the root causes" of inequality.[30]

After the Supreme Court's decisions, the people of Michigan amended their state constitution in November 2006 to prohibit race-based admissions preferences in state universities. Following the change in law, the Law School abandoned its race-conscious policy and adopted race-neutral admissions criteria. And it appears that race-neutral means have accomplished diversity at the Law School. Its website now touts that 42 percent of the Law School class of 2025 is made up of students of color, the highest number to date.[31]

The fight over affirmative action continues to this day. At the time of this writing, the Supreme Court is considering whether the "Harvard plan" is still permissible—in litigation brought by rejected Asian students against the University of North Carolina and Harvard. Michigan filed a brief in support of its fellow universities.[32]

At the end of Justice Thomas's opinion in *Zelman v. Simmons-Harris*, the Cleveland voucher case, he noted that the public schools had failed poor black children.[33] For him, the best way to fix the diversity problem in higher education was the "constitutional way": by improving public schools and providing vouchers in the meantime.[34]

Jesse Tompkins lost his case against Alabama State. Both the district court and the Eleventh Circuit upheld the "whites only" scholarship program.[35] That scholarship program was the result of a previous case, *Knight v. Alabama*. In that case, the district court had ordered Alabama State to increase its white student population in order to address a perception—"deserved or not"—that historically black schools were inferior. The district court had concluded that "increasing the number of white students at [historically black colleges] helps eliminate that perception."[36] In making this point, the district court was responding to Justice Thomas's statement in a previous case: "It never ceases to amaze me that the courts are so willing to assume that anything that is predominantly black must be inferior."[37]

CHAPTER 4

The Professor and the Patient

Gonzales v. Raich

Once the pain started, relief was almost impossible to find. She usually felt the first pangs in her back—like someone was twisting a knife. But then it would spread like a snake down her legs and up her neck. Angel Raich dreaded it, and so did her two children. Angel was a single mother, and when the pain started, both of her children suffered alongside her.

Angel knew she had to get help. Otherwise, how could she be the mother she had always hoped to be? Therefore, in 1995, Angel started seeing doctors. The pain always started in the right side of her body, she told them. First, the doctors prescribed opiates. They deadened the pain, but violent vomiting took its place. And when one doctor gave up—they always did—she'd find another, hoping the new doctor would find some solution the others had missed. They never did.

Then it got worse. She woke up one morning with pain shooting down her body. Her right leg looked and felt like Jell-O. It was bright red and cold to the touch. Angel was scared. She tried to walk, but she couldn't. She started crying—she could not move her body from the waist down. And the pain was excruciating. Angel felt like her life was a living hell.

The only solution the doctors could think of was to put Angel in a wheelchair. The pain grew worse, and she grew desperate. Every part of her five-foot-four inch, one-hundred-pound body ached. The pain overwhelmed her thoughts. She could not concentrate on anything else. She could hardly think. Eventually, even sleep eluded her.

Angel couldn't take it anymore. She knew of only one way to end it, and that was to end it all. She had lost her will, her hope, and her desire to live. In August 1997, at the age of thirty-one, Angel tried to kill herself. Like all the previous attempts to end her pain, her suicide attempt did not succeed.

Since everything else had failed, Angel started praying. She promised God that she would do His work if He gave her back her legs. She even promised that she would try not to complain about the pain.

In late 1997, Angel visited a new doctor. At the beginning of the appointment, a nurse whispered a question to her: "Have you thought about using medical marijuana?" Angel was offended. She answered sternly, "I absolutely won't. It is wrong." Angel didn't even drink. Illegal drugs were out of the question.

She tried more prescription drugs. The result was the same: vomiting or severe allergic reactions.

Then, one night, Angel found her eight-year-old daughter crying. She asked, "Mommy, why can't you do what other mommies do? Why can't you play with me?" That sent Angel over the edge. She *had* to get out of her wheelchair. She heard the nurse's words again in her mind and considered that perhaps they were an unexpected answer to her prayer. Eventually, Angel gave in and tried some marijuana she got from a friend. The marijuana helped, but it wasn't the solution she was looking for. Her friend's marijuana was from the street. She was told that medical marijuana was different, and she decided to give it a try.

To Angel, medical marijuana was clearly a gift from above. As she puffed on it, she felt the drug relax her muscles and the pain start to recede. She couldn't believe it. Slowly, her strength and courage came back. After several months of using medical marijuana, she was able to walk. Next, she started attending physical therapy. She was even able to sleep. By 1998, Angel was living her life again. She became a member of the Oakland Cannabis Buyers' Cooperative. The organization provided Angel and thirteen other approved patients with their highly regulated medical marijuana.

During this time, Angel started dating the co-op's lead lawyer, Robert Raich. Rob, forty-five, had spent most of his adult life fighting to legalize medical marijuana. He had begun his efforts as a college student at Harvard, working on a Massachusetts bill to legalize medical marijuana. After law school, he worked for the federal government for a short while before starting his own legal practice in California.

To Angel, Rob seemed like the perfect teammate and spouse. They soon got married, and Angel started to settle into normal family life.

But life was about to change, and this time not for the better. The United States government sued the co-op to stop it from distributing marijuana in violation of federal drug laws. Judge Charles Breyer (the brother of Supreme Court Justice Stephen Breyer) sympathized with the government's argument and stopped the sales. Ultimately, in *United States v. Oakland Cannabis Buyers' Cooperative*, the Supreme Court agreed. The Supreme Court held that there is no medical exception to the Controlled Substances Act for medical marijuana.[1] This meant that cooperatives like Angel's were no longer allowed to supply people like Angel their marijuana.

Angel knew she couldn't go back to the way things were. Left with no alternatives, she turned to the streets. For Angel, this was unfamiliar territory, and the marijuana dealers knew it. Sometimes they robbed her. Other times, they just ripped her off. She paid a premium for the best she could find, but her street supply was often laced with other drugs and contaminated with everything from mold and fungus to pesticides and rat droppings. It was nothing like the highly regulated medical marijuana she could get from the co-op. For a mother, buying from dealers involved difficult choices, like which bills to ignore that month and which food to go short on.

Simply put, Angel's turn to the streets was a disaster. She was not equipped to be a common criminal. At some point, she learned that people could grow their own marijuana. Angel thought this was her solution. After all, she was good with her house plants. Could marijuana really be that much harder? Yes. Marijuana is no ordinary house plant. It needs space and ventilation. Even when Angel succeeded, she couldn't grow enough to meet her medical needs.

Back Angel went to the doctor and explained the problem. The doctor believed that without the marijuana, Angel's condition would rapidly decline, so he found a creative solution. If he issued a doctor's recommendation, under California law a grower was allowed to provide marijuana to Angel for free. Typically, the grower was a fellow sufferer who had the land and expertise to grow the marijuana. Angel thought her problems were solved.

She wasn't the only one to have found this solution. Diane Monson, also from California, suffered from a spinal disorder that caused intolerable spasms in her back. Like Angel, Diane had struggled for years to find a remedy. From 1989 to 2002, her doctors tried everything. But their prescriptions were ineffective at best, harmful at worst.

In 2002, Diane found her cure. As a last resort, her doctor prescribed medical marijuana. It solved her problems, just as it had Angel's. And unlike Angel, Diane succeeded at growing her cure: six marijuana plants in all. She grew the plants in her front yard. But that brought a different problem her way.

On August 15, 2002, Diane heard a knock on the door. The words that followed surprised her: "Police! Open up." Her local sheriff and the DEA had noticed the six plants in her yard. When they asked her about the plants, she told them she had a prescription. The local sheriff found Diane's prescription and told the DEA that her plants were legal under California law, and that he, therefore, supported her right to grow them. The DEA agents had a different view. The plants were still illegal under federal law, so they wanted to destroy them. Her sheriff balked and asked the DEA agents to leave her alone.

The situation grew tense: the sheriff called the local state prosecutor. The prosecutor agreed with the sheriff and ordered the local deputies to protect the marijuana plants from the DEA—at gunpoint if necessary.

Three hours into the standoff, the DEA agents reached out to the United States Attorney (the lead federal prosecutor in the area). The federal prosecutor called the state prosecutor and demanded that the local police stand down. Ultimately, the state prosecutor felt like he had no choice. And so, grudgingly, the local police backed off. The DEA agents seized and destroyed all six of Diane's cannabis plants. When Diane woke up that morning, she had had no idea her plants were illegal; now the only cure for her debilitating pain was gone.[2]

When Angel heard about Diane's predicament, she panicked. After the lawsuit against the co-op, Angel had become a national figure. She had been on national television, and she was on the record saying she could not follow any federal law that would stop her from using medical marijuana. Angel had tried to educate others by giving interviews, attending conferences, and teaching classes. She thought she was paying back the gift God had given her. But now, that notoriety made her a target. With the DEA having destroyed Diane's plants, Angel worried she was next.

Angel had a solution: sue the federal government. But how? First, Angel's legal team recruited Diane to be a part of the lawsuit. Next, the team ran the idea past Boston University law professor Randy Barnett, a rising superstar in the legal field. Rob Raich had previously recruited Professor Barnett to be part of the Oakland Cannabis legal team. Now Rob asked Barnett what he thought about a new lawsuit on behalf of Angel and Diane.

Professor Barnett is one of the leading proponents of the judicial theory of originalism. In fact, he has spent his career arguing that the Constitution, under its original meaning, does not provide the government with carte blanche to interfere with the lives of ordinary Americans.

When Professor Barnett heard about Angel and Diane's situation, he immediately signed on to the lawsuit. He saw the seizure as a major overreach by the federal government: California had passed a law explicitly allowing medical marijuana, and federal agents were interfering with state sovereignty. He believed this federal meddling was unconstitutional. This was the perfect case to test the federal government's power. And he now had two appealing clients with compelling stories.

When Angel met Professor Barnett, she immediately knew she could trust him. He was warm, caring, and, most important, brilliant.

After studying the case, Barnett constructed various theories. The one he liked the most hinged on the Commerce Clause. According to the Constitution, Congress can only regulate "commerce among the several States," otherwise known as *interstate* commerce.[3] Congress claimed to be using that power over interstate commerce to ban marijuana, but Angel and Diane were hardly engaged in commerce at all, let alone interstate commerce. They were not buying or selling marijuana. The marijuana they used was grown only in California, it was grown only for their personal consumption, and it did not cross state lines. Does the power to regulate interstate commerce include the power to ban marijuana grown and consumed in one state? Barnett didn't think so.

But this theory had a big problem: a sixty-year-old Supreme Court case called *Wickard v. Filburn.* In the late 1930s and early 1940s, a farmer named Roscoe Filburn grew wheat on his farm to feed his animals. He didn't sell the wheat out of state—in fact, he didn't even sell it to his neighbors. He produced 462 bushels of wheat on 23 acres, and that wheat never left his property. But to stabilize wheat prices in the Great Depression, the federal government had passed an act that limited the wheat per acre a farmer could grow. The government reasoned that less wheat in the market would help prices rise.

The act allowed Roscoe to produce only 223 bushels of wheat. The other 239 bushels he grew were subject to a penalty of 49 cents per bushel, or $117.41—a substantial amount of money back then. Rather than pay the penalty, Roscoe sued the federal government. He won in the lower court, but the government appealed to the Supreme Court.

At the Supreme Court, Roscoe pointed out that the limit on wheat production, as applied to his situation, violated the Commerce Clause. After all, his wheat was grown entirely within the state of Ohio and fed only his family and animals.

The government responded that Roscoe's wheat was still relevant to interstate commerce because the wheat that Roscoe grew himself was wheat he didn't have to buy on the open market. Of course, one farmer's wheat production isn't going to move the market, but the Supreme Court sided with the government anyway. This was a surprise. As the Court admitted, it had never allowed Congress to regulate activity "where no part of the product is intended for interstate commerce." Why the change? The Court accepted the government's theory that homegrown wheat could affect the supply and pricing of wheat in the market. Roscoe's bushels of wheat didn't matter on their own, but if farmers across the country started doing the same thing, the government would lose some of its power to set the price of wheat nationwide.

That was all the argument the government needed to get the Court to rule in its favor. The Constitution has a clause allowing Congress to make laws that are "necessary and proper" to carry out its powers. If Congress couldn't carry out its power to affect national prices without controlling backyard wheat supplies, then it must be allowed to control those supplies, too. The Court found that the individual wheat quota was "necessary and proper" in order for Congress to control interstate commerce, and thus constitutional. Roscoe had to pay up.[4]

Professor Barnett recognized that *Wickard* was an obstacle to his case, but perhaps not an insurmountable one. Unlike Roscoe, whose wheat fed livestock that could be considered part of a national market, Angel and Diane were using the marijuana only for their own medicinal purposes. That made *Wickard* distinguishable. If Barnett succeeded in getting the Court to draw a line there, perhaps it would help rein in what he believed was an out-of-control federal government.

By October 2002, the team was ready to sue. Complaint in hand, they went to the local federal courthouse and filed their case. They asked the court to stop the federal government from exceeding its power and seizing privately grown medical cannabis. In other words, they asked the court to tell the federal government to leave Angel and Diane alone.

When a lawyer files a case in federal court, a judge is assigned to the case at random. Angel and Diane's case was assigned to District Judge Martin Jenkins. District court judges are the lead judges on cases—the ones who handle trials and give initial decisions. When

Judge Jenkins drew the case, he had been a federal judge for five years; President Clinton had appointed him in 1997. Before his appointment to the federal bench, Judge Jenkins had been a state court judge for eight years. But perhaps the most interesting fact about Judge Jenkins's biography is his brief tenure in the National Football League as a defensive back for the Seattle Seahawks. After two games, however, he decided that he preferred a career in the law, so he retired from the NFL and enrolled at the University of San Francisco Law School.

Angel and Diane were probably glad of another fact about Judge Jenkins—he was known to be compassionate. One day, when he was working at a homeless shelter handing out lunches and blankets, a homeless man commented on how much he liked Judge Jenkins's shoes. The judge sat down on the curb and took them off. "These were new to me yesterday," he said. "Now they are new to you."[5]

Judge Jenkins was also known as someone who would follow the law. Unfortunately for Angel and Diane, this fidelity ultimately prevailed. Judge Jenkins recognized Angel and Diane's serious medical need and California's interest in providing marijuana to patients like them. He understood the "severe harm and hardship" a ruling against them would pose. But he believed that the law, and the *Wickard* wheat case in particular, required him to rule against them. To his thinking, this precedent dictated that the Controlled Substances Act was constitutional even when it reached purely intrastate conduct. As a result, Judge Jenkins denied Angel and Diane's request to stop the federal government from taking their medical marijuana.[6]

But this was only the first step in Angel and Diane's legal journey. They filed an appeal, which went to the Ninth Circuit. There, they found a sympathetic audience. At federal courts of appeals, litigants ordinarily find themselves in front of three-judge panels. The three judges that Angel and Diane drew were Harry Pregerson, Richard Paez, and Arlen Beam.

Judge Pregerson was a former Marine who had been injured during World War II. He was first appointed to the district court by President Lyndon Johnson. President Jimmy Carter then appointed him to the Ninth Circuit. Judge Pregerson had a reputation as one of the most liberal judges on the court and was described by an advocate as "one of the most successful social engineering judges in the country."[7]

Judge Richard Paez had also spent some time as a trial judge; he had been nominated to the district court by President Clinton as the first Mexican-American district court judge in Los Angeles. He spent only six years there before President Clinton tapped him again, for the Ninth Circuit.[8]

Finally, Judge Arlen Beam was born in rural Nebraska. He had served in the United States Army during the Korean War and achieved the rank of captain. Like his two colleagues, he had also served as a federal district court judge—appointed by President Ronald Reagan. But he wasn't in that position for long; President Reagan appointed him to the Eighth Circuit one year later. He was a visiting judge on the Ninth Circuit when this case was drawn.[9]

Ultimately, Judges Pregerson and Paez found that purely "intrastate" cultivation and use of marijuana for personal medical purposes was different from drug trafficking, and that cultivation does not raise "the same policy concerns regarding the spread of drug abuse." They ruled for Angel and Diane.

How did they get around *Wickard*? The Supreme Court cases after *Wickard* had settled on a general rule: Congress could regulate intrastate commercial activity so long as it had a "substantial" effect on interstate commerce. The majority started there and made two points. First, any effect Angel and Diane might have on interstate commerce was incidental, not substantial. Second, the regulated activity was not commercial at all—Angel and Diane only wanted to grow marijuana for personal use. No sellers, no buyers, no commerce.

Judge Beam disagreed. He pointed out that Angel and Diane's conduct was not much different from Roscoe's. Roscoe, too, was growing a crop for his own personal use, but that didn't stop Congress from getting involved. Sure, Roscoe grew wheat and Diane grew marijuana, but why should that make a difference? As Judge Beam pointed out, both goods have a commercial market—one just happens to be illegal at the federal level. Growing marijuana for personal consumption affects the marijuana market just as growing wheat for personal consumption affects the wheat market. To Judge Beam, the two situations were almost identical. Like Judge Jenkins, he believed *Wickard* required him to rule for the government. But he was in dissent, so he didn't stand in the way of Angel and Diane's success. They were relieved and happy. They thought they had their lives back. Their happiness, though, was short lived.

The government was not done. It was determined to get the Supreme Court to review the case. So it brought out its ace in the hole, Solicitor General Paul Clement. There is little debate that Paul Clement is the gold standard among appellate advocates. He has been called the greatest Supreme Court advocate of all time. Blessed with a photographic memory, Clement never brings notes to argue his cases. No matter the case, his presence and intellectual prowess demand the thoughtful attention of judges. Even in the Supreme Court, Clement commands a level of respect afforded to very few advocates. David, meet Goliath.

The Supreme Court rejects most requests for review. If you roll the dice, the odds of any one case being selected are less than 1 percent. But those odds shoot up when the government makes the request. Why? The government does not seek Supreme Court review often, and when it does, it's usually for a good reason. The justices pay special attention to government requests, and this case was no exception. Rob and Professor Barnett argued that the Supreme Court should not take the case, but they were also realistic. They told Angel and Diane to be ready for the fight to go to the national stage.

Sure enough, the Supreme Court decided to hear the case. Angel and Diane were going to Washington.

After the briefs were filed in the Supreme Court, Rob and Professor Barnett prepared for argument. Recognizing the obstacle that they faced in *Wickard*, they planned a two-pronged attack. First, they would argue that the Supreme Court could leave *Wickard* in place and still rule for Angel and Diane. How? *Wickard,* they argued, involved quintessential economic activity—commercial farming. Angel and Diane were not engaged in any commercial activity. The quantities of marijuana involved here were minuscule when compared to Roscoe's 462 bushels of wheat. Second, the government in *Wickard* demonstrated there was a "substantial aggregate effect" on interstate commerce. Here, it had made no such showing.

While Barnett's ultimate goal was to overturn *Wickard*, he knew he had to do what was best for his clients, and that the Supreme Court is reluctant to overturn its prior cases. That's why Barnett's first line of attack was to clarify *Wickard* and distinguish it—to show why it did not apply here. But he also recognized that the government would try to fit his case within the *Wickard* rule, so he was prepared to ask the Court to overrule it.

There was one additional issue looming over the case: Who would argue it? Rob wanted Barnett to argue the case before the Court, but others on the team disagreed. Arguing a case in the Supreme Court is a big deal. The law firm that had assisted Rob and Barnett with the brief had plenty of experienced lawyers. Professor Barnett, on the other hand, had never argued a case before the Supreme Court, as the law firm pointed out to Angel and Diane.

Nonetheless, for Angel and Diane, the choice was easy: Barnett would represent them before the nation's highest court.

To Professor Barnett, this was not just another argument. He sincerely believed in narrowing the scope of federal power.

Barnett knew he had to prepare like this was the Super Bowl. He set up various practice arguments. The first was at Georgetown's Supreme Court Institute. The lawyers on the panel destroyed him. They asked him "slippery-slope" questions he couldn't answer. This case is about medical marijuana in California, but how far would a ruling for the plaintiffs go? Where the Constitution is concerned, what's the difference between medical and non-medical marijuana? What's the difference between "legal" marijuana in California, and illegal marijuana in any other state? And why stop at marijuana? If the federal government can't ban homegrown marijuana, does that mean it can't ban homemade methamphetamine? Professor Barnett knew that if his answer to that last question was "yes," he was in trouble. But he didn't know what else to say.

Professor Barnett was despondent. Three weeks before oral argument, and he could not answer the tough questions. The next day, he happened to be having lunch with a federal judge in D.C. Explaining the problem he had in the moot court, Barnett found himself making a new and different argument to distinguish state-authorized medical marijuana from other hypothetical situations. With this theory in hand, he traveled to Oklahoma City for his second moot court. There, three excellent professors challenged him, but they did not ask the slippery-slope questions—whether the government could regulate things like basement meth labs. He did fine, but he needed to be pushed on the slippery-slope issue.

The third moot court was sure to do that. Professor Barnett scheduled it at Harvard, where he had gone to law school. On the panel were his torts and property professors from his first year there.

The Harvard professors hit him hard, but this time he was prepared. He said Congress could regulate purely intrastate activity if it was essential to their broader regulatory scheme—but Angel and Diane's medical marijuana was not. Because the argument differed from the briefs, it confused the panel, but it did answer the slippery-slope questions. Barnett knew he would have to make his argument more clearly before the Court. But now he felt ready to do so.

As argument day approached, Angel and Diane grew nervous. In their minds, this was their chance to help many people who needed medical marijuana. What if they lost? What if it was taken from them, and others like them, forever? The marijuana made their lives worth living. They both knew they were not equipped to become criminals to obtain their cure. They were at wits' end when argument day arrived—November 29, 2004.

The weather was crisp and the sky was blue as Angel and Diane approached the Court. The Supreme Court building looked like a marble palace against the clear sky. One thing stood out to them—the pledge inscribed above the sixteen marble columns, "Equal Justice Under the Law." They hoped it applied to them.

As they walked through security, Angel and Diane noticed the magnificent entrance and the imposing statues aligning the main corridor. But they were shocked when they entered the chamber where the argument would be held. It was tiny. The advocates, and even the clients themselves, were much closer to the justices than they had anticipated. Even Judge Jones's courtroom had seemed bigger. They took their seats and waited.

As the justices entered the courtroom, everyone rose. Chief Justice Rehnquist was ill, so the next most senior justice, John Paul Stevens, presided over the argument. Solicitor General Clement went first. His argument appeared to go smoothly, and Angel and Diane realized that, to the justices, this case was about much more than the two of them.

Sure, Angel and Diane were just growing a little bit of marijuana, but if they could do it, couldn't tens of thousands more? According to one brief, California had more than one hundred thousand cancer patients; if they could all use medical marijuana, wouldn't that affect the marijuana market overall? Wouldn't allowing Angel and Diane to use the marijuana they grew force judges to allow communes to grow and use marijuana in bulk? Plus, why should judges decide whether marijuana has medicinal value? Wouldn't the FDA know better? If marijuana truly had medical benefits, why not get the FDA to reclassify it so physicians could prescribe it? And, of course, why shouldn't *Wickard* control this case?

Barnett stood up, ready for each of these questions. His answers came back to the key theory: homegrown marijuana was not interstate commerce. In fact, it was not economic activity of any kind. Under the Supreme Court's recent "federalism decisions," it did not matter whether noneconomic activity had a substantial effect on commerce. Such activity could not be restricted as a means of regulating interstate commerce.[10] If the justices bought that argument, he would win.

They didn't seem convinced. Every justice who questioned Barnett seemed antagonistic to his theory. Angel and Diane left the courthouse full of doubt. They were afraid that, once again, their ability to cope with their pain and illness would be taken from them. Even more, they feared that this case would take it from everyone else.

Now the waiting game began. They had no idea when they would get a decision. Months passed, and then on June 6, 2005—a full six months later—it happened. The nine justices took the bench and announced the result. Angel and Diane lost six to three.

Justice John Paul Stevens announced the decision against them. His opinion was joined by Justices Souter, Kennedy, Ginsburg, and Breyer. This majority held that Angel and Diane's activities were "economic"—according to a 1966 edition of Webster's dictionary, which defined "economic" as "the production, distribution, and consumption of commodities."[11] Just as wheat was a commodity, so, too, was marijuana. Therefore, there was no difference between this case and *Wickard*: if Congress could regulate the intrastate production of wheat to protect the interstate market, it could do the same with the intrastate production of marijuana.

What shocked Angel and Diane more than the vote tally was who voted against them—all the justices people had told them were liberal. Why wouldn't these justices be sympathetic to their plight? Weren't those the justices who were supposed to favor the "little guy"? Why would Justice Ruth Bader Ginsburg vote against them? At the very least, they had thought they could count on her.

Equally shocking to Angel and Diane, but not to Rob and Barnett, were the justices who voted with them. Justice Scalia was not with them, but Justice Thomas was. Justice O'Connor and Chief Justice Rehnquist also sided with Angel and Diane in a separate opinion.

Justice Thomas agreed with Barnett's argument. There was simply no interstate commerce here. Angel and Diane's privately grown marijuana never crossed state lines—what was "interstate" about that? As for "commerce," Justice Thomas pointed out that Angel and Diane did not purchase the marijuana. He explained that at the time of the nation's Founding, "commerce consisted of selling, buying, and bartering, as well as transporting for these purposes." Since Angel's and Diane's conduct wasn't truly commerce according to the original meaning of the Constitution, it was beyond the power of Congress to regulate their conduct. It was that simple. After all, the federal government was established as a government of "limited and enumerated powers."

Justice Thomas concluded with a note of sympathy for Angel and Diane. In his view, it was clear that California had devised a drug policy that provided "much-needed respite to the seriously ill." In their rush to embrace federal power, he claimed, the justices in the majority forgot that states have a unique prerogative "to decide for themselves how to safeguard the health and welfare of their citizens."

Could Congress override these state prerogatives through its legislative powers? Sure, according to Thomas, but only by exercising one of its specific powers enumerated in the Constitution. If Congress wanted to rely on the Commerce Clause, it had better be regulating interstate commerce. And that wasn't the case here, Thomas argued.

Justice Scalia agreed to some extent, but he had a broader reading of Congress's power under the Constitution. Why? The Constitution has a clause that gives Congress the ability to make laws that are "necessary and proper" for carrying out its other powers. In Justice Scalia's view, this clause boosts Congress's power: not only could Congress regulate interstate commerce, but it could also regulate local activity it deemed necessary in order to make its regulation of interstate commerce effective.

Congress's goal here was simple: completely eradicating marijuana from interstate commerce. As Justice Scalia saw it, marijuana grown at home for personal use "is never more than an instant from the interstate market." Whether it was for medicinal use that was lawful under state law was irrelevant—marijuana could easily find its way into cross-country trade. Congress could reasonably conclude that its regulatory scheme would be undercut if this type of marijuana was allowed to be grown. That was enough for Justice Scalia to decide that regulating intrastate marijuana was necessary and proper.

Justice Thomas thought this reasoning went too far. He argued that simply having "some conceivable" connection to interstate commerce is not enough for Congress to step in and regulate homegrown medical marijuana. California had strict controls in place to make sure the medicinal marijuana would never reach the broader market, and those controls seemed to be working—no one argued that the use of medical marijuana had in fact undermined Congress's regulatory scheme. So it simply was not "necessary" to regulate Angel and Diane's medical marijuana. Nor was it "proper." The Constitution did not give Congress the power to ban marijuana in California—that sort of power had long been left to the states. In Justice Thomas's view, it was improper for Congress to use the Commerce Clause to accomplish something it otherwise could not.

Angel and Diane were distraught. They believed they had lost their lifeline. But Barnett had some good news. There was one topic that the Supreme Court had sent back down to the court of appeals: whether Angel and Diane had a "substantive due process" right to medically necessary drugs. It was a long shot, but the fight could continue. Still, they had lost on the major issue. Had the team won this case, the people of California could fill their prescriptions in peace, under their carefully crafted state law. No longer.

Things did not go as the team hoped after the Supreme Court case. Angel and Rob had a falling out. Diane, an extremely private person, decided that she was done being in the spotlight and withdrew from the lawsuit. In the end, Angel lost her final fight in the Ninth Circuit. Her journey through the American justice system was over, and she still felt far from justice. Nearly two decades later, Angel's life continues to be a testament to human resilience. In her years fighting a brain tumor, she has endured setbacks, inconveniences, and pain as a consequence of shifting and inconsistently enforced cannabis laws. Since she is allergic to many standard pain medications, surgeons told her to smoke marijuana in her car in the hospital parking lot before surgery to avoid the pain. She still lives in California and continues to fight illness to this day.

Rob described Justice Thomas's opinion as the best piece of legal craftsmanship he had ever read. He was shocked it did not convince the other justices. To Rob, this case remains a no-brainer, and he hopes in the future to bring another challenge. He has been encouraging states to legalize medical marijuana in the hope that if a consensus builds among the states, the Supreme Court will take another look.

Barnett was disappointed but not surprised with the vote. He had known from the beginning that it would be an uphill battle, but he had also known that as long as he had Justice Thomas in his corner, he had a fighting chance. The fact his clients also got the votes of Chief Justice Rehnquist and Justice O'Connor meant he had beaten the spread.

CHAPTER 5

Standing Alone

Doe v. United States

S enior year in high school is stressful and exciting. For a lot of young people, it is the first time they contemplate leaving the comfortable confines of their home. "Jane Doe" was no different. She had worked hard to balance her studies, extracurricular activities, and a job. She was smart, athletic, and determined to make a difference.[1]

While many young people with her record might dream of attending an Ivy League school, Jane had other ideas. Growing up in a military family, Jane understood that life was about more than transcripts and report cards.

Like many high school seniors, she received brochures pitching some of the nation's best schools. One stood out. Like the others, it was academically elite. But it promised more. The brochure described an institution founded on "Duty, Honor, and Country," and featured glossy pictures of women in uniform and leadership.[2]

Jane was hooked: her new dream was to attend the United States Military Academy, more commonly known as West Point.[3]

Originally established as a fort, West Point sits on the shore of the Hudson River and spans almost sixteen thousand acres. The gray buildings interrupt the greenery above the Hudson, but the campus is not an eyesore. The understated buildings, secluded behind an imposing fort wall, have a beauty of their own. Looking at the school from the river, one can see the grandeur of the fort. More important, that grandeur reminds cadets that the school is no ordinary college.

West Point has an illustrious history. No Army post in the country is older. In 1778, George Washington considered West Point to be the most important strategic location in the United States, so he ordered that a fort be built there. In 1779, during the height of the Revolutionary War, he moved his headquarters there. The Army has kept troops there ever since.[4]

As president, the former general knew the importance of training the nation's future leaders. Therefore, President Washington proposed opening a military academy at West Point. While placing a fort there was easy for General Washington, President Washington had a hard time convincing others to make it the nation's premiere military academy. Ultimately, Secretary of State Thomas Jefferson scuttled President Washington's plans. But when he himself became president a few years later, Jefferson recognized Washington's wisdom, and West Point Academy was born.[5]

Today, the excellence that Washington envisioned pervades the academy. The school counts among its alumni two presidents (Ulysses S. Grant and Dwight D. Eisenhower), numerous generals, CEOs, astronauts, Rhodes Scholars, and even one of the greatest college basketball coaches of all time—Mike Krzyzewski (affectionately known as Coach K).[6]

The more Jane learned about West Point, the more she wanted to attend. She knew it would provide the academic rigor she sought and a true physical challenge.[7] After graduation, she would have the honor of serving her country. Jane was confident she could succeed if she got into West Point, so she turned her attention to the application process.

Getting into a military academy is not like applying to other elite institutions. Jane needed a nomination from a politician. Luckily, Jane's qualifications would impress anyone—she was near the top of her class and participated in multiple extracurricular activities. After seeing her record, her congressman was happy to nominate her. One of her senators followed suit and listed Jane as the top candidate in her state![8]

On June 30, 2008, she accepted admission to the United States Military Academy and signed an oath of allegiance committing her to serve for eight years after she graduated, including five years on active duty. In exchange, her tuition, books, and room and board were fully paid for by the United States.[9]

Jane's class numbered about thirteen hundred cadets; about two hundred of them were women.[10] That small number did not discourage her. She knew that with her work ethic, intelligence, and agility, she could succeed at West Point.

And succeed she did. She flourished from the start. Indeed, one faculty evaluation said that Jane had "what it takes" and that she was "one of the most professional and internally motivated cadets I've worked with." The evaluation predicted that "she will excel as an Army officer." It finished with this endorsement: "I would gladly recruit her to serve on my team, regardless of the mission." Perhaps the highest praise a student at West Point could receive—and that was when Jane was only in her first year at the academy.[11]

Despite her success, all was not well with Jane. She felt like harassment was part of the culture at West Point, and she believed that to succeed she would have to conform to "male norms." She also felt pressure to match the male cadets' physical capabilities.[12]

Even though she was excelling in the classroom, she contemplated leaving after her first year. She started to suffer from anxiety and had trouble sleeping. For her sleeping problems, she was prescribed medication. That medication, however, came with its own set of problems, including impaired awareness and memory loss. True to form, Jane gutted it out. She was committed to graduating and becoming a soldier.[13]

Then, one night, things changed. Jane took her sleep medication before going to bed, as was her routine.[14] At one o'clock in the morning, she heard a knock. It was a friend, "Robert Smith," who said he needed someone to talk to and asked if she would walk with him.[15] She agreed, even though it was a violation of school rules to be out so late.

Smith was a former combat veteran who had enrolled at West Point. He had already completed a tour of duty, so he was older and more seasoned than most cadets.[16]

Smith told Jane that he suffered from post-traumatic stress disorder, and that, rather than take medication or seek counseling, he drank alcohol to deaden the pain.[17] Jane may have wondered why Smith confided in her rather than his girlfriend, but if she did, she didn't say anything.

They eventually made their way into an academic building. Smith took out some alcohol and started drinking. When he offered Jane some, she accepted—a dangerous, toxic combination with her sleep medication.[18]

Jane slowly drifted off into a state of unconsciousness. Then the unthinkable happened. Smith forced her onto the cold, concrete floor in the boiler room and raped her.[19]

Jane woke up in her bed with dirt in her hair, bruises on her lower back, and blood between her legs. She could hardly remember the attack.[20]

She didn't know what to do, but a friend recommended she go to the on-campus health center. There, the nurse informed her that she was suffering from vaginal tearing.[21]

After she built up the courage, she privately confronted Smith. He smiled and claimed the sex had been consensual. Jane knew otherwise; she felt horrified and violated. She believed he had taken advantage of her, and she let him know it. He apologized and admitted to being a "creep." His excuse: the alcohol took over, and he must have lost control.[22]

When Jane saw her psychiatrist, he referred her to the Sexual Assault Response counselor. The counselor told her she had two options: file an unrestricted report with her name and the name of her attacker or file a restricted report that would keep the parties' identities confidential. She chose the latter option because she feared for her prospects in the Army if she publicly accused another cadet. She might be labeled a troublemaker or even a liar, and that would impact her career in the Army. She also worried that she would be punished for drinking and being out after curfew.[23]

The rape impacted Jane profoundly. She felt isolated, and her anxiety went through the roof. To top it off, she was approaching the completion of her second year, and she needed to make a decision: if she left at that point, before her third year at West Point, she would not have to pay the military back for the first two years. With her anxiety skyrocketing, she decided she could not bear the financial risk of staying and possibly quitting later. She gave up on her dream and left. On August 10, 2010, she told West Point she was leaving, and on August 13, 2010, West Point gave her an honorable discharge.[24]

Being the fighter she is, Jane did not give up. She went to another college and graduated. But her emotional struggles have not subsided and probably never will.[25]

After graduating from college, Jane decided to sue West Point. Luckily, an elite veterans' legal clinic, housed at Yale Law School and staffed by student volunteers under the tutelage of a law professor, took her case.[26]

The clinic filed several claims on her behalf, including one under the Federal Tort Claims Act. In that claim, Jane asserted that the superintendent of West Point and the commandant of the cadets were aware of numerous acts of sexual violence at West Point but did nothing. How did she know they were aware of the assaults? Because, she said, there had been congressional hearings about the previous incidents and various internal investigations. If that was not enough, the media had also covered the incidents and investigations.[27]

Rather than control the environment that allowed these sexual assaults to occur, she claimed, the leadership fostered it. In doing so, they "failed to comply with [Department of Defense] directives intended to reduce rape and sexual assault."[28] In sum, Jane claimed that the leadership's negligence created a culture where rape was possible, and many victims felt too intimidated to seek justice.[29]

She filed suit with the hope that she would be given the chance to prove her allegations in court. If this suit was against a normal college, that would not have been a problem. But the United States Military Academy was different.

When our country was founded, we broke away from many English legal traditions, including the notion that "the king can do no wrong." But even as we rejected that maxim, we kept immunity for our government. However, as government became more involved in daily life, the public demanded that some of that immunity be removed. Specifically, the government could no longer be allowed to injure people with impunity. Thus, in the 1946 Federal Tort Claims Act, Congress allowed people to bring tort suits for any personal injury that resulted from the negligence "of any employee of the Government while acting within the scope of his office or employment."[30]

That should help Jane, one would think, but in 1950 the Supreme Court had created a new rule in *Feres v. United States*. *Feres* involved three separate lawsuits. In the first, a soldier had perished in a fire at his barracks because of an allegedly defective heating plant. In the second case, an Army doctor had performed surgery on a soldier and left a 30-inch-long, 18-inch-wide towel inside the soldier's abdomen. The towel was later discovered in his stomach, the label still clearly reading "Medical Department U.S. Army." In the final case, a soldier had died because of allegedly negligent medical care by unskilled physicians. The Supreme Court recognized that the plain language of the Claims Act—which had been passed just a few years before these lawsuits—would allow each of these members of the military to sue. Nonetheless, the Court made a policy determination: the victims should not be able to sue "where the injuries arise out of or are in the course of activity incident to service."[31] This language is found nowhere in the statute.

Despite this lack of textual foundation, in 1983 the Supreme Court extended the rationale of *Feres* in *Chappell v. Wallace*. There the Court held that military personnel could not recover damages even when their superiors violated the Constitution. In that case, five black Navy men claimed their superiors discriminated against them because of race. Officers assigned the men the worst duties, excluded them from training, gave them poor performance evaluation, and punished them severely for any violation. In dismissing the lawsuit, the Supreme Court explained that *Feres* rested on functional considerations: if subordinates could sue their commanding officers, the whole military discipline system would crumble.[32]

With this precedent, Jane's lawsuit faced an uphill climb. Ultimately, the district judge felt cabined by this case law and dismissed her case. At the United States Court of Appeals for the Second Circuit, she met the same fate. The court of appeals said that *Feres* barred her lawsuit because the rape was "incident to her service."[33]

Jane's lawyers sought certiorari in the United States Supreme Court. They argued that *Feres* should be overruled or limited so that people like Jane could bring their claims. While a petitioner needs five justices to win a case, she only needs four to vote to take the case. Jane, though, got only one vote—from Justice Clarence Thomas.

When the Supreme Court declines to take a case, usually the justices remain silent about their reasoning. But Justice Thomas chose to write a decision explaining why the Court should have taken Jane's case. First, he pointed out that Jane should have been able to proceed with her case under the plain language of the Federal Tort Claims Act. The act allowed recovery for negligence, and it did not bar service members from seeking recovery except for "combatant activities . . . during time of war."[34] The rape obviously was not a combatant activity. That should have been the end of it. Instead, in an act of "judicial legislating," the Supreme Court had created an additional bar to recovery in *Feres*. And for "70 years," the Supreme Court had followed that precedent to the detriment of people like Jane.[35]

Justice Thomas went on to point out the perverse results this had created. "Under our precedent, if two Pentagon employees—one civilian and one a servicemember—are hit by a bus in a Pentagon parking lot and sue, it may be that only the civilian would have a chance to litigate his claim on the merits."[36] If nothing else, he argued that the Court should take Jane's case to clarify what precisely is "incident" to military service: because the Court made the phrase up, there is no statutory language defining it, and without a definition, lower courts have struggled to apply the rule. Justice Thomas pointed out that one lower court had barred the lawsuit of a service member who had been injured when skiing behind a recreational boat that belonged to the military, while another service member was allowed to go forward with a claim that he had been injured by the negligent operation of an Army van. Without guidance, there was no consistency.[37]

Referring to Jane's case in particular, Justice Thomas noted that "one might be concerned to find out that a student's rape is considered injury incident to military service."[38] Yet, that is what the court of appeals had held. The opportunity was ripe to bid *Feres* farewell—but only Justice Thomas was willing to do so.

CHAPTER 6

Beauty and the Beast

McKee v. Cosby

From the time she was a young child, Kathrine McKee had dreams that were larger than life. Each time Kathy and her best friend went to a theater in her hometown of Detroit, they would watch movies all day, idolizing the stars on the silver screen. Doris Day was her favorite actress. Hours after the credits rolled, young Kathy wondered what it would be like to be Doris Day.[1]

By age twelve, Kathy was ready to graduate from audience member to actress. Well, almost ready. Her dressing room was the Hudson's Department Store, the small bar next door was her stage, and the bar's patrons—mostly pilots and stewardesses—were her adoring fans. Even though she was barely a teen, McKee's act was good enough to convince some stewardesses that she was at least twenty. In fact, they encouraged her to apply for a job to join them. And perhaps more important, they also invited her to the land of her dreams, California.[2]

When McKee turned sixteen, she thought it was finally time. She dropped out of school and headed west to California. She had saved up enough money for one night at a hotel. To truly live like the stars, there was only one option: the Beverly Hills Hotel. But there was a problem. After her first night, McKee was going to be homeless if she did not find a place to stay.[3]

Then McKee remembered a friendly stewardess who had offered to host her if she ever found herself in California. When McKee reached out, the answer was not exactly what she had hoped: she couldn't stay the night, but she could come to a party the stewardess was hosting. With nothing to lose, McKee said yes.[4]

Luckily, John Rose, whom McKee met at the party, immediately took a fancy to her. When Rose heard she was on the cusp of homelessness, he invited her to stay with him. McKee wasn't exactly in a position to refuse. Nor did she want to when she learned where he lived—the Hollywood Hills above Sunset Strip. Plus, she really liked Rose; he was a genuinely kind person, and he liked her, too.[5]

One weekend, Rose invited McKee to Las Vegas, so off they went. When they arrived, they booked a room, and Rose began gambling. McKee, on the other hand, wanted to see the city. Once she stepped out on the Las Vegas Strip, she immediately fell in love with the glitz and glamor. Then a sign caught her eye. A show was looking for go-go dancers. McKee thought she should audition. After all, wearing fancy outfits and dancing sounded like fun, so she put her name on the list.[6]

By the time McKee returned to the hotel, Rose had lost all the money he brought to Las Vegas. He did not even have money to pay for their hotel room. If anything, Rose's losses only increased McKee's resolve to audition. So off she went, dressed in her best cocktail dress. But once McKee arrived, she knew she was out of her league. Everyone there was a professional—dressed in leotards, dance shoes, the whole nine yards. McKee, on the other hand, didn't even know what the audition entailed. But then the choreographer called her name and asked her to dance. McKee may not have dressed the part, but she knocked him dead. The choreographer hired her on the spot, gave her an advance payment, and told her to be ready to work the next day. McKee went back to the hotel and paid for the room with Rose. When he left for Los Angeles the next day, McKee stayed behind.[7]

Though her mother was black and her father was white, McKee told employers that she was "Jewish, Italian, or East Indian."[8] In the early 1960s, being a mixed-race young woman in Las Vegas wasn't easy. McKee hoped that when she became a star, she could start to break down racial barriers so other talented women could follow in her footsteps.

While her position as a go-go dancer was a good one, McKee wasn't satisfied. In 1966, when she saw an advertisement for a lead show girl, she applied. This was a highly coveted position, but McKee was sure she was good enough. And she was. Once hired, McKee reportedly became the first black show girl in Las Vegas (though that wasn't known at the time).[9] In this role, McKee was larger than life—wearing exquisite costumes in major theatrical productions.

People took notice. One was the world-famous Sammy Davis Jr., who was immediately drawn to her. With McKee's dynamic personality and good looks, it was hard not to be. In 1970, he hired her to join his roadshow, and over the course of seven years, they performed at nightclubs all over the world. During that period, they spent time with the other members of the "Rat Pack"—Frank Sinatra, Dean Martin, Peter Lawford, and Joey Bishop. For a girl from Detroit, things were heading in the right direction at a rapid pace.[10]

The Rat Pack introduced McKee to new opportunities. She started making cameo appearances on various shows, including *Good Times* and *Sanford and Son*.[11] In 1971, she appeared on *The Bill Cosby Show* and became friends with Bill Cosby and his wife.[12] "It was my dream come true," McKee said.[13] She was becoming the actress she had dreamed of for so many years.

McKee even appeared on *The Tonight Show* starring Johnny Carson, with whom she said she had a secret love affair.[14] As she put it, "[I]n show business, . . . it's very common to be in and out of affairs, unless you're married. You're in the limelight, people are after you, men are chasing after you. And these were wonderful, lovely men. They treated me wonderfully."[15] Carson was one of them, and McKee enjoyed her friendship with him.

Then, in 1974, her life changed. McKee was still touring with Sammy Davis Jr., and one of their shows took them back to her hometown of Detroit. Davis left after the show, but McKee stayed behind to visit family.[16]

McKee heard from her friend Bill Cosby, who happened to be in town at the time. He invited her to join him at a party and asked her to pick up some ribs from a local barbecue restaurant and bring them with her. She did.[17]

When McKee got to Cosby's room, he was still in his bath robe and had a wool cap on. This was not unusual. Cosby was known for being in a bath robe, cigar in mouth. He often wore one on set. He invited her in. As soon as she entered, he closed the door and tossed the ribs aside. Cosby then overpowered McKee and raped her. "He was a different man. It felt like a different person performing that act," she said.[18]

McKee was shocked and terrified.[19] She couldn't believe that a man she considered a friend would do something so horrible. She wanted to leave right away, but she felt she couldn't. To McKee, Cosby was just "another powerful person in Hollywood who just felt he could take what he wanted from women."[20] If she reported him, who would believe her? Cosby was one of the most beloved men in America—people considered him "America's dad."

While McKee considered how to escape the horrific situation, Cosby proceeded as if nothing had happened. He still expected

McKee to join him at the party, which she did. But he barely spoke to her the rest of the night. At the first opportunity, she left.[21]

Like many rape victims, McKee wondered what she could have done differently. "I was mad at my own self for not saying, 'What the f—-?' Why didn't I stop it and get him away from me? But it happened too fast. I was absolutely flabbergasted. And I had the guilt. I questioned myself, 'Why did I go there? Why did I bring him those ribs?' Maybe he thought that's what I wanted too?"[22]

McKee was determined not to let this awful incident sink her career. She thought of the Frank Sinatra song, "Pick Yourself Up."[23] It was not easy, but she hoped that if she didn't think about the rape, it wouldn't bother her.[24] She tried her best to deny the reality of her feelings and focus solely on succeeding. And she did. In 1975, McKee appeared on one of the first episodes of *Saturday Night Live* with Richard Pryor.[25] By 1979, McKee was the star of a local talk show *Good Morning L.A.*[26]

Successful as ever, McKee began to plan her future in show business, an industry she never wanted to leave. Wisely recognizing that no one's time in the spotlight lasts forever, McKee eventually moved behind the camera and began a successful career in casting. She served as a casting assistant on the movie *61** about Mickey Mantle and Roger Maris. The film ultimately won an Emmy Award for outstanding casting.[27]

McKee also became a mother. She had a baby boy, Khristopher, and wanted to raise him closer to home. "I wanted to settle down. My son is a gift from God. That was a blessing in disguise for me. I never imagined how great it could be to be a parent. My priorities changed," McKee explained.[28] She and her son moved back to Detroit, where she could raise Khrisopher, help her aging parents, and care for her sister with cerebral palsy.[29]

In her hometown, McKee embraced anonymity. She began teaching at a local college and offering acting and professional development classes in the community. She also launched her own successful casting agency.[30]

But McKee never forgot that awful night in Detroit in 1974.

Decades later, when other women started reporting Cosby's crimes, McKee's trauma flooded back with unexpected force. What McKee had tried to block from her mind was now staring her in the face. She had always assumed her attack was an isolated incident. But now she knew she wasn't alone.[31]

McKee became especially enraged by how Cosby and his people retaliated against these women. Hadn't he already taken enough from his victims? McKee knew Cosby had to be stopped, and she was confident that truth and justice were on her side. But the time to bring criminal charges had expired. So McKee's only option for justice was in the court of public opinion. In December 2014, McKee spoke with Nancy Dillon of the *New York Daily News* about the rape. On December 22, 2014, Dillon published McKee's story.[32]

Cosby didn't take the allegations lightly. Instead, he implemented a "scorched-earth strategy" against his accusers, and McKee was no exception.[33] After the *New York Daily News* story, Cosby's lawyer sent a letter to the paper accusing McKee of being a liar and engaging in "reckless conduct." The letter claimed that the newspaper had "recklessly labeled as 'rape' an alleged sexual encounter in the 1970's during which . . . the accuser never objected, never said no, did not attempt to end the encounter, went to a party that night with her alleged attacker (and drove him to the party in her own car), and remained his friend and traded on his name for 40 years."[34] The letter also accused the paper of failing to investigate McKee's allegedly damning background. "To say that Ms. McKee is not a reliable source is a gross understatement. Ample published information readily available to the *Daily News* completely undermines this story."[35]

McKee was undeterred by this attempt to besmirch her character. Instead, in December 2015, she filed a complaint (later amended) alleging that Cosby had engaged in defamation by having his lawyers falsely call her a liar in the press. As a result of Cosby's lawyer's work, some of the defamatory information was "published and disseminated broadly to the world at large, through the internet, television, and through other newsprint organizations to a very broad community."[36] Cosby's goal, she alleged, was to discredit her "and to damage her reputation for truthfulness and honesty, and further to embarrass, harass, humiliate, intimidate, and shame" her.[37] McKee wanted her day in court to prove that she was telling the truth and that Cosby and his hired guns were liars.

But an old Supreme Court case makes it hard for anyone in the public eye to sue for defamation. In *New York Times v. Sullivan*, the Supreme Court said that public figures can recover for defamation only if they show that the defendant acted with "actual malice." In other words, the plaintiff needed to show the defendant actually knew for a fact that the statement was false or else recklessly disregard that it probably was false.[38] This standard is "almost impossible" to meet.[39]

McKee found herself in the crosshairs of the *Sullivan* decision. According to the Supreme Court, a person who "voluntarily injects" herself into a controversy can become a public figure for a "limited range of issues."[40] And the trial court had found that by talking to a reporter about Cosby's assault, McKee had done just that. She had become a "limited-purpose public figure."[41] Thus, the trial court dismissed the action. The Court of Appeals agreed and said that by speaking "with a reporter, McKee thrust herself to the forefront of this controversy, seeking to influence its outcome."[42]

McKee's only remaining option was a Hail Mary pass: to seek review by the Supreme Court. In her petition to the Court, McKee argued that her minimal interactions with a reporter did not make her a "public figure." She did not ask the Court to overrule *New York Times v. Sullivan*. Her petition claimed only that the lower courts had applied that precedent incorrectly.[43]

Unfortunately for McKee, the Supreme Court does not typically review cases merely because a lower court made an error. Generally, the Court hears cases only when the law is unclear, or if a party asks the Court to overrule precedent. McKee's petition didn't do that. The Court declined to hear McKee's case.[44]

Unlike the rest of the Court, Justice Thomas wasn't ready to let the case go without comment. He agreed that the Court should not wade into a dispute about whether McKee was a "limited-public figure." But, he said, it was time to revisit *New York Times v. Sullivan*—the case that had led the lower courts to dismiss McKee's suit.

Specifically, Justice Thomas explained that the Constitution allowed the states to define defamation. That was true from the Founding until the Supreme Court announced the decision in *New York Times v. Sullivan* in 1964. Justice Thomas wrote, "*New York Times* and the Court's decisions extending it were policy-driven decisions masquerading as constitutional law."[45]

In *Sullivan*, the Supreme Court applied its novel "actual-malice" standard to public figures (in that case, an elected official). Various subsequent decisions expanded the new standard's scope to include "private persons who 'thrust themselves to the forefront of particular public controversies in order to influence the resolution of the issues involved.'"[46] But none of this "judge-made law" was grounded in the original meaning of the Constitution.

As he often does, Justice Thomas then recounted the history of American law, which contradicted the very premise of *New York*

Times v. Sullivan. At the time of the Founding, the common law deemed false statements against public figures to be "more serious and injurious" than those against private figures. But it allowed people to make a personal attack against a public figure "so far as it . . . respect[ed] his fitness and qualifications for the office," and so long as it was true.[47]

The Supreme Court had distorted all of that, Justice Thomas explained, by "displacing state defamation law." And federal courts shouldn't take power away from the states for policy reasons alone. As he wrote, to the contrary, "States are perfectly capable of striking a balance between encouraging a robust public discourse and providing a meaningful remedy for reputational harm."[48] And merely being "a limited-purpose public figure" shouldn't have prevented McKee from having her day in court.

Since *McKee v. Cosby*, Justice Thomas has consistently called for the Court to overrule *New York Times v. Sullivan*. Instead of "insulat[ing] those who perpetrate lies," he believes that "we should give them only the protection the First Amendment requires."[49]

He continues to issue solo opinions each time the Court denies litigants the opportunity to revisit *Sullivan*. In one such case, the Southern Poverty Law Center labeled a Christian nonprofit organization "an anti-LGBT hate group." As a result of that label, Amazon barred the group from receiving donations through AmazonSmile, costing the group a significant amount of money. In response, the nonprofit sued, noting that while it opposed "homosexual conduct" based on its religious beliefs, it "has never attacked or maligned anyone" for engaging in that type of conduct. In short, the nonprofit asserted that the "hate group" label was defamatory and had caused them material harm. But since the organization was considered a "public figure," it could not meet the "almost impossible" actual-malice standard to sue for defamation.[50]

Justice Thomas doesn't criticize *New York Times v. Sullivan* simply because it is unsupported by the text of the Constitution and American history. He also opposes the real-world harms to people like McKee for which *Sullivan* is responsible. So long as someone—a high school football coach, for example—has some degree of prominence in even a small community, that person has essentially no recourse against false accusations.

Justice Thomas did not forget about McKee. Two years after her case was rejected, Justice Thomas reminded the Court, in another solo opinion, that *Sullivan* had denied McKee the right "to defend her reputation in court simply because she accuse[d] a powerful man of rape."[51]

CHAPTER 7

The Picture

Brumfield v. Cain

To anyone else, January 6, 1993, looked to be an ordinary day. But for Betty Smothers, it was a day she had dreamed of for years. After work and a quick rest, thirty-six-year-old Betty was going house hunting. A mother of six, she was determined to provide a stable home for her children—Warrick (eighteen years old), Derrick (sixteen), Summer (fourteen), Bricson (eleven), Travis (ten), and Samantha (nine). Betty dreamed of owning a home they could all be proud of, one they could keep in the family for generations. She couldn't wait to find one for them.

Saving for the down payment had not been easy. Betty had served as a Baton Rouge police officer for fourteen years, but her job did not pay well enough to provide for her children in the way she wanted. Her $36,000 salary barely put food on the table for her six kids, so she often worked extra shifts as a security guard. As her oldest grew, she worked even more so he could attend the local Catholic high school. She believed firmly in the power and value of education.

Betty knew there was more to parenting than money. Even as a single mom, she was determined to give her kids her undivided attention every minute she wasn't working. A track star in high school, Betty volunteered at her local track club so she could coach her children and get to know their friends. Every one of her kids recognized her effort and adored her for it. Betty was a generous and loving mother, and nothing was more important to her than her children.[1]

Twenty-year-old Kevan Brumfield chose a different path. He had worked only three months in an honest job in his life. He could make more money dealing drugs, so why bother?[2]

Sometime in 1987, Brumfield's and Betty's lives crossed for the first time. Betty was working security at a grocery store when Brumfield, then a teenager, walked in. He began shoplifting, but Betty caught him. She did not arrest him or turn him in. Instead, Betty gave Brumfield a second chance, making him put back what he had taken and then letting him go. She hoped to teach him a lesson, not derail his life. As Betty's oldest son, Warrick, said, she was "always giving people second chances to do right."[3]

But Brumfield did not capitalize on his second chance. Instead, he continued his life of crime, committing one illegal act after another. Shortly after his encounter with Betty, Brumfield was involved in the fatal shooting of a drug dealer. In 1992, he was convicted for attempted possession of cocaine and for trying to steal a gun. Instead of detaining Brumfield until his sentencing, the judge released him.[4]

Neither the conviction nor the pending jail term deterred Brumfield. Even while awaiting sentencing, he returned to crime. On Christmas Day, Brumfield robbed Anthony Miller at gunpoint and stole his gold chain, jacket, and all the cash he was carrying. After Brumfield stripped Miller of his possessions, he put a gun to Miller's head and pulled the trigger. Fortunately for Miller, the gun misfired. Miller survived, and Brumfield got away.[5]

Just seven days later, Brumfield approached Edna Marie Perry and her young daughter. He put a sawed-off shotgun to Edna's face and grabbed her purse. Edna pleaded with him to let her keep the pictures of her deceased son that she carried in her bag. Brumfield answered, "Bitch, you dead." Luckily, he left her alive, making off with only the purse and the memories.[6]

Two weeks, two robberies. And Brumfield wasn't finished. On January 6, while riding around with a couple of friends looking for a "hustle," he hatched a plan to steal a grocery store's nightly deposit. He and one of his companions, Henri Broadway, would hide in the bushes at the night deposit spot; the third friend would act as the getaway driver.[7]

While Brumfield was plotting, Betty Smothers was, as usual, working. That day, she reported to the police department for a 10-hour shift. Kimen Lee, the owner of the grocery store, asked Betty to escort her to the bank to make the nightly deposit. So, with her boss's permission, Betty drove her police cruiser to the grocery store and picked Lee up. She was excited. She was just hours away from touring the houses she dreamed of buying.

Betty never made it to her appointment with the realtor. Shortly after midnight, she and Lee arrived at the bank. As Lee leaned out of the passenger door to make the deposit, Brumfield and Broadway opened fire. Brumfield shot seven times; Broadway shot five. Betty was riddled with bullets, almost all from Brumfield's gun. Lee was also hit multiple times, but she managed to take control of the police cruiser and drive to a nearby convenience store for help.[8]

Even though he hadn't managed to grab any cash, Brumfield bragged to a friend that he had just killed "a son of a bitch."[9] Meanwhile, one of Betty's fellow officers had to call the Smothers' house and tell Warrick that his mother had been shot and officers were on the way to the house. Warrick's mind was spinning—he knew that things were worse than the officer made it sound on the phone. But how much worse?[10]

When the first officer arrived, well after midnight, he asked Warrick, and only Warrick, to accompany him to the hospital. When he arrived at the hospital, he saw his mother lying outstretched and motionless on a bed. Warrick noticed that she was wearing the pearl earrings he had given her. They were stained with her blood. He stared at his mother's lifeless body and thought that he had just lost his "best friend, soul mate, and guardian angel."[11]

Warrick, a talented running back, had turned eighteen just two days earlier. He had been looking at college football programs. In fact, that coming weekend, he had planned to visit the University of Alabama with his mom. Instead, he buried her.[12]

Derrick, Summer, Bricson, Travis, and Samantha had just lost their mother, but Warrick wouldn't let his brothers and sisters lose more. He thought about the life his mom had given the six of them. She had kept them off the streets. She had kept them dedicated to their studies. And she had paid for Warrick to go to a Catholic high school, where she thought he would receive a better education. Without her, how would they survive?

In the hospital, during what must have been the darkest, longest night of his life, Warrick sat with his mother's body and realized that his life as he knew it was over. Brumfield's crime had thrust Warrick into the role of father to his younger five siblings. Whatever his dreams had been, he had to take care of his brothers and sisters now, too. If it was necessary, Warrick decided, he would forgo college and give up on the NFL. Warrick was his mother's son. No matter the cost, Warrick would do everything he could to give each of his brothers and sisters their best shot at success.[13]

While Warrick was contemplating life without his mom, Betty's fellow officers were tracking down her killer. The trail led to Kevan Brumfield. They arrested him, and he confessed at the station, detailing how he'd come up with his "hustle," waited in the bushes for Lee and

Betty, and fired the seven fatal shots with his .38. This time, Brumfield was not released on bail, but that didn't stop him from attacking another police officer while he was in prison awaiting trial.[14]

While Brumfield spent his time committing assaults in jail, Warrick spent his time piecing together a future for his family. His siblings pushed back on his decision to give up on college and a football career. Warrick's two sisters and three brothers, as young as they were, had a certain maturity about them. Betty's five youngest children knew that it was best for Warrick to go to college, and they told him so. A close friend of the family also urged Warrick not to give up on his dreams and stay home, but rather to go to college and become someone who could provide. That way, the friend said, Warrick would set the tone for the entire family.

It was not an easy decision. Warrick was still grieving. Every night that his mom had worked, he had slept in her bed until she got home.[15] The night of her murder, he had an upset stomach. He called his mom, and she told him to come to the Piggly Wiggly convenience store, where she would buy him some medicine that could help settle his stomach. He was tired, so he told her he would wait for her to get home with the medicine. She never did.[16]

As Warrick reflected on all that had happened, he remained convinced that he had to let go of his college dreams and care for his siblings. Without their mother, who else would take care of them?

That's when Warrick's grandmother stepped in. She told Warrick that it was his mother's dream for him to get a college scholarship and graduate with a degree. To make sure Warrick's siblings were getting along while he was away at college, she could move in with them. So, with his grandmother's help and her blessing, Warrick finally accepted his scholarship offer from Florida State.[17]

At five foot nine, Warrick Dunn was not your typical Division I running back, let alone at one of the most elite football programs in

America. That did not stop him from quickly becoming a superstar. Nothing would.

Despite making stunning plays on the field, Warrick rarely smiled or was happy off of it. He thought about his mom every day, and he kept her bloodstained pearl earrings in a box on his dresser. Those earrings reminded him that she would have wanted him to graduate and care for his siblings. He wanted to make her proud.

So Warrick rarely went out with his teammates or friends in Tallahassee. Instead, he studied and talked to his siblings. From more than four hundred miles away, he was trying to stitch his family's life back together. Warrick spent most evenings on the phone, checking in on his brothers and sisters. When he had parenting questions, Warrick went to his coaches. His brother Derrick (the second oldest) was taking the lion's share of the responsibility in raising the others. But as the oldest, Warrick felt he had to make sure everything was all right. He knew the responsibility for his siblings rested with him. Warrick's ultimate plan was to graduate and provide for his siblings with either his football skills or his education. He was not a typical college student, to say the least.[18]

One more thing made Warrick different from his peers. While most students enjoyed summer vacation, Warrick returned home after his sophomore year for Kevan Brumfield's trial.[19] A jury of Brumfield's peers convicted him for the murder that he had confessed to and bragged about. The jury sentenced Brumfield to death. The people of Louisiana had rendered their judgment.

But that was far from the end of the matter. For Betty's family and their community, closure would be a long time coming. Why? Because while Warrick and Derrick were shouldering the immense responsibility of caring for their siblings, Brumfield was trying to evade his responsibility for the murder of their mother.

For the next two decades, Brumfield fought all aspects of his conviction using every possible legal avenue. First, he appealed his conviction in state court in Louisiana, claiming that the judge's rulings at trial were wrong, that the judge had improperly instructed the jury, and that his own counsel had made too many mistakes. He also claimed, ironically, that his upbringing by a single mother in a tough environment was responsible for his behavior. The Supreme Court of Louisiana rejected his appeal in 1998. Brumfield then tried to take his case to the United States Supreme Court. But in 1999, the Court denied his petition for review.

In 2000, Brumfield sought relief in state court by filing a habeas corpus petition alleging numerous errors by the state trial court.[20] A habeas petition is a long shot. The great writ, as it is known, has a storied heritage but a narrow role. Originally, it was only meant to protect people who were being unlawfully detained. The habeas corpus petition was never meant to be a judge-run do-over, a way to circumvent the people's judgment. Thus, while the petition is often filed, it is granted only in the rarest of circumstances.

Brumfield requested and received "multiple extensions of time" from the state court to amend his habeas petition.[21] His final petition, submitted in 2003, raised many of the claims he had raised before but added a new, very significant, claim, one that had not been available to him at his trial ten years before: in 2002, in a case called *Atkins v. Virginia*, the Supreme Court had held that it was unconstitutional—cruel and unusual punishment—for the state to execute mentally retarded individuals.[22] So Brumfield added to his 2003 amended petition the claim that he was mentally retarded and therefore ineligible for the death penalty.

The Louisiana trial court denied Brumfield's petition, finding that he had not made a sufficient showing of mental retardation, and in 2004 the Louisiana Supreme Court refused to review the trial court's determination. Brumfield then turned to federal court for yet another bite at the post-conviction apple.

Federal court review is even more difficult than state review. That did not used to be true. In the 1950s, the Supreme Court expanded the habeas writ to cover many things it never had covered before. But as the prison gates opened, Congress became concerned, so eventually it passed a law narrowing habeas review. Congress's goal was to stop federal courts from second-guessing their state counterparts and to provide victims with closure sooner. Brumfield claimed he was one of those rare people who should be granted federal relief.

This time, Brumfield wanted a hearing in federal court to show that he was mentally retarded. But again, he was in no hurry. After Brumfield filed his petition, his lawyers requested a postponement of the hearing so they could find experts to attest to Brumfield's retardation. The federal court granted the request.[23]

While Brumfield spent his time challenging every aspect of his conviction, Warrick returned his focus to his family, his classes, and football. Despite everything going on around him, he earned good grades, made it through four years of college, and graduated a star of the football team. Indeed, even though Warrick could have gone to the NFL after three years in college, he stayed four. Why? To fulfill his mother's dream by making sure he received his college degree.

At the end of his college career, Florida State retired Warrick's jersey—an honor awarded to very few college athletes. The Tampa Bay Buccaneers selected him as the twelfth pick in the NFL draft.

But Warrick's heart was still broken. Caring for his siblings, attending Brumfield's trial, attending college, and playing football, he had never really had a chance to grieve his mother's death. Warrick's emotions often welled up, though he pushed through them and continued to perform. He was angry and sad. Since Betty's death, he had tried to be the man she wanted him to be, but that did not mean he could enjoy his success or feel happy.[24]

Warrick was not alone. His three youngest siblings were struggling, too. Even with their grandmother watching after them, two were flunking out of school. Warrick decided that they had to come to Tampa Bay and live with him. He took them out of the Baton Rouge public schools and enrolled them in the local Catholic high school in Tampa Bay. He wanted to ensure they stayed on the right path. So Warrick now had two jobs—NFL player and single parent.[25]

Warrick became a star, ultimately becoming only the twenty-second running back in NFL history to rush for ten thousand yards. But no matter what he accomplished, he could not find happiness. Finally, a friend convinced him to see a counselor. He started opening up about that tragic night, its impact on him, and how it had stolen the joy from his life. Working with the counselor, Warrick figured out that he was never going to get past that tragic night until he spoke with his mom's killer.[26]

In search of closure, Warrick decided to visit Brumfield on death row.[27] Warrick hoped that since Brumfield had confessed, maybe he would answer some of Warrick's questions. He wanted to understand what could lead a person to inflict so much misery on another. What had Brumfield been thinking about when he pulled the trigger? Had he wondered if he was killing someone's mom? Someone's spouse? Someone's daughter?

But when Warrick finally came face to face with Brumfield, he didn't find closure or understanding. Brumfield immediately told him, "I didn't kill your mother. They got the wrong guy."[28] Maybe Warrick should not have been surprised by such a statement, given that Brumfield had been fighting his conviction for fourteen years. But he was stunned all the same. This was a man who had bragged about the killing and admitted to it in a videotaped confession. All these years, and Kevan Brumfield was still denying responsibility.

Yet Warrick was not going to leave empty-handed. He wanted Brumfield to know what he had wrought. So Warrick read a statement he had prepared ahead of time. He told Brumfield what he had taken from Warrick's family. Tears streamed down Warrick's face as he recounted the consequences of Brumfield's actions. He finished by reading a poem from his sister, Summer, titled "The Feeling of a Hurt Soul."[29]

Warrick got up to leave. Before going, he decided to share with Brumfield one of his favorite quotations from the Reverend Dr. Martin Luther King Jr.: "The ultimate measure of a man is not where he stands in moments of comfort and conveniences, but where he stands at times of challenge and controversy."[30] Then he turned and left.

Before Warrick could leave the prison, Brumfield's attorneys asked to meet with him.[31] They asked Warrick to help with their appeals. He couldn't. While Warrick may have found it within himself to forgive Brumfield, that forgiveness did not extend to allowing the man to escape the sentence handed down by his peers. Warrick promised to pray for Brumfield, but he could not support changing Brumfield's ultimate sentence after a fair trial and "a million appeals."[32]

This latest challenge seemed far-fetched to Warrick. The state courts had found Brumfield mentally competent, and that was not something that the federal courts would lightly set aside. After all, federal courts only set aside findings of fact if those findings are clearly unreasonable. And Warrick was certain the state court's findings were not only reasonable but correct. It was obvious to him, having been face to face with Brumfield, that Brumfield was mentally competent.

So, without Warrick's support, Brumfield's lawyers made a last-ditch effort to get their client off death row. They called him "mentally retarded" and filed an amended petition in federal court on October 1, 2007—more than fourteen years after the murder.

A federal magistrate judge was the first one to review the petition. He found that the state trial court's decision not to grant a hearing on the evidence was reasonable. On habeas review, that is typically the end of the road. But the magistrate judge decided to consider Brumfield's new evidence and said he was entitled to a hearing. Three years later, in 2010, the district court held what has become known as an "*Atkins* hearing" to determine whether Brumfield was in fact mentally retarded. Brumfield presented two experts who claimed he was mentally disabled. The State of Louisiana presented three experts saying he was not. Two years later, the district court sided with Brumfield and found him "mentally retarded."[33] Brumfield had finally gotten the relief he sought.

The State of Louisiana, however, was unhappy with the result, and it appealed the decision to the United States Court of Appeals for Fifth Circuit, which unanimously reversed the district court's ruling. The appellate court held that the district court had erred in concluding that the state court should have held an *Atkins* hearing. Indeed, there was evidence in the record that Brumfield could perform his daily life activities and maintain relationships. If anything, Brumfield was a sociopath and had attention deficit disorder, but he was not "mentally retarded" in the sense *Atkins* meant. According to the state court, he had not pointed to sufficient evidence in the record to justify holding a hearing about whether he was "mentally retarded." Since this determination by the state court was reasonable, the appellate court held, a federal court was not allowed to second-guess it. Thus, the court reversed the district court and reinstated the death penalty.[34]

Brumfield sought Supreme Court review again. This time, the Court agreed to take his case. It was argued on March 30, 2015, twenty-two years after Brumfield had shot and killed Betty. Because the Court had announced the right to habeas corpus for death-row inmates with intellectual disabilities in *Atkins*, it wasn't obvious what standard courts should use in deciding whether to grant a hearing. The Court struggled with this problem at oral argument: Does the standard come from state law or federal law? If state law, what was Louisiana's standard? How would Brumfield prove his disability? Could Brumfield introduce evidence not in the record of the original case to show that he was intellectually disabled, since an *Atkins* claim is a new kind of claim?[35]

The Supreme Court handed down the opinion on June 18, 2015. Justice Sotomayor wrote for the five-justice majority and found that the state court made an unreasonable determination of the facts regarding Brumfield's mental capacity, that the federal district court was correct to hold an *Atkins* hearing, and that the facts adduced at that hearing proved that Brumfield was intellectually disabled. For these reasons, he could not be executed. The majority dedicated just one sentence of its opinion to the crime Brumfield had committed, and not a word to the consequences of that crime.[36]

Justice Thomas dissented.[37] He was joined by Chief Justice Roberts, Justice Alito, and Justice Scalia. Justice Thomas pointed out that the case was a "study in contrasts": "On the one hand, we have Kevan Brumfield, a man who murdered Louisiana police officer Betty Smothers and who has spent the last 20 years claiming that his actions were the product of circumstances beyond his control. On the other hand, we have Warrick Dunn, the eldest son of Corporal Smothers, who responded to circumstances beyond his control by caring for his family, building a professional football career, and turning his success on the field into charitable work off the field."

The majority may not have discussed the crime and the victims, but Justice Thomas did. For him, this case was not just about Brumfield.

It was about Betty Smothers, her children, and the people of Baton Rouge. Movingly, empathetically, he described the crime in detail. In an unusual move for a judicial opinion, Justice Thomas spent a section describing how the Smothers family had picked up the pieces and moved on. He started by pointing out that "Brumfield's argument that his actions were the product of his disadvantaged background is striking in light of the conduct of Corporal Smothers's children following her murder." He then described the effect of the crime on the family and how the various members had sought to cope. Justice Thomas also recounted Warrick's remarkable charitable work—his Homes for the Holidays program, which has become famous. Justice Thomas described how Homes for the Holidays decorates and completely furnishes homes obtained by single mothers, and how Warrick created many other charities, including ones dedicated to service members and victims of Hurricane Katrina, and a grief program for victims of crime. He commended how, while Brumfield relentlessly complained about his circumstances, Warrick took control of his.

Justice Thomas's discussion of the crime and its effects on the victim's family was unorthodox for a Supreme Court opinion—so much so that the other three dissenting Justices did not join this section of the opinion. Indeed, Justice Alito wrote separately to emphasize that, while the Smothers children were "inspiring," this section was not essential to the legal analysis in the case.[38]

Of course, the facts were only part of the story. Justice Thomas's dissenting opinion also explained why he believed the majority's legal analysis was misguided. The other three dissenting justices joined this part of the opinion, in which Justice Thomas explained that the statutory standard for setting aside factual findings of the state court is high, and Brumfield had not met it. There was more than enough evidence in the record, Justice Thomas noted, to show that Brumfield was not intellectually disabled. One doctor testified that Brumfield had an IQ over 75 (borderline, not indicative one way or the other) and had not demonstrated any impairment in adaptive skills. The doctor added that Brumfield simply appeared to have "no conscience" and an antisocial personality disorder. But neither of those things make him intellectually disabled. Another doctor scored Brumfield's IQ even higher. Ultimately, Justice Thomas argued that Brumfield had failed to rebut the state court's factual findings or show they were anything other than "eminently reasonable." To reach the opposite conclusion, Justice Thomas said, the majority had to use sleight of hand: the majority "[took] a meritless state-law claim, recast it as two factual determinations, and then award[ed] relief despite ample evidence in the record to support each of the state court's *actual* factual determinations."

Justice Thomas concluded with strong words addressed to the majority:

> What is perhaps more disheartening than the majority's disregard for both [the habeas statute] and our precedents is its disregard for the human cost of its decision. It spares not a thought for the 20 years of judicial proceedings that its decision so casually extends. It spares no more than a sentence to describe the crime for which a Louisiana jury sentenced Brumfield to death. It barely spares the two words necessary to identify Brumfield's victim, Betty Smothers, by name. She and her family—not to mention our legal system—deserve better.

Then, in an unprecedented move, he included a picture of Betty Smothers in an appendix.[39]

Warrick and his family were not happy with the Supreme Court's decision. (But they believe it is appropriate to include the faces of victims, including their mother, in the record.) The majority's decision meant the saga would continue. Once again, more than two decades after the murder, Brumfield was back in court for a hearing to determine his final sentence.

Warrick prepared to speak once again at Brumfield's new sentencing hearing. At the hearing, Warrick told the court that he had met with Brumfield and that he did not believe Brumfield was mentally disabled. He also told the court that the judicial system had failed his mother and her entire family by concluding that Brumfield was disabled. "The system is . . . horrible. I do not believe in the justice system because this is not justice," Warrick said.[40] The state court finally sentenced Brumfield to life in prison.

After the hearing, Kimen Lee, the grocer who had survived the attack despite being shot four times, noted that she continues to live with the incident every day. And Warrick's family members still struggle to understand why Brumfield would do such a thing, despite coming from a challenging background. The prosecutor who handled the case said, "We do have intellectually disabled people in our country. This man is not one of them. This is the gravest injustice I have ever seen."[41]

Warrick and his family hoped that this final sentencing would be the end of Brumfield's intrusion into their lives. Regardless of what Brumfield does next, he no longer has power over Warrick's emotions. Warrick took that power back in 2007, when he offered Brumfield the gift he had never asked for—forgiveness.[42]

CHAPTER 8

Streets of Terror

City of Chicago v. Morales

D antrell Davis, with a radiant smile and an electric personality, had his whole life ahead of him. Even at seven years old, his charm and smile could take over a room. He was his momma's boy.

Dantrell and his mother, Annette, lived in the Cabrini-Green public housing project on the outskirts of downtown Chicago. Across the street from Dantrell's building sat his elementary school. Even though it was only one hundred feet away, Annette insisted on walking Dantrell to school every day.

October 13, 1992, started like any other day. Dantrell woke up, and Annette made him breakfast. Then Dantrell got ready for school.

That same day, Anthony Garrett woke up seeking revenge. A member of a local gang, he set himself up at a window on the tenth story of a high-rise building across the street from where Dantrell and his mother lived.

At approximately 9:00 a.m., Dantrell walked outside, holding his mother's hand. At the same time, Garrett loaded his illegal rifle, aimed at a group of rival gang members standing in front of Dantrell's building, and fired.

Garrett was a terrible shot. Not a single gang member was hit. But a bullet fatally struck Dantrell. It all happened so fast that his mom couldn't shelter him. Nor could the police officers across the street who were guarding the school. Nor could the volunteer parent patrol that tried to keep the little students safe from the gangs as they walked to school. Despite these adults' efforts, Dantrell was gone.[1]

Sadly, Dantrell's story was one that was all too common in Chicago. Indeed, in 1992 alone, fifty-seven children under the age of fourteen were murdered.[2] Dantrell was number forty-four. And sadly, he wasn't even the first student from his school murdered that year. In March, nine-year-old Anthony Felton had been killed by a stray bullet while playing on the blacktop next to the school.[3]

The children knew what was going on around them. Six-year-old Sean A. R. Williams wrote an essay called "Trapped in My House." He explained, "The houses in my neighborhood look so pretty, but I don't see my neighborhood much. I only go outside when I get in the car or go to school."[4]

Another essay, penned by thirteen-year-old Demetrius Jones, offered this assessment: "I feel as though the world and the people may come to an end. No one seems to care about the children or the future."[5]

At an age when children should not have a care in the world, many of these little boys and girls were prisoners in their own home. Why? Because their parents had to lock them inside for their own safety. One mother of four summed it up like this: "I wish you could see the rust that has accumulated because they cannot ride their bikes." Stray bullets were not the only cause for concern. The parents knew that the gangs would recruit, harass, or harm their children at the first opportunity.

Even the parents' protection could not always shield the kids from the gang recruitment, which was often carried out on the side-walks near the schools. The gang members weren't shy about recruiting youngsters. They frequently started with children who weren't even ten years old. And once the children were in the recruiting process, parents could do little to stop it. Those who put up any resistance faced threats or worse. And for most families in these low-income areas, moving away was not an option. A generation of children was growing up imprisoned by the violence of their city.[6]

Of course, grown-ups weren't immune to the gunfire or the harassment, either. Like their children, they were afraid to go outside.

When the Chicago city council held hearings about the problem in 1992, many concerned citizens showed up to testify. One, D'Ivory Gordon, said, "When I walk out my door, those guys are out there." They "watch you," she explained. "They know where you live. They know what time you leave, what time you come home. I am afraid of them." She had even started carrying a kitchen knife to protect herself. She told the council that they must "clean these corners up. Clean these communities up and take it back from [the gangs]."[7]

Elderly Susan Mary Jackson said the same. "We used to have a nice neighborhood," she lamented. "We don't have it anymore." She was scared to go out, day or night. She told the council, "I don't go the store because I am afraid. At my age if they look at me real hard, I be ready to holler."[8]

Another resident said he

> never had the terror that I feel every day when I walk down the streets of Chicago. . . . I have had my windows broken out. I have had guns pulled on me. I have been threatened. I get intimidated on a daily basis, and it's come to the point where I say, well, do I go out today. Do I put an ax in my briefcase. Do I walk around dressed like a bum so I am not looking rich or got any money or anything like that.[9]

The citizens and the city council had had enough. The year Dantrell was shot, the city's four largest gangs—the Gangster Disciples, the Vice Lords, the Latin Kings, and the Latin Disciples—could already claim the allegiance of more than 19,000 members, and the city's 40 other major street gangs perhaps 19,000 more.[10] The smaller gangs tended to be more violent because they had less territory and could not afford to lose it. All of the gangs, however, fought over turf, dealt drugs, vandalized homes and neighborhoods, and robbed and intimidated residents. Between 1987 and 1994, Chicago police recorded 63,141 gang-related criminal offenses.[11] Those were the ones that were reported.

In response, the city council considered a time-tested solution: a loitering ordinance. The proposed ordinance prohibited gang members from "loitering" in public places without an apparent purpose and allowed police to order gang members to disperse when they did.

Not everyone supported the ordinance. The legal director of the ACLU protested that the law was too vague and would be abused by police officers. Other civil rights groups agreed with the ACLU, and battle lines rapidly formed.

On June 18, 1992, the city council met to consider the proposed bill. The *Chicago Tribune* described the resulting council debate as "one of the most heated and emotional" in recent memory.[12] Several councilmen warned that the ordinance would be used to target racial minorities. Others, including some representing the hardest-hit districts, insisted the measure was absolutely necessary. As one of those councilmen said, "This [ordinance] doesn't allow the police to go hog wild. But we're tired of seeing the rights of gangbangers get protected when . . . a mother can't send her children outside for fear of them getting shot to death in a drive by shooting." In the end, the ordinance's champions prevailed, by a vote of 31–11.[13]

If a gang member did not comply with the order to disperse, the police could arrest him for a misdemeanor. The punishment was not stiff—a fine of up to $500, up to six months' imprisonment, and/or community service. But it would be, the city hoped, a useful tool for police to help protect neighborhoods, avoid further gang enrollment, and, perhaps, stop turf battles before they started.

The police immediately set forth guidelines to make sure the enforcement was not arbitrary or discriminatory. First, the regulations required police to keep files on known gang members. Second, before ordering them to disperse, the police needed probable cause to conclude that loiterers belonged to a gang. Third, dispersal orders could only be issued in areas identified by community members as having a history of "demonstrable" problems. These included "hot spots" such as schools, where gangs often recruited. Fourth, Chicago allowed only officers who had specialized training and familiarity with the gangs—in effect, the Gang Crime section and special tactical units—to issue the dispersal orders. Finally, if an officer made arrests under the ordinance, that officer had to fill out an incident report giving the specific reasons for each person's arrest.[14]

In late August 1992, the law went into effect. Together, police officers and community members began identifying the areas where gangs congregated to sell drugs, recruit children, and fight with other gangs. Then, newly empowered police officers deployed, directing suspected gang members to disperse.

Stymied on the streets, the gang members fought back in court. One, Daniel Washington, was a member of the Vice Lords. Officers had seen him loitering in the street and yelling at passing vehicles, stopping traffic, and preventing pedestrians from using the sidewalk. When an officer issued a dispersal order, he did not move. The officer tried again. He refused again, so he was arrested. Another, Jose Renteria, was a member of the Satan Disciples. When an officer saw him on a street corner with other gang members, she issued a dispersal order. When she came back to the corner about twenty minutes later, Renteria was still there with his friends, so she arrested him. After their arrests, Renteria and Washington both argued that the ordinance violated the Constitution.

Even as the legal challenges continued, the Chicago police were able to issue eighty-nine thousand dispersal orders and arrest more than forty-two thousand people for violating the ordinance. By 1995, city-wide homicide rates had dropped by 9 percent, and gang-related homicides had dropped 26 percent.[15]

Unfortunately for Chicago, the promising successes on the streets did not extend to the courtroom. Of the twelve cases heard in trial courts challenging the ordinance, four judges upheld the ordinance, while eight struck it down. When the matter finally reached the Illinois appellate court, it noted the "obvious connection between gang crime and loitering." Even so, the court sided with the gang members and held the law unconstitutional in a December 18, 1995, ruling.[16]

The issue was the ordinance's language. According to the court, it was vague, creating two problems. First, the vague language did not give Chicagoans enough warning about what exactly was prohibited. Second, it gave the police too much power to engage in arbitrary and discriminatory enforcement.

When the appellate court struck the ordinance down, the police had to stop enforcing it. Predictably, gang-related violence started to escalate again. In 1996, the first year of non-enforcement, gang-related homicides rose 7 percent, though other homicides continued to fall.

But Chicago didn't give up the fight. Instead, it took its case to the Illinois Supreme Court. Like the appellate court before it, the Illinois Supreme Court recognized that gangs were "an expanding cancer in our society and their illegal activities endanger the safety of many law-abiding citizens." Nevertheless, it struck down the ordinance as unconstitutionally vague.[17]

Even as the ordinance had met defeat in the courts, it was growing more popular with Chicagoans, who asked the city's lawyers to take the fight all the way to the United States Supreme Court. In May 1998, the city council passed a resolution, by a 25–8 vote, urging the Supreme Court to take the case. Those voting in favor of the ordinance included a majority of the council members representing high-crime wards.[18] The people of those wards had seen the peace that the ordinance brought, and they saw the gangs coming back in its absence.

The city marshaled support in preparation for the appeal—a coalition including community activists, other cities, states, and law enforcement groups, plus the United States solicitor general—to challenge the Illinois Supreme Court decision as badly out of touch with the needs of average Chicagoans and the dangers facing inner cities. The residents of these high-crime areas, they pointed out, simply wanted to live in their neighborhoods without fear of losing their children or their lives to the gangs.

With these groups' backing, the city of Chicago asked the United States Supreme Court to take up the case. In its petition, the city explained why it needed the ordinance. First, the city noted that "although gang members blatantly engage in drug deals and other crimes on the public way in full view of neighborhood residents, they stand about pretending to be innocently loitering once the police arrive." Without the ordinance, police had no way to disperse gang members who had been dealing or fighting only moments before. "Second, the mere presence of a large collection of brazen, lawless, and violent gang members and others on the public way intimidates residents, who become afraid even to leave their homes." The gang loitering ordinance, the city explained, gave the police a necessary tool to combat these significant problems.

The city also noted that enforcement of the ordinance had coincided with a drop in crime. The ordinance had empowered the police and the community to take their city back from the gangs. Finally, the city argued that, while the Illinois courts had struck down the gang-loitering ordinance, other states' courts had allowed similar ordinances to be enforced.[19]

But the opponents of the ordinance pushed back, demanding that the Supreme Court resist the "neighborhood empowerment" crusade. There was no reason to hear the case, they said, because the Illinois Supreme Court had gotten it right. These groups asked the Court to protect the people from the arbitrary and discriminatory enforcement this ordinance supposedly allowed. The Court could do that by declining to review the Illinois Supreme Court's ruling.[20]

Despite the opposition, the Supreme Court granted the city's request to hear the case. On December 9, 1998, almost three years after Illinois courts had halted enforcement of the law, the Supreme Court finally heard the appeal.

It was an uphill battle from that outset. At oral argument, the justices pressed Chicago's advocate, Lawrence Rosenthal. They were worried that the ordinance would catch too many innocent people in its dragnet. What's more, some justices worried that it would unnecessarily restrict people's freedom of movement.

Justice Kennedy asked how an innocent person was supposed to know whether he was loitering with gang members. Rosenthal explained that the law did not make it illegal to loiter with gang members. Rather, it only made it illegal to loiter with gang members once an officer had issued a dispersal order.

Did the police have to tell the non-gang members the reason for the dispersal order, Justice Breyer wanted to know. No, Rosenthal said. Neither the ordinance nor the Constitution required such a disclosure. He then pointed out that when the police clear a street for the president, they have no obligation to provide their reasoning to the public.

Justice O'Connor wanted to know if cities had considered including an intimidation element in the law. In other words, she wondered whether loitering should be a crime only if the city could prove the loiterer was also intimidating those around him. Rosenthal pointed out that Chicago already had a law against intimidation, but the law was ineffective because most people were too terrified to testify against the gangs.

The justices continued to press Rosenthal about law-abiding people getting arrested for being in the wrong place at the wrong time. Rosenthal had a response: "What is critical [is] respondents can't identify a single case where that actually happened, and the legislative findings explain why. In these communities, law abiding people are afraid to use their public spaces. People are afraid to stand with gang members because gang members do not want law abiding people in their midst."

Throughout the argument, Rosenthal tried to make clear that the ordinance only allowed the police to arrest someone for failing to obey a dispersal order—not for loitering itself. He finished by emphasizing that the order had been passed because the "law-abiding people" of Chicago wanted it and felt it was necessary to make their city livable.

After Rosenthal's argument ended, Harvey Grossman got up to speak for the challengers of the ordinance. He argued that the language of the ordinance was unconstitutionally vague.

Chief Justice Rehnquist and Justice Scalia pointed out that an officer's command to move on was perfectly clear. Grossman resisted, arguing that to defy such an order and win in court, a citizen would have to prove that the person he was standing with was not a gang member. And that, Grossman said, would be "an impossible burden." When pressed, Grossman conceded that no one could be charged with merely loitering. Rather, everyone who was charged under the law was actually charged with failing to obey a dispersal order.

Justice Breyer asked Grossman how Chicago was supposed to address the violence. Grossman responded that the ordinance should have specified that the person must be loitering with an unlawful purpose—to deal drugs, to commit prostitution, and so forth. Grossman concluded by conceding that the city's numbers were accurate but added that in 1997, two years after the appellate court's decision halting the ordinance, gang-related homicides had dropped 19 percent.

In rebuttal, Rosenthal pointed out that gangs remained a significant problem and that the other laws on the books weren't working. In 1999, drive-by shootings were up 40 percent. He also reemphasized the limits of the law: loitering wasn't a crime in itself—only failing to obey a dispersal order while loitering with gang members. And, he noted, the only non-gang members likely to be loitering with the gangs were their recruits. With that, argument concluded.

On June 10, 1999, the Supreme Court announced its decision. By a 6–3 vote, it found Chicago's ordinance unconstitutionally vague. Justice Stevens wrote the majority opinion.[21]

The majority said the ordinance lacked sufficient guidance for law enforcement. According to the majority, whether an officer believed a person was loitering—that is, standing around with no apparent purpose—might be arbitrary. A gang member and his father might be lurking near a stadium to rob a fan, to catch a glimpse of baseball star Sammy Sosa, or to discuss the weather, but the police could order them to move on just the same. The "no apparent purpose" standard was too subjective and too deferential to the officer on the scene, the majority asserted. In other words, what might be an apparent purpose to one officer might not to another. They believed that the law lacked the standards that were needed for consistency. Had the city limited the ordinance to loitering with a "harmful purpose or effect," though, the majority opined, it would have been fine.

Some in the majority wanted to go further. They would have held that there is a constitutional right to loiter and that the "freedom of movement" is as much a part of our liberty as it is of "our heritage." But Justice Stevens could get only Justices Ginsburg and Souter to agree to this proposition.

Justice Scalia dissented. He took direct aim at the three justices who argued there was a constitutional right to move about as desired. He noted that the "citizens of Chicago were once free to drive about the city at whatever speed they wished," but at some point they had enacted speed limits to provide for safety. Similarly, people were at some point free "to stand around and gawk at the scene of an accident." Chicagoans, however, eventually "discovered that this obstructed traffic and caused more accidents." So they passed a law authorizing officers to order people to disperse. And with regards to the loitering ordinance, Chicagoans were once again willing to give up some freedom in exchange for safety. This, Justice Scalia said, was "a small price to pay for liberation of their streets."[22]

As Justice Scalia explained, "[I]n our democratic system, how much harmless conduct to proscribe is not a judgment made by the courts." He went on to note that a city may forbid "all sorts of perfectly harmless activity by millions of innocent people" including "riding a motorcycle without a safety helmet . . . starting a campfire in a national forest, or selling a safe and effective drug not yet approved by the Food and Drug Administration." The citizens of Chicago chose to restrict their own freedom to "hang out" with gang members "to eliminate pervasive gang crime and intimidation. . . . This Court has no business second-guessing either the degree of necessity or the fairness of the trade."[23]

Finally, Justice Thomas wrote a separate dissent, joined by Chief Justice Rehnquist and Justice Scalia. "By invalidating Chicago's ordinance," he lamented, "the Court has unnecessarily sentenced law-abiding citizens to lives of terror and misery."

Justice Thomas's opinion made two points: First, there is no constitutional right to loiter. And second, any citizen on the street—let alone a trained police officer—could understand what loitering meant, so the ordinance was not vague.

Justice Thomas then recounted the terror and misery of Chicago's citizens, including those who lived in fear of leaving their own homes. Quoting a Department of Justice report, he explained that gangs had "virtually overtaken certain neighborhoods." In so doing, the report explained, the gangs "contribut[ed] to the economic and social decline of these areas and caus[ed] fear and lifestyle changes among law-abiding residents."

"Gangs fill the daily lives of many of our poorest and most vulnerable citizens with a terror that the Court does not give sufficient consideration, often relegating them to the status of prisoners in their own home." The gangs also crippled small businesses by demanding protection money or making their customers "hostages within their homes."

The ordinance, Justice Thomas wrote, was simply the city of Chicago's attempt to address "the devastation wrought by this national tragedy." Innocent people, many of them children, were endangered simply because these gangs claimed turf and then fought to the death to protect it. Chicago had addressed these problems by simply "returning to the basics."

Chicago's ordinance, like many others before it, just allowed the police to maintain the public peace: "The ordinance does nothing more than confirm the well-established principle that the police have the duty and the power to maintain the public peace, and, when necessary, to disperse groups of individuals who threaten it." Laws like Chicago's prohibiting "loitering and vagrancy have been a fixture of Anglo-American law at least since the time of the Norman Conquest." Justice Thomas cited many of these old laws. In response to the plurality's supposed discovery of a new constitutional right to loiter, Justice Thomas pointed out that the written Constitution contained no such right. Nor, as he explained, did anyone at the Founding think there was any such right.

Then, Justice Thomas turned to the vagueness issue. The ordinance, he explained, was anything but vague. First, it did not criminalize "loitering, per se." Rather, it penalized loiterers who failed "to obey a police officer's order to move along." This didn't vest excess discretion in law enforcement officers, he argued. Instead, it allowed them "to fulfill one of their traditional functions. Police officers were not, and never have been, solely enforcers of criminal law. They wear other hats—importantly, they have long been vested with responsibility for preserving the public peace."

Indeed, police officers in most jurisdictions have a responsibility "to maintain the public peace." As part of this authority, Justice Thomas observed, police have "long had the authority to order groups of individuals who threaten the public peace to disperse." As an example of this, he cited the 1887 police manual from New York. Even the American Bar Association's *Standards for Criminal Justice* pointed out that police often have the power to order people not to loiter. To carry out these duties, the police must have sufficient discretion. Officers frequently must make "spur of the moment" decisions in the field. If they are wrong, the courts can determine whether the error was in effect an honest mistake or an abuse of the officer's authority. And if officers act in bad faith, they can be punished.

According to Justice Thomas, this is the traditional way of handling things—and for good reason. Police officers often exercise discretion in enforcing the law. Forbidding them from doing so "cannot be reconciled with common sense, longstanding police practice, or this Court's Fourth Amendment jurisprudence." As Justice Thomas saw it, the Chicago ordinance sufficiently balanced guidance and discretion, and was not vague.

Justice Thomas concluded with these words:

> Today, the Court focuses extensively on the "rights" of gang members and their companions. It can safely do so—the people who will have to live with the consequences of today's opinion do not live in our neighborhoods. Rather, the people who will suffer from our lofty pronouncements are people like Ms. Susan Mary Jackson; people who have seen their neighborhoods literally destroyed by gangs and violence and drugs. They are good, decent people who must struggle to overcome their desperate situation against all odds, in order to raise their families, earn a living and remain good citizens. . . . By focusing on the imagined "rights" of the two percent, the Court today has denied our most vulnerable citizens the very thing that Justice Stevens elevates above all else—the "freedom of movement." And that is a shame.[24]

•••

Since the ruling, Chicago still suffers from gang violence. In 2021, Chicago had 3,561 shooting incidents and 797 homicides, approximately 64 percent of which were gang related. Most of the violence occurs on the South and West Sides of Chicago, where the gang presence is very high. And the majority of these violent crimes occur outside and in public places.[25]

CHAPTER 9

The Sharecropper's Son

McDonald v. City of Chicago

F annie Lewis wasn't the only Midwesterner to begin her life in the South. From 1910 to 1970, six million other black Americans made the same journey. Often traveling with little more than a few dollars in their pocket and the clothes on their back, they went north to cities with great histories: New York, Toledo, Boston, Detroit, Muskegon, Saginaw, Chicago.

What moved them was hope: Word of jobs and a better life. Letters from cousins and brothers, telling of good pay and steady work. The dream of an apartment, a house, running water, a toilet, and lightbulbs. More important, many of them went with hopes of a better life for their children.

Otis McDonald was one of these men. He was born in 1933, the son of Louisiana sharecroppers and the grandson of slaves.[1] At the age of sixteen, he left, bound for Chicago. But in spite of what Otis had heard, work was still difficult to find, even in Chicago, and what he did find was not much better than in the South. So Otis decided to take a drastically different course: the Army. There, he thought, he would find a meritocracy. When Otis enlisted, though, he found the military didn't live up to his hopes, either. So he only served one term with the 42nd Anti-Aircraft Artillery Battalion.[2]

After finishing his service, Otis returned to Chicago. Even for a veteran, work was hard to find, especially when, like so many boys in the rural South, Otis had left school at fourteen. Finally, he found a job as a janitor at the University of Chicago.[3] Meanwhile, Otis had met his wife, Laura. Pushing a mop put a roof over the McDonalds' heads. Just in time, too—the McDonalds had one baby, and another on the way.

But Otis didn't believe that the journey he'd begun in Louisiana was supposed to end with him pushing a mop to pay a landlord. He imagined something better for his wife, for his children. He imagined a home in a community he could be proud of. The community where he decided to build his dream was Morgan Park.[4]

A neighborhood on Chicago's far South Side, Morgan Park was one of the most integrated areas in Chicago. And most important, it was a good place to raise a family. In order to give his dream a firm foundation, Otis began taking night courses at Kennedy-King College, one of Chicago's public colleges. Otis loved to learn, and he was motivated. After a couple of years, this man who had never earned a high school diploma received an associate's degree in engineering. Bit by bit, he worked his way up from janitor to supervisor, and finally to maintenance engineer. His colleagues elected him union president.

Otis's new degree and hard work put money in the McDonalds' pockets and an opportunity to buy a house in their hands. After saving enough for a down payment, in 1972 the McDonalds found a place in Morgan Park: a two-story house, with a garage for the car and a basement. By now, the McDonalds had three children—two girls and a boy. They could use the space. And the basement gave Otis—who had grown up in the swamps of Louisiana, served in the

Army, and loved to hunt—a place where he could display his hunting rifles with pride.

But even with a hard-earned home, a degree, and a job, the McDonalds weren't living the dream yet. Something sinister was happening on Chicago's South Side, and it was spreading to Morgan Park.

For the McDonalds, it began with a bicycle.

Their boy, Kevin, had left it on the front lawn, and someone had snatched it. A bit annoying, but not a big deal. Carelessness on their part. Kids' stuff. The McDonalds did not pay it much mind. But shortly after the bike theft, Otis and Laura McDonald returned from the grocery store to discover that someone had broken into their home. This time, their electronics were gone.[6]

The break-in scared Laura. Taking something from the yard was one thing. But robbers entering the house was something different. The electronics were gone, of course. But the thieves had also taken the peace and safety she'd felt inside those walls. New electronics they could buy. But recovering a feeling of security was harder.

When the police left, she looked up at Otis with tears in her eyes and her bottom lip trembling. How could this happen to them?[7]

Their three high schoolers were thinking about something else: revenge. They wanted to find the culprit, and the way gossip swirled through Morgan Park, they figured they could. But Otis and Laura warned in no uncertain terms that their children were *not* to take the law into their own hands. The McDonalds had fought hard and traveled far for the life they now led. Things might not be perfect, but they believed in the system and wanted to give it a shot. Their kids listened, and the robbery faded into the background of their lives.[8]

But other children felt the tug of the street, too, and unlike the McDonald children, they followed.

The truth was that robberies, muggings, and killings were mounting nationwide. And few cities suffered more than Chicago. When

Otis first came to the Windy City, crime was at almost its lowest point in the twentieth century. But then, in the 1970s, the homicide rate nearly tripled.[9] And it kept climbing. Why? No one quite seemed to know. Maybe it was heroin, followed later by crack cocaine. Maybe it was the growing gang problem. Or a population boom, or lost jobs and collapsing families.[10] Whatever the cause, crime began to eat Chicago from the inside out.

The people of Morgan Park did not escape. For the McDonalds, the third incident was not far behind the first two. This time, the robbers didn't stop at the TV or the stereo. Instead, they went to the McDonalds' bedrooms and rifled through their belongings. Gone were Laura's jewelry and Otis's hunting guns. The worst theft of all was that of Otis's prized possession—an Ithaca rifle with Chinese engravings, a trophy Otis had won hunting. Otis had hoped to pass the rifle along to his children.[11]

Luckily, this time the police found the robber. When the McDonalds learned his identity, they were crestfallen. It was one of the boys from the neighborhood. Other houses in Morgan Park continued being robbed even after that boy was arrested. The arrest made barely a ripple. The neighborhood that had once seemed to be their bridge to a better life was crumbling before their eyes.[12]

So Otis did something he never thought he would have to do: he installed block glass in the basement windows and ugly deadbolt-barred doors in the front. The warm little home had become a little fortress.[13] Their neighbors did the same. Some of the warmth went out of the neighborhood. But at least Laura could sleep soundly again.

For a time, the crime ebbed, and Otis and Laura's two oldest children left for college. Unfortunately, the reprieve didn't last long.

When Laura and her youngest daughter returned from church one Sunday, their front door was wide open. In front of the house was a neighbor, loading something into a truck. Laura figured out it was a robbery in progress. She called Otis at work, and he told her to call the police and stay away from the house.[14] So much for the deadbolt and block-glass.

Laura was angry. She knew the young man who was robbing them. How many times had he played in their home? Eaten with her children? She had cared for that boy like she'd cared for all the neighborhood kids. Why would he do this to them?[15]

After this break-in, Otis took the next step: purchasing a house alarm and monitoring service. But for Laura, these safety measures did not bring peace. Now she felt like she had to be constantly alert. She saw her concern reflected all around her. Once-beautiful buildings now had graffiti, fences went unrepaired, and weeds were growing through the sidewalk. No one seemed to care anymore about the neighborhood they called home.

Things were only getting worse. Across Chicago, gangs were claiming street corners and city blocks as their own, openly intimidating the residents who lived there. One day when Otis was driving home from a friend's house, a figure stepped into the middle of the road. Otis slammed the brakes. It was a young man with a black square cap on sideways, dark shades over his eyes, and heavy jewelry around his neck. As he glowered at Otis, another man approached the car, rapping on the window. Otis knew this was not a good situation, so he only cracked the window two inches. He knew he had to keep himself calm.

As Otis lowered his window, the man was already shouting. "You almost hit my homey, mother f——-." The man continued to yell, and Otis saw him reach for his waistband. As the man pulled out the gun, he yelled, "Old man, I'm gonna END you." Otis reacted quickly. Before the young man could get the gun up, Otis slammed the accelerator, throwing the would-be shooter off balance. The tires screeched, the man fell, and Otis sped away. But he knew he couldn't count on being so lucky next time.[16]

Petty robberies and minor drug transactions were one thing. Gangs and shootings were another. Otis and Laura's once-beautiful South Side neighborhood was going the wrong way, but they weren't going to surrender Morgan Park without a fight.

But the people of Morgan Park did have allies: the police. Across the nation, muggings, shootings, and drugs continued to plague cities and neighborhoods. While legislatures passed loitering laws, reformed bail, and added new punishments, the police experimented with new tactics. Among these was community policing.

Chicago decided to give it a try, and one of the pilot programs was located in Morgan Park.[17] Otis began attending the local meetings. There, local beat cops would offer reports, crime statistics, and updates to community members, and the community members would share concerns, tips, and information with the police. Together, they worked to save Morgan Park.

Otis became a regular. He recruited his neighbors to come. Indeed, he began running the meetings himself. But that came with its own set of costs—Otis began receiving threats from the local drug dealers.[18]

While the cooperative helped, it didn't stop the crime. One night, while Otis and Laura were sleeping, someone broke into their garage. Luckily, a neighbor was up and called the police. The police found the man hiding under Laura's car.[19]

Otis and Laura were thankful their neighbor had spotted the man, but a criminal hiding under their car was unacceptable. If not for Otis's eagle-eyed neighbor, something much worse than a robbery could have happened. With the gang encounter still fresh in his mind, Otis realized he couldn't wait for the police to get the situation under control. He had spent six decades bettering himself and his family, and he wasn't about to be helpless now.

A painful truth became clear. While the police were working hard, Otis might awaken to discover a burglar or mugger in his own home. And then, if he called the police, it might be too late for him and Laura. Otis needed a handgun—something he could keep by his side that was easy to use on a moment's notice. The next time someone broke into their house, the McDonalds' neighbors might not see it. And worse yet, the police might not make it in time. Otis knew the best way to protect his family, after all his other attempts had failed, was to have a handgun by his side.[20]

But Chicago had a law banning handgun possession, even in private homes. Otis understood that this did not stop the criminals from having guns. As he saw it, the law only stopped law-abiding individuals like himself from possessing handguns. Otis vented his frustration to anyone who would listen.

His hunting buddies, in particular, were all ears. They turned him onto a couple gun-rights organizations—the Illinois State Rifle Association and the Second Amendment Foundation. Otis attended a rally where his friends introduced him to the organizations' leadership. They talked to Otis about filing a lawsuit. He immediately said yes. They paused, then asked if he was sure. Did he want to think about it? No. Get him the right lawyer, and he would do the rest. They promised him only the best and introduced him to Alan Gura.

Alan was not just any lawyer. Even before he'd graduated from law school, he had begun cutting his teeth fighting for individual rights. As a student, Alan had been searching for part-time work when a flier from the Institute for Justice caught his eye. IJ asserted that it was a privilege of every American to earn a living doing honest work, and that that right was protected by the Privileges or Immunities Clause of the Constitution's Fourteenth Amendment. So when the city of Denver—under the thumb of a taxi monopoly—denied the local chairman of the NAACP the right to drive a taxi, IJ sued. But IJ needed help. And Alan needed a job.

That first battle had fired in Alan a passion for protecting the rights of all Americans. Since that first battle, he had struck out on his own and specialized in Second Amendment litigation. As it turned out, he was good at it. In fact, he had carried his fight all the way to the Supreme Court, where his challenge to D.C.'s gun restrictions was now pending in *District of Columbia v. Heller*.[21] When Otis met Alan, he knew he'd found the right lawyer to advocate for his right to protect his family.

For his part, Alan knew immediately that Otis was the right plaintiff. Otis had poured his soul into his South Side community, fighting for its future every inch of the way. Otis was smart. He was hardworking. He was a family man. And now, Otis needed help.

Alan could also see that Otis had grit. Otis would need it to withstand the criticism that was sure to come. Usually, popular culture makes heroes of people who champion individual rights. But it tends to treat the Second Amendment differently.

Otis wanted to start immediately, but Alan explained they needed to wait. Timing was everything. He was waiting for a decision in *Heller*.

Heller was poised to make history. It was the first time the United States Supreme Court had considered whether the Second Amendment protected an individual's right to keep a handgun in the home.

As the nation awaited the *Heller* decision, Alan counseled Otis to be patient. He was confident that the Supreme Court would find that the federal government could not ban the possession of handguns, but if he filed Otis's case before the decision in *Heller* came out, it would be dismissed.

Otis did not want to wait. Each day that passed was another day when an unarmed, law-abiding citizen in Morgan Park might find herself at the mercy of an armed intruder. But Otis consulted with his trusted nephew, Fred Jones. Fred was not only smart and savvy, he was also a lawyer. Fred confirmed Alan's advice—that patience here was a virtue. So, while he waited, Otis turned to study. He wanted to understand the shape of the legal battle ahead. On Fred's advice, Otis read Supreme Court decisions. He read books. He read everything he could get his hands on.[22]

As Otis studied, he began to glimpse the contours of Alan's strategy. Until he won *Heller*, no future case could succeed. But by itself, *Heller* wouldn't be enough to help the people of Morgan Park.

Otis learned that the Second Amendment originally only applied against the *federal* government. At the Founding, the American people worried that a faraway federal government would trample on their rights. After all, they had just fought for freedom from a faraway monarch. They didn't want to replace one monarch with another, so many of them insisted on protections for certain rights that the federal government should not be allowed to touch. As a condition for approving the new Constitution, they demanded a Bill of Rights. After the Constitution was ratified, they got their wish: ten amendments protecting them against the federal government—and the federal government alone.

Since the federal government controls the District of Columbia directly, Alan could call on the protections of the Second Amendment directly to challenge the District's handgun law. A victory there would show that the Second Amendment protected an individual's right to own a gun as much as a militiaman's right.

But that would only be the first step—showing that the protection applied against states and local governments like Chicago's was more complicated. After demonstrating *what* the Second Amendment protected, Alan would have to show that those protections applied against the states as well. That's where Otis's suit would come in.

After the Civil War, Americans realized that state laws could oppress people—in particular, the black men and women who until recently had been held in bondage. So the United States passed the Fourteenth Amendment. That Amendment was supposed to give the people—black as well as white—many of the same protections from state governments as the Constitution gave them from the federal government.

But in the years after the Civil War, the nation balked. The first line of the Fourteenth Amendment forbade states (and their local city governments) from passing laws that would abridge "the privileges or immunities of the citizens of the United States." This was the part of the Constitution Alan had used to fight for the NAACP chairman's right to drive a taxi in Denver, and it seemed the clearest way to extend the Bill of Rights' protections against the states. Enforcing the rights of freed blacks in the face of Klan violence, though, proved difficult. At the same time as violence against black Americans was escalating, the Court was cutting back the protections contained in the Privileges or Immunities Clause of the Fourteenth Amendment.

The first time the Court had limited the power of the Fourteenth Amendment was in the *Slaughter-House Cases* in 1873.[23] That set of cases held that "privileges or immunities" referred only to a set of "federal privileges"—not to the whole Bill of Rights. Then came *United States v. Cruikshank* in 1876.[24] In that case, the Supreme Court held that a white militia that had brutally murdered approximately 165 black Louisianans had not deprived those black citizens of the privileges or immunities of citizenship—to peaceably assemble or to keep and bear arms. Thus, the Supreme Court threw out the militia members' convictions. The *Cruikshank* case was going to be a stumbling block for Otis.

Since then, the Court had eventually begun to apply—or "incorporate"—the protections in the Bill of Rights against the states, but it did so one by one. And rather than consider whether it had been wrong in *Cruikshank* and the *Slaughter-House Cases*, the Court had picked a vehicle that Alan (and Otis) found rather odd—"substantive due process." The Due Process Clause of the Fourteenth Amendment provides that no person shall be deprived of "life, liberty, or property, without due process of law."[25] Many scholars and originalists believe that the Due Process Clause provides people only with process, not substantive rights. For example, the Due Process Clause guarantees that a person gets his day in court before he can be deprived of his life, liberty, or property, but the Due Process Clause didn't create its own set of rights—such as a "right to loiter." It only guarantees that the appropriate process be followed.

To Alan, the proper way to incorporate the Bill of Rights was through the Privileges or Immunities Clause. Alan believed this approach was both legally cleaner and more historically accurate.[26]

In a perfect world, Alan would have insisted on making only the Privileges or Immunities Clause argument. But it isn't a perfect world. He knew that it would take a lot to convince five justices to overturn the years of precedent that had turned the Privileges or Immunities Clause into an afterthought with no teeth. So he planned to file Otis's suit, seeking incorporation under either clause.

Alan didn't like this approach, but he knew he had an obligation to Otis to advocate as effectively as possible. Still, it bothered him profoundly for several reasons. First, he believed that the courts had a duty to get things right no matter the consequences. Second, he worried that if judges could find substantive rights where none exist, they could do anything: When things got tough, people's rights would be at stake. Just as easily as judges could find rights, they could deny them.

Then, on June 26, 2008, the Supreme Court decided *Heller*. Alan knew the decision was coming down that day, and he was at the courthouse; he was both anxious and confident. When he received a copy of the decision, the first thing he noticed was the length—it was very long. He immediately started flipping through the crisp, white pages in the booklet. When he found the Court's ruling, he saw it confirmed what he had fought and argued to show: that the *federal government* was not allowed to ban a lawful person from keeping a handgun in their home. But were the states? Alan would soon find out.

Indeed, before Alan even finished reading his copy of *Heller*, he was on the phone with his co-counsel, who was waiting on the steps of the federal courthouse in Chicago. The Chicago law was almost identical to the District of Columbia's. It was time to show that the Second Amendment applied against the states as well. Fifteen minutes after *Heller* was announced, Alan called his co-counsel: "File."[27]

Alan knew it was not going to be easy to convince the lower courts to adopt a theory that had been rejected many times before. He was right. The district court rejected his claim out of hand. On to the appellate court he went. Unfortunately, the appellate court had a similar view: in a unanimous decision, the United States Court of Appeals for the Seventh Circuit ruled against Otis. It found that the Supreme Court had routinely rejected incorporation of the Second Amendment through the Privileges or Immunities Clause—pointing to *Cruikshank* and other cases like it.

Alan and Otis had expected that. So they sought certiorari, and the Supreme Court granted their petition. The Court also granted the NRA's parallel petition from another case. Alan planned to spend most of his time before the Court arguing that the best way to incorporate the right to bear arms was through the Privileges or Immunities Clause. At the same time, the NRA would argue that it should be incorporated under Substantive Due Process.

As the day approached for argument, Otis was excited. He had never been to the Supreme Court, and now it was hearing *his case*. Otis, a grandson of slaves, who had served his country, obtained a degree, and made a better life for himself, his family, and his community, had taken his fight to the nation's biggest stage.

When he entered the chambers, Otis noticed that the justices would enter on an elevated dais. He saw his nephew Fred in the lawyers' section of the courtroom. As he was looking at the artwork around the courtroom, the justices entered, and Alan stood up to present his argument.[28]

To say that the argument was not easy would be a massive understatement. From the outset, almost all the justices indicated that they were not willing to reconsider their privileges or immunities jurisprudence. Why? Two reasons. First, they had already incorporated most of the Bill of Rights through substantive due process. Why shift gears now? Second, they feared what other unenumerated rights the Privileges or Immunities Clause might bring into the Constitution. Alan did his best to convince them. As he pointed out, "wonderful historical guideposts" indicated exactly what the clause was meant to protect. But it seemed like an uphill fight. Justice Thomas, as was his custom, remained silent at argument.[29]

When the arguments concluded, Otis and Alan waited again. Three months later, on June 28, 2010, they returned to the Supreme Court to hear the decision announced. Otis was outwardly confident, but he had his doubts. No case was a sure thing; his case studies had taught him that much. As he waited nervously, he admired the majestic courtroom. Even though it was not big, it had a commanding aura about it. The justices entered and took their assigned seats. They then announced the decision.

Otis had won! Four justices found that the Second Amendment was incorporated against the states through Substantive Due Process, as the NRA had argued.[30] They refused to revisit their privileges or immunities jurisprudence. Only one justice, Clarence Thomas, found that it was incorporated through the Privileges or Immunities Clause.[31] Otis read all the opinions, including the dissents, but he studied Justice Thomas's opinion closely and read it several times.

Justice Thomas used his opinion to provide a history lesson. First, he pointed out that the Court's substantive due process jurisprudence is a "legal fiction." He reiterated what Alan and Otis already knew: "a constitutional provision that guarantees only process" does not define any substantive rights; to think otherwise "strains credulity." Second, he made clear that the Founders had envisioned rights being incorporated against the states through the Privileges or Immunities Clause. He covered that history in detail. Then he turned to the subject at issue: guns and the states.

Justice Thomas started, again, with history. Leading up to the Civil War, the South had been worried about a slave rebellion. "Slaves and free blacks represented a substantial percentage of the population and posed a severe threat to the Southern order if they were not kept in their place." As Justice Thomas noted, these fears were not unfounded. There were "two particularly notable slave uprisings" that had had a strong influence on Southern opinion, leading Southern legislatures to restrict the rights of slaves and free blacks "to speak or to keep and bear arms for their defense." If authorities in those states found slaves or free blacks with firearms, they would be taken to a justice of the peace for severe punishment, which included "whipping on the bare back, not exceeding thirty-nine lashes" unless they could give a clear explanation of how they came to possess the gun.

After the Civil War, "Southern anxiety about an uprising among the newly freed slaves peaked." This led to "systematic efforts in the old Confederacy to disarm more than 180,000 freedmen who had served in the Union Army, as well as other freed blacks." Some states

Susette Kelo with her lawyer, Scott Bullock, in front of the Supreme Court on the day *Kelo v. City of New London* was argued. *Courtesy of the Institute for Justice*

Susette Kelo and her little pink house, which the city of New London sought to take from her by eminent domain. *Courtesy of the Institute for Justice*

The empty lot where Susette Kelo's house once stood. *Photograph taken by the author in 2022*

Cleveland parents demonstrating in front of the Supreme Court building in support of the Ohio student voucher program on the day of the argument in *Zelman v. Simmons-Harris*. *Courtesy of the Institute for Justice*

Bill Batchelder, the "godfather" of Ohio's voucher program, at issue in *Zelman v. Simmons-Harris*. *Courtesy of Alice Batchelder*

The University of Michigan Law School, which defended affirmative action admissions policies in *Grutter v. Bollinger*. *Courtesy of Flavinista. Reprinted under the Attribution-ShareAlike 4.0 International (CC BY-SA 4.0) Creative Commons License, available at https://creativecommons.org/licenses/by-sa/4.0/legalcode.*

The U.S. Military Academy at West Point, where "Jane Doe," the plaintiff in *Doe v. United States*, was an outstanding cadet. *Photograph by U.S. Military Academy Public Affairs Office*

Angel Raich at a press conference after the oral argument in *Gonzales v. Raich*. *Courtesy of Angel Raich*

Angel with medical marijuana plants. *Courtesy of Angel Raich*

Angel speaking in front of the Supreme Court building on the day *Gonzales v. Raich* was argued. *Courtesy of Angel Raich*

Angel Raich learning of the Supreme Court ruling in her case. *Courtesy of Angel Raich*

Kathy McKee, the plaintiff in *McKee v. Cosby*, with Sammy Davis Jr. *Courtesy of Kathy McKee*

The page from the Appendix to Justice Thomas's dissent in *Brumfield v. Cain* where he included the picture of Betty Smothers, who was murdered by Kevan Brumfield. *Courtesy of the Baton Rouge Police Department*

Warrick Dunn, Betty's oldest son, signing autographs as an All-Pro NFL running back on a USO tour aboard the U.S.S. *Ronald Reagan. Photograph by Mass Communication Specialist First Class Chad J. McNeeley*

Otis McDonald, the grandson of slaves who sued the city of Chicago for his right to own a handgun, speaking before the Supreme Court building, with lawyer Alan Gura to our left, Otis's nephew Fred Jones standing behind him, and lawyer Alan Gottlieb to our right. *Courtesy of the Second Amendment Foundation*

Otis McDonald with his team of Second Amendment attorneys. Left to right: David Sigale, Adam Orlov, David Lawson, Colleen Lawson, Alan Gura, Alan Gottlieb, Richard Pearson, and Otis McDonald. *Courtesy of the Second Amendment Foundation*

David Baugh, who defended Klansman Barry Black's right to burn a cross on First Amendment grounds. *Courtesy of David Baugh*

Ku Klux Klan members with a burning cross in 1921. *Denver Library Digital Collections*

The People's Justice

passed laws banning blacks from possessing firearms—known as "black codes." In addition, ex-Confederate soldiers and militiamen "forcibly took firearms from newly freed slaves." Justice Thomas emphasized that, as the majority had made clear, "if the Fourteenth Amendment had outlawed only those laws that discriminate on the basis of race or previous condition of servitude, African-Americans in the South would likely have remained vulnerable to attack by many of their worst abusers: the state militia and state peace officers."

At the time, many Americans had looked to the federal government to provide a solution. For example, "a memorial from the colored citizens of South Carolina" asked for, among other things, "constitutional protection in keeping arms." And the federal government attempted to resolve the problem by issuing military orders banning Southern arms legislation. But abolitionists wanted more—they wanted all "rights, privileges, and immunities granted by the [C]onstitution of the United States" to be "extended to all." As Frederick Douglass, the famed abolitionist and orator, had pointed out, absent a constitutional amendment to enforce the right to bear arms against the states, black Americans would never be on truly equal footing. All this, Justice Thomas explained, culminated in the passing of the Fourteenth Amendment's Privileges or Immunities Clause.

When Otis finished reading the opinions, he got up to leave the Court. The Americans who had passed the Fourteenth Amendment had sought to give all Americans—and especially freedmen—the right to protect themselves. And now, 144 years later, it was the grandson of one of those freedmen who had finally vindicated that right. Furthermore, the justice who had dared to tell their story was himself the descendant of slaves. Now, no man or woman need wait on the government for protection in his or her own home. Though the battle against lawlessness would continue, the descendants of slaves throughout the United States would no longer be powerless to protect themselves. In fact, thanks to Otis, no American would.

Otis felt such a burst of happiness that he couldn't help but smile. As he exited the Court, he stepped into the limelight. He thanked everyone he could think of—his family, his lawyers, and the other plaintiffs. Then he concluded, "Last, but not least, I am very grateful to the justices of the high court for having the courage to right a wrong, which has impacted many lives long ago, and this will protect many lives for many years to come. In my opinion, self-defense has been validated!"[32]

CHAPTER 10

Causation or Correlation?

Brown v. Entertainment Merchants Association

"I t's going to be like F—-ing *Doom*," said one teenager.[1] As he wrote in his journal, "I must not be sidetracked by my feelings of sympathy . . . so I will force myself to believe that everyone is just another monster in *Doom*."[2] His friend agreed: "I find a similarity between people and *Doom* zombies."[3]

Then, on April 20, 1999, the two teenagers proceeded to play out the video game *Doom* in real life. They entered Columbine High School and tragically shot and killed thirteen people and injured another twenty-one.[4]

At the time, *Doom* was known for its graphic violence—and it was one of the most popular video games ever made. Needless to say, it sparked controversy even before Columbine. The founder of Killology Research Group dubbed it a "mass murderer simulator."[5] The United States Marine Corps had modified a version of *Doom II* to train Marines and simulate missions. The Marines believed that games like *Doom* helped soldiers "prepare themselves mentally for the rigors of combat."[6]

The Columbine shooters were not the only mass shooters who had played violent video games. Less than a year before, an Oregon student had gone into a school and fatally shot four people and injured twenty-three more. The year before that, another *Doom* enthusiast had shot and killed three students and wounded five in his Kentucky high school. He was fourteen years old and "frighteningly accurate" with his shots.

Nor was *Doom* the only violent video game popular among teens. *Grand Theft Auto* was another. When *Grand Theft Auto: Vice City* was released in 2002, it became a bestseller right away, selling 4.4 million copies in the United States alone.[7]

In *Vice City*, the player has just been released from prison after serving fifteen years for murder. Now back in the mafia, he must break into the South American drug trade, by any means necessary. When he's not "working," the player can go outside and beat pedestrians to death—for fun.

When the cops come to get the player, he can choose to run to a car, pull a woman out, punch her, and steal her car. When the police finally catch him, the player can kill them—in the bloodiest fashion possible. Gore, guts, crime, and death are the main "thrills" of this game.

In 2005, players discovered that they could also access a hidden feature of the game. With a few lines of code, a player could unlock a "sex game," which allowed him to have sex with another character.[8]

In 2003, one teen played out *Grand Theft Auto* in real life. Alabama police arrested the teen for car theft and brought him to the station for booking. The teen attacked the officer booking him, stole his gun, and shot him. Fleeing down the hall, he saw a 911 dispatcher and shot her in the head for no reason. He grabbed car keys on his way out and hopped in a police car. Before these crimes, he had no criminal record. He was nothing more than a gamer. His game of choice? *Grand Theft Auto*.[9]

American Marines said *Grand Theft Auto* reminded them of combat they had seen during the invasion of Iraq. One said, "It felt like I was living it when I seen the flames coming out of windows, the blown-up car in the street, guys crawling around shooting at us."[10]

In response to these shootings by gamers, Iowa State psychology professor Craig Anderson started studying the impact of violent video games on American youth.[11] As personal computers took over in the 1990s, companies started producing games for them, like *Doom*. They also began building devices, such as Xboxes and PlayStations, exclusively for games. Kids no longer had to bike to the local arcade to play. They didn't have to save up their quarters. Now, so long as they had a computer or gaming console, kids could play video games for hours on end, holed up in their basements.

As the games became more graphic, violent, and easily available, they also became more addictive. In the 1990s, boys played on average four hours a week, while girls played two hours. By 2004, boys averaged thirteen hours a week and girls five hours.

That same year, the latest installment of *Grand Theft Auto—Grand Theft Auto: San Andreas*—became America's bestselling video game. Video games in general were selling at an amazing rate. In 2003 alone, approximately 239 million video games were sold in the United States (approximately 2 games for every household).[12] And by 2009, 90 percent of American kids were playing video games.[13]

Anderson, along with two other professors, produced a paper on the impact of violent video games. "The scientific debate about whether there are harmful effects of media violence is over," Anderson wrote. "Early exposure to violent media (including violent video games) causes an increase in later aggressiveness."[14]

Their report built on other studies. In 2001, United States surgeon general David Satcher had warned that the link between screen violence and aggression was stronger than the link between secondhand smoke and cancer.[15] Other reports had found that playing violent video games led to aggressive thoughts, antisocial behavior, delinquency, and poor school performance. The more children played violent games, the more desensitized to violence they became. Some of the games also had racist and sexist undertones. Sometimes, they weren't even undertones.[16]

The video game industry took notice and copied the movie industry, instituting a voluntary rating system. Games designed specifically for adults were given a Mature rating (M). But without the force of law behind them, these voluntary ratings did little to stop kids from acquiring those games. In a 2006 study, the Federal Trade Commission found that 69 percent of thirteen-to-sixteen-year-olds could successfully purchase M-rated games. "Even among those retailers with programs in place to restrict sales, 55% of the unaccompanied children were able to buy M-rated games."[17]

Leland Yee, a California state senator who had a doctorate in psychology, worried about the impact these games were having. Dr. Yee understood that playing a video game is different from passively listening to music, reading a book, or watching a movie or television show. In the game, the child is an active participant. He's part of the action and, unfortunately, the killing. The child chooses whether to kill and how to kill. It especially troubled him that eight-year-olds were playing the very same games that the military was using to train its soldiers for the "rigors of combat."

Dr. Yee studied the problem, talking to experts and reading their research, including the Anderson report. Then, on February 15, 2005, he proposed a law limiting children's access to violent video games. He was not trying to ban the games. His only goal was to make sure that children could not buy violent games without their parents' awareness and permission. Given the worries around these games, Dr. Yee believed that the least the government could do was help parents maintain the power of discretion regarding what their children should play.

Dr. Yee's law defined a violent video game as a game in which a player kills, maims, dismembers, or sexually assaults an image of a human being. In addition, for the game to qualify as "violent," a reasonable person had to believe that the game "appeals to a deviant or morbid interest of minors" and that it was "patently offensive to prevailing standards in the community as to what is suitable for minors." Finally, the game had to lack "serious literary, artistic, political, or scientific value for minors."

The law required video game makers to label these games as suitable only for people eighteen and over. And even then, the law still permitted a child under eighteen to buy the game if accompanied by a parent. The prohibition only applied to sales to *un*accompanied minors.[18]

On September 8, 2005, the California House approved the bill by a 66–7 vote. That same day, the California Senate approved it by a 22–9 margin. The bill had strong support not only from medical associations, but also from groups like the National Association for the Advancement of Colored People (NAACP), parent-teacher associations, and the Girl Scouts.[19]

The video game industry, however, was not a fan. By 2005, it had grown to a $7 billion-a-year enterprise centered in California. The industry had some sway, and it used it to put pressure on Governor Arnold Schwarzenegger. The industry hoped it would find an ally in the governor. After all, before entering politics, Schwarzenegger had starred in dozens of violent movies. And some of these movies, like the *Terminator* series, had spawned their own violent video games.

Despite pressure from the industry, the governor sided with Dr. Yee and California's parents. On October 7, 2005, he signed Dr. Yee's bill into law. "What this bill does is get parents involved in the decision-making process," Schwarzenegger explained. "I am a parent myself, and I think it's extremely important that we know what our kids watch and what games they play."[20]

The law was set to go into effect on January 1, 2006. But ten days after its signing, the Video Software Dealer Association and Entertainment Software Association sued to stop it from being enforced. Two days after that, they filed an emergency motion asking the court to stop California from enforcing the law. They argued that the law was unconstitutionally vague and a violation of their free speech rights.[21]

The news hit the papers and caught the eye of California deputy attorney general Zackery Morazzini on his way to the office. Morazzini wasn't much of a gamer himself—he'd grown up in northern California, where kids spent most of their free time outside. But Morazzini was a dedicated public servant, a passionate lawyer, and up for a challenge. And this case struck him as both fascinating legally and important for the people of California. As soon as he arrived at the office, he asked his supervisor if he could take the lead on the case.

After being assigned the case, Morazzini conferred with the stakeholders to decide the litigation strategy. This meant several meetings with the governor's team and representatives like Dr. Yee. They decided that they did not want to contest the idea that the games were speech. Instead, they decided to argue that this law was no different from a law banning minors from buying *Playboy* and other pornographic magazines.

Now California had to prove this to the district court. Morazzini devised a twofold strategy. First, he would introduce the studies that Dr. Yee and others had relied upon, which demonstrated the impact of violent video games on children. Second, they needed to show the court, in detail, what the children were playing. Morazzini knew an image would truly be worth a thousand words. So he bought copies of commonly available video games, and he and his colleagues spent their lunch breaks in the AV room playing and recording them.[22]

After submitting the gameplay snippets and the studies to the district court, Morazzini made his legal arguments. The video game makers did the same. Then the court rendered its decision.

The court's analysis began with the issue of vagueness. If the law was too vague, it might chill lawful speech because producers would be unsure what speech was lawful and what wasn't. In other words, producers (and even retailers) might hesitate to sell a game to a minor, even if its violence shouldn't trigger the California act's restrictions. To determine whether a video game producer could accurately discern whether the law applied to it, the court compared two of the video games the parties had submitted to the court.

The court's analysis started with *Postal 2*. As its name suggests, *Postal 2* involves a player who has "gone postal" and wants to kill everyone. As part of the game, the player kills not only police officers, but also unarmed children, and tortures animals. A player can shoot someone in the leg—and then throw gasoline on him and set him on fire. The player can urinate on him and say, "Now the flowers will grow." One feature of the game allows the player to use a cat as a silencer by putting a gun up the cat's rear.

After viewing the game, the district court found that *Postal 2* qualified as a "violent video game" under the law—and that the maker would easily know that it did.

Next, the court looked at *Full Spectrum Warrior*. That game, developed in part by the U.S. Army, involves a player who is in command of two squadrons of U.S. soldiers. The players plan and execute missions in a fictional Middle Eastern country that involve killing the enemy and saving downed airmen and the players' own wounded soldiers.

As the district court observed, while the game involves violence, it would be "hard to say that the U.S. military operations appeal to the deviant or morbid interests of minors." And, the court found, the game also has some political value. Because of these characteristics, a video game maker would know, the district court wrote, that the law would not cover *Full Spectrum Warrior*.

Consequently, the district court concluded the law was not vague.

Nonetheless, the district court granted the video game association's motion because it found that the law violated the First Amendment.[23] In doing so, the district court relied upon a decision written by well-known Seventh Circuit judge Richard Posner.[24] In that case, Judge Posner had found unconstitutional an Indianapolis ordinance that required a parent's approval before a minor could play a violent video game in an arcade.

Judge Posner started his opinion by recognizing that sexually explicit (obscene) materials were not protected by the First Amendment. He also wrote that "protecting people from violence is at least as hallowed a role for government as protecting people from graphic sexual imagery." Despite these traditions, Judge Posner rejected the ordinance. Shielding children from violent images until they are eighteen, the judge speculated, would have a "deforming" effect because "it would leave them unequipped to cope with the world as we know it." He then went on to compare violent video games to violence in literature. Even with the interactive nature of video games, Judge Posner opined, any distinctions between them and books were "superficial." Therefore, he concluded, the First Amendment should be read to invalidate the Indianapolis law.[25]

The district court relied on this decision and similar ones to say that "limitations on a minor's access to violent expression" were subject to the highest scrutiny available under the law. It found that Anderson's research linking the video games to violence was not conclusive enough to withstand this scrutiny. Therefore, the law violated the video game makers' First Amendment rights. On December 21, 2005, the court ordered California not to enforce the law.[26]

That order was preliminary. Next, the parties each asked the district court to make a final ruling in their favor. Eventually, on August 6, 2007, the district court ruled for the video game makers and granted their motion to permanently bar California from enforcing the law.[27] Morazzini promptly filed an appeal to the Ninth Circuit, asking the court of appeals to reinstate the law.

On October 29, 2008, the parties argued the case before the Ninth Circuit. As luck would have it, the Ninth Circuit heard the argument at the University of the Pacific's McGeorge School of Law, a leafy campus in Sacramento dotted with redwood trees, which was also Morazzini's alma mater.

When argument began, Morazzini contended that California should be allowed to regulate the availability of violent video games to children just as it does sexually explicit material. Both violence and sex appealed to minors for the wrong reasons. Furthermore, California was not trying to ban the games entirely, but only make sure that parents had a say in what their kids were exposed to.[28]

In making his case, Morazzini relied heavily upon an obscenity case called *Ginsberg v. New York*, concerning a New York law prohibiting the sale of sexually explicit ("obscene") materials to minors under seventeen years old. The Supreme Court had upheld the law and said, "[T]he power of the state to control the conduct of children reaches beyond the scope of its authority over adults." When a state finds a minor's "exposure to such material" to be "harmful," it may regulate it to protect the "well-being of its children." First, as the Court found, doing so enhances a parent's ability to "to direct the rearing of their children," which "is basic in the structure of our society." Second, a state also has "an independent interest in the well-being of its youth." And obscenity is not protected like other speech; it is not an infringement of the First Amendment for a state to regulate its purchase by minors.[29]

The Ninth Circuit did not buy California's argument. Even the state had agreed that video games are "a form of expression protected by the First Amendment." And California's law sought to restrict the purchase of video games based on their content—the violent nature of the games. The *Ginsberg* decision had only carved out a narrow exception to the First Amendment for sexually explicit materials. Since California was not trying to regulate sexually explicit materials, but rather violent ones, the Ninth Circuit decided it had to apply the highest level of scrutiny to the law. Like the district court before it, the Ninth Circuit concluded that California's law could not meet this exacting standard because they found the evidence of the harmful nature of video games inconclusive. The court also wondered whether parental controls within the new gaming systems would better accomplish the state's goal.[30]

Even years into the fight, Morazzini wasn't discouraged. He had known lower courts would be cautious. Now was time for the decisive appeal.

To improve the chances of getting the Supreme Court to take the case, Morazzini knew he needed to reach out to other states and organizations like the American Pediatric Association. Almost all of them said yes. With the backing of these parties, California filed a petition seeking Supreme Court review. The Supreme Court granted the petition and scheduled argument for November 2, 2010.[31]

In the interim, experts submitted amicus briefs on both sides. On average, the experts who backed California, such as Craig Anderson, had considerably more experience and had performed more studies on the impact of violent video games on children.[32]

A diverse set of states also came to California's aid with a powerful amicus brief. Under the leadership of Louisiana solicitor general Kyle Duncan (now a federal judge), the states that signed included Louisiana, Connecticut, Florida, Hawaii, Illinois, Maryland, Michigan,

Minnesota, Mississippi, Texas, and Virginia. This was one of the rare cases that saw California on the same side as Texas.[33]

Meanwhile, mail from the American public was flooding Morazzini's office. Letter after letter told Morazzini about the harm violent video games were doing to California's children. Concerned Californians, parent associations, and faith-based groups were worried for their boys and girls. "Keep fighting," they encouraged Morazzini. "Don't give up."[34]

The video game industry knew the stakes were high. They launched a public relations campaign to convince the American people that they had nothing to fear from violent video games—not an easy task in the wake of traumatic mass shootings.[35]

They also chose Paul M. Smith of the Jenner & Block law firm to argue the case before the United States Supreme Court. Smith was not just any lawyer, but an elite advocate who had argued numerous Supreme Court cases, including many involving commercial speech. Morazzini had a tremendous amount of respect for Smith as both a zealous advocate on behalf of his clients and a gentleman. Importantly, these two lawyers demonstrated one of the great hallmarks of the legal profession at its best: they disagreed with each other without being disagreeable.[36]

Finally, the day of argument arrived. Morazzini arrived at the great marble courthouse knowing it would be an uphill battle, but he was hopeful. Chief Justice Roberts called the case, and argument began.

As soon as Morazzini started speaking, Justices Scalia and Ginsburg intervened to try and pin down the difference between violent video games and violence in literature. Morazzini argued that the California legislature had reviewed substantial evidence showing that violent video games that were both "deviant" and "patently offensive" were "especially harmful to minors," which made them different than literature.

Next, the justices pressed him on why interactive games were different from movies. Movies, Morazzini argued, do not depart from the norms of what "children have been historically exposed to."

Next came questions about age. What might be inappropriate for a seven-year-old might be fine for a seventeen-year-old, yet the law didn't make any distinction between the two. Wasn't that a problem? In response, Morazzini agreed with Justice Breyer's observation that none of the violent video games have "serious literary, artistic, political, or scientific value," even for eighteen-year-olds. And since that was the case, they had no value for children under that age, either.

Moving to the issue of vagueness, the justices wanted to know how the video game industry was supposed to know which games were covered by the law. Morazzini pointed out that the video game industry already rated its games based on the level of violence involved, so it was clearly capable of engaging in such evaluations.

Finally, Morazzini noted that parents could still buy violent video games for their children. That, in a way, was California's main point. "Under *Ginsberg*," Morazzini explained, parents "are entitled to direct the development of the upbringing of their children in the manner they see fit." The law's purpose was to ensure that "parents can involve themselves in the front end" of the purchase. Parental controls on the computer system wouldn't suffice because "a simple internet search for bypassing parental controls brings up video clips instructing minors and young adults how to bypass the parental controls."

Smith took the podium next to argue on behalf of the video game industry. Smith contended that the California law restricts "expressive works based on their content." Chief Justice Roberts, who was the first member of the Court to speak, wanted to know why video games' interactive nature did not make them different from books and movies. When Smith argued in response that California did not have scientific evidence demonstrating that books and movies were different in how they affected children, Chief Justice Roberts pointed out that in *Ginsberg*, the Supreme Court hadn't insisted on scientific evidence—it had relied on common sense.

Justice Ginsburg then observed that the magazines the Supreme Court had allowed to be restricted in *Ginsberg* were "rather tame" when compared to the violent video games. Smith responded that, in *Ginsberg*, the Supreme Court was not trying to determine if particular materials were appropriate for children, but rather was trying to determine what materials properly fit within the definition of obscenity.

Justice Breyer wanted to know why it wasn't common sense to say that a state may restrict a child from buying a game where he "tortures and imposes gratuitous, painful, excruciating violence upon small children and women." He pointed out that the American Psychological and American Pediatric Association had sided with California and said the restriction was a good idea.

Smith argued that there was no evidence that parents needed help restricting their children's access to video games. In response, Breyer pointed out that parents usually have jobs and can't monitor their children twenty-four hours a day. California was just trying to help them. When Smith again suggested that parental controls could be used, Chief Justice Roberts noted that children could easily bypass those "in about 5 minutes."

Justice Breyer and Chief Justice Roberts pressed Smith on why violence didn't merit regulation while obscenity did. Smith argued that there simply was "not a violence exception to the First Amendment."

Justice Alito asked whether literature was really the most accurate parallel. He pointed out that the American Founding Fathers could never have envisioned video games, much less video games in which children could "dispose of [their] enemies in a meat grinder." Smith argued that new types of media, like radio or television, come along all the time, and society often overreacts to them at first.

Justice Alito asked Smith whether he would argue that "there is nothing that a state can do to limit minors' access to the most violent, sadistic, graphic video game that can be developed." Smith admitted that, in his view, there was *nothing* a state could do. Chief Justice Roberts then asked if the state could, at the very least, require that these games be placed on a high shelf out of the reach of small children. Smith said no.

Justice Scalia suggested that the games were too expensive for most children to buy, so the risk of a child's acquiring a game without a parent's aid wasn't that great.

When Morazzini got up for rebuttal, he told the justices that while the games may cost $60, they could also be rented for less, meaning children could likely afford them without their parents' knowledge.[37] Finally, the lively argument was over, and the waiting began.

The Supreme Court did not announce its decision until June 27, 2011, the final day of its term. California lost. Justice Scalia wrote the opinion for the Court, finding that the law violated the First Amendment. Justices Kennedy, Ginsburg, Sotomayor, and Kagan agreed with him.

Starting from first principles, Justice Scalia observed that the First Amendment protects most speech. That means that the government lacks the power "to restrict expression because of its message, its ideas, its subject matter, or its content." Several specific, narrow exceptions exist, like for obscenity. But beyond these preexisting exceptions, rooted in "long tradition," states cannot create new ones.

California was therefore not permitted to shoehorn violent speech into a preexisting exception or analogize it to one. Justice Scalia pointed out that California was trying to "make violent-speech regulation look like obscenity." But the Supreme Court's "cases have been clear that the obscenity exception to the First Amendment does not cover whatever a legislature finds shocking, but only depictions of 'sexual conduct.'" Thus, because "speech about violence is not obscene," it did not matter that California's law "mimic[ked]" the obscenity law upheld in *Ginsberg*.

For Justice Scalia, the fact that the law specifically regulated speech directed at minors didn't matter. As the Supreme Court had said before, "Speech that is neither obscene as to youths nor subject to some other legitimate proscription cannot be suppressed solely to protect the young from ideas or images that a legislative body thinks unsuitable for them." There was no history in America of protecting children from violent images, Justice Scalia asserted. And to back that claim, he noted that little children are often read *Grimm's Fairy Tales*, and when they reach high school, they are assigned books such as *Lord of the Flies*.

The fact that video games were interactive, or new, didn't change anything. All good literature, Scalia wrote, is interactive. As early as 1969, "young readers of choose-your-own adventure stories have been able to make decisions that determine the plot by following instructions."

Since the speech at issue was protected by the First Amendment, that meant California's law would have to withstand the highest scrutiny to survive. And this it could not do. The studies California relied upon were, in Justice Scalia's opinion, "not compelling." While the state had offered evidence of correlation between the games and negative outcomes, it had not shown causation. In other words, the state had failed to "prove that violent video games *cause* minors to *act* aggressively."[38]

Justice Alito, joined by Chief Justice Roberts, had a different concern: they found that the law was too vague and thus did not provide the "fair notice that the Constitution requires."

Justices Alito and Roberts disagreed with the majority about whether California could ever ban such games. While the majority treated video games as no different than movies or books, Justice Alito argued that it had too quickly disposed of the idea that video games might be different "from anything that we have seen before." Before lumping the new technology in with books, Justice Alito said, the Court "should make every effort to understand the new technology. . . . There are reasons to suspect that the experience of playing violent video games just might be different from reading a book, listening to the radio, or watching a movie or a television show." And the Court should not discount the views of "federal and state legislators, educators, social scientists, and parents" so easily.

"Today's most advanced video games," Justice Alito observed, "create realistic alternative worlds in which millions of players immerse themselves for hours on end." And the technology would keep improving. One day, Justice Alito hypothesized, technological advances might allow players to feel pain "by wearing a special vest or other device," or even to experience "the splatting of blood from the blown-off head of a victim."

These games were not tame, even compared to violent movies or books. In some games, points were "awarded based, not only on the number of victims killed, but on the killing technique employed." One game, *School Shooter*, allowed a player to "reenact the killings carried out by the perpetrators of the murders at Columbine High School and Virginia Tech."

If that wasn't bad enough, in one game the objective was "to rape a mother and her daughters," and in a different game, "to rape Native American women." In another, "players engage in 'ethnic cleansing' and can choose to gun down African Americans, Latinos, or Jews."

Add a troubled teen to the mix, and he can learn "in an extraordinarily personal and vivid way what it would be like to carry out unspeakable acts of violence." As Justice Alito saw it, the Court did not need to go as far as it had to "squelch" the legislature's ability to deal with what some consider "a significant and developing social problem."

Even so, Justice Alito hesitated to affirm the law. While some violence might merit banning games, not all violence did, and California's law was not specific. A video game reenacting a school shooting was one thing. But what about cartoon violence like in *Looney Toons*? Or reenacting the Allied landings on D-Day? A game based on World War II might involve "killing" and "maiming," but was shooting a digital depiction of a Nazi the same as murdering a digital pedestrian for sport? California's law didn't say. Instead, it referred video game makers to "community standards." But those standards weren't obvious, either. Average people might differ greatly over what violence is acceptable for children of one age or another. Justice Alito concluded that California could enact a constitutional law if it was more specific in what it banned.[39]

Justice Thomas and Justice Breyer dissented from the decision of the Court. Each wrote his own opinion.

For Justice Breyer, common sense and the word of the experts mattered most. He wrote that the First Amendment yielded to the compelling need for the state to help parents protect their children from harm, which had, in his view, been sufficiently demonstrated by "considerable evidence." The evidence also showed that video games helped people develop habits. "Why else would the Armed Forces incorporate video games into its training?" And while the military had good reasons to use video games to train adults for combat, parents might justifiably hesitate before allowing their own children to be subjected to the same experience. For anyone who doubted the evidence, he attached an appendix to his opinion listing the "peer-reviewed academic journal articles on the topic of psychological harm resulting from playing violent video games."[40]

For Justice Thomas, the original meaning of the Constitution was what mattered. He did not think the expert debates, analogies to obscenity, or concerns about vagueness were relevant. Indeed, to him, the question wasn't whether the First Amendment protected depictions of violence. Rather, it was whether the First Amendment was intended to apply to children the same as adults. And there, the answer was clearly no.

The "practice and beliefs of the founding generation," Justice Thomas observed, "establish that 'the freedom of speech,' as originally understood does not include a right to speak to minors . . . without going through the minors' parents or guardians."

"It would be absurd," he said, to think that the Founders believed the Constitution guaranteed a right to speak to someone else's child without the parent's permission.

Justice Thomas then cataloged considerable evidence demonstrating that "the founding generation believed parents had absolute authority over their minor children." He started by pointing out that in colonial New England, the father was thought to rule the family with absolute authority. And after the Revolution, parents continued to have authority over their children "including control over the books their children read."

As many in the Founding generation understood, children "lacked reasoned decision-making ability" and had "malleable minds." It was the parents' duty to regulate what their children saw and read and how they were educated. "In short, home and family bore the major responsibility for the moral training of children and thus, by implication, for the moral health of the nation."

That "control over children's lives extended into the schools." Teachers understood that parents had the ultimate authority over their children and their children's education.

"The law at the time reflected the founding generation's under-standing of parent-child relations." Laws did not allow boys to "enlist in the military without parental consent." Other laws set age limits for marriage without parental consent.

States continue to have laws that assist parents, Justice Thomas added. Some states prohibit people from luring or enticing "a minor away from the minor's parent." Most states still have laws that condition a minor's ability to marry, join the Army, or stay out late on a parent's consent.

Justice Thomas concluded by noting that "this Court has never held, until today, that 'the freedom of speech' includes a right to speak to minors (or a right of minors to access speech) without going through the minors' parents." Parental consent laws were desirable and permissible at the Founding and remain that desirable and permissible today, so California's law should have been allowed to stand.[41]

While the other justices debated what sorts of depictions of violence the First Amendment might protect, Justice Thomas saw that the original meaning of the Constitution gave a simpler, common-sense answer: a parent has the right to regulate the type of speech to which her child is exposed.

● ● ●

After the decision, Dr. Yee wanted to amend the law immediately and take a second shot. But Morazzini counseled caution. To overcome the stringent standard established in the Court's ruling, California would need more evidence—evidence clearly showing not just correlation, but causation between violent video games and real-world acts of violence. A second shot would have to wait.[42] Even so, Morazzini, who had been "naïve" about video games when he started litigating the case, had learned a great deal about them. He sympathized with Dr. Yee's desire to try again. Playing ultra-violent video games was clearly bad for minors' development. Children shouldn't be playing these games at all, he thought. Or, at the very least, the parents should know and supervise them.[43]

Since *Brown v. Entertainment Merchants Association*, the video game industry has continued to grow. In 2021, it pulled in revenue of $180 billion.[44] Meanwhile, defenders of violent video games continue to insist that the games don't cause children to commit violent acts. Rather, they say, certain children are already predisposed to kill.[45]

Yet the controversy over violent video games persists. After the shooting in Newtown, Connecticut, parents in the neighboring city collected and burned video games in protest.[46] Meanwhile, Congress pushed for tougher gun-purchase laws and considered legislation pledging millions of dollars to reexamine the relationship between video game play and violence. Congress never authorized the funding.[47] But a report from the Connecticut Office of the Child Advocate in 2014 found that "heavy or addictive video game use can have 'a deleterious impact on social emotional functioning.'"[48]

Video game makers have also developed other products that raise concerns for parents. One, so-called "loot boxes," allow players to pay real-world dollars to purchase randomized in-game upgrades. The randomization makes these purchases akin to playing a slot machine. Often, the players buying these loot boxes are young children. In an effort to curb this practice, Senator Josh Hawley, with the bipartisan endorsements of Senators Richard Blumenthal and Ed Markey, proposed legislation to restrict these purchases in 2019. As Senator Blumenthal put it, Congress must show that children "are not cash cows" to be "exploit[ed] for profit."[49] The bill was never voted on.[50]

More recently, agencies have taken measures on their own. In December 2022, the federal government settled with Epic Games, the maker of the hit video game *Fortnite*. Why? Because, the government alleged, *Fortnite* was designed to allow children to make in-game purchases without parental approval. The game is also allegedly designed to trick users into making purchases. Rather than fight the allegations, the video game maker settled for $245 million.[51]

CHAPTER 11

A Good Neighbor?
State Farm v. Campbell

E ven more than most people, Curtis and Inez Campbell knew
that life is never easy.
Curtis's first wife had been murdered. His second wife left
him after he had a stroke. His third wife died of cancer. When he married Inez, his fourth wife, he hoped his bad luck had finally run out.[1]

Inez, for her part, had experienced a bitter divorce. Even after
they married, the Campbells had to go through a foreclosure on their
home and a repossession of one of their cars because of the actions
of Inez's ex-husband.[2]

Finally retired, and with their past hardships behind them, the
Campbells looked forward to a good and peaceful life together. On
Memorial Day weekend, 1981, the Campbells were returning from a
wedding reception, driving through Sardine Canyon in Utah. As the
name suggests, the canyon is quite narrow, and the road had only one
lane running in each direction.[3]

While driving through the canyon, the Campbells came upon a
slow-moving, six-van caravan. Mr. Campbell crossed the line and
tried to pass the entire caravan at once. While he was passing the
vans, he saw a car coming toward him. He sped up, crossed back over

the line in the nick of time, and narrowly avoided a collision. But the driver of the oncoming car, Todd Ospital, had to veer onto the shoulder to avoid hitting Campbell. He overcorrected in his effort to get back on the road and hit one of the vans head on, which was driven by Robert Slusher.[4]

The resulting accident was horrible. Ospital, a college freshman, died at the scene, while Slusher suffered serious injuries that left him permanently disabled. The Campbells were not hurt, but the accident would haunt them for the rest of their lives.[5]

Investigators descended on the scene. State Farm, which insured the Campbells, sent out Ray Summers to interview witnesses and collect evidence. After completing his investigation, Summers concluded that Mr. Campbell was at least partially to blame. Slusher's out-of-pocket medical bills alone were more than $20,000. Summers worried that when Slusher and the Ospitals sued Campbell, he would lose big. The Campbells' policy limit was only $25,000 per person and $50,000 per accident, so the Campbells would be on the hook for any damages exceeding that limit.[6]

Summers presented the report to his supervisors. One supervisor objected to the report and instructed Summers to change the report to say that Mr. Campbell was not at fault. When Summers disagreed, his supervisor told him to "do what you're told."[7] Fearing for his job, Summers followed the order. After he changed the report, State Farm removed him from the case.[8]

That was just the beginning of the lies and deception. When the inevitable lawsuit against Mr. Campbell came, he asked State Farm to hire him a lawyer. The company reached out to one of its regular lawyers, Wendell Bennett, who took over the case. Bennett claimed to have won more than one hundred trials in this part of Utah. In reality, he had tried fewer than ten cases and had lost most of them.[9]

Slusher had sued both Mr. Campbell and Ospital's estate, claiming they were to blame for his injuries. Ospital's estate also sued Campbell, claiming he was actually responsible. Bennett answered the complaint on the Campbells' behalf, claiming that Ospital was to blame for the accident. As would become known only later, a State Farm official had told the claims adjuster on the case to lie and say "that Ospital was 'speeding to visit his pregnant girlfriend.'"[10] But there was no pregnant girlfriend, and both the adjuster and the company knew that the fault lay with Mr. Campbell.[11]

Before trial, Bennett had to confront the evidence, including documents and eye-witness testimony, which demonstrated that "a consensus was reached early on by investigators and witnesses that Mr. Campbell's unsafe pass had indeed caused the crash."[12] Even State Farm's hired expert said that Mr. Campbell did not allow sufficient time to pass the caravan.[13]

On various occasions leading up to trial, the Ospitals' attorney, Rich Humphreys, offered to settle with the Campbells to avoid forcing the Ospitals to relive their son's death at trial. When State Farm rejected his initial offer, Humphreys followed up with the Ospitals' offer to accept the policy limit of $25,000. Failing to accept this offer, he pointed out, would expose the Campbells to considerable personal liability.[14]

Again, State Farm refused his offer. At that point, Humphreys gave them one last chance and offered to settle the Ospitals' death claim against Campbell for less than $25,000. He told State Farm that if it didn't accept, he was going to settle with Slusher. When State Farm continued to balk, Humphreys followed through on his promise. Thereafter, both Slusher and the Ospitals trained their sights on Mr. Campbell and argued he was to blame for the accident.[15]

Bennett and State Farm assured the Campbells that they had nothing to fear with a trial because they were not at fault. They also told the Campbells that even if a jury found them liable, they would not have to pay since a verdict would not exceed the policy limits. They didn't tell the Campbells that there were numerous eyewitnesses lined up to testify against them.[16]

When the trial began and the Campbells heard the testimony, they were perplexed. Why hadn't anyone told them about the witnesses? Bennett assured them there was nothing to worry about.[17]

But then the jury returned a verdict finding Mr. Campbell 100 percent at fault. The damages: $253,957—more than $200,000 over the policy limit. Mr. Campbell was shocked. He asked Bennett what would happen next. "Put a for sale sign on your property," Bennett responded.[18]

The Campbells were distraught. Bennett had assured them that he would represent their interests, that they didn't need counsel of their own, and that they would not be exposed to liability. But now the verdict would cost them everything.[19]

They "spent many, many nights never sleeping . . . discussing what [they] would do." People close to Mr. Campbell described him as "personally very devastated," "fragile," and "greatly distressed." They were worried he would suffer another stroke.[20]

News of the verdict quickly spread. The local State Farm office even posted a newspaper account of the story as a warning to its clients. The message: increase your policy limits with us or this could happen to you.[21]

In the meantime, State Farm appealed and continued to fight the verdict. Left with few options, the Campbells decided to seek advice from another attorney—especially since they believed that State Farm had abandoned them. The attorney advised them that if Slusher and the Ospitals collected on the judgment, the Campbells would lose everything. So the Campbells' new counsel demanded, as the Ospitals and Slusher had earlier, that State Farm pay the entire verdict. State Farm refused.[22]

The Campbells started looking at their assets to try and find a way to pay without going into ruin. There wasn't one. So their attorney tried something unusual. He reached out to Humphreys, the lawyer on the other side of the lawsuit. Humphreys sympathized with the Campbells. During the lawsuit, he had seen firsthand how badly State Farm was acting. As an insurance-law expert, he also recognized that the Campbells had a valid "bad-faith" claim against State Farm, meaning that rather than give the Campbells the protection their policy had paid for, State Farm had sacrificed the Campbells to protect its own bottom line. He came up with a plan that would benefit everyone: if the Campbells would file the bad-faith claim and share the proceeds, the Ospitals and Slusher would forego their claims against the Campbells. They all agreed. That ended their dispute, and a new partnership began, with Humphreys at the lead.[23]

Humphreys filed the Campbells' bad-faith suit against State Farm. They claimed that State Farm (1) failed to properly investigate the accident, (2) unreasonably refused to settle the case, (3) misrepresented the Campbells' exposure to the Campbells, and (4) acted in its own interests and against the Campbells'. They also sought damages for fraud, emotional distress, and damage to their reputation. Finally, the Campbells asked for punitive damages, which are meant to punish the defendant for its actions.[24]

After Humphreys filed the lawsuit, he was surprised that State Farm did not come to the table. He knew that once a bad-faith suit was filed, the case would be escalated within the company. And in his experience as an insurance defense lawyer, he had often found that a company's higher-ups could be more willing to compromise than the ground-level adjusters and lawyers assigned to the case. He had believed that once the higher-ups saw that the Ospitals and Slusher had an iron-clad verdict, supported by overwhelming evidence, and that State Farm was facing serious bad-faith exposure, the company's executives would be anxious to settle. Yet much to his surprise, the top executives did not intervene, and he continued to get the same response: No. The policy limit was all State Farm would pay.[25]

State Farm was now fighting two lawsuits—one for the accident and one for bad faith. State Farm did change its tune eventually when it lost the accident suit at the Utah Supreme Court in 1989. Out of appeals, and thus out of options, State Farm paid the entire amount of the judgment. So after eight years, State Farm had ponied up the policy limit plus the $135,000 the Campbells owed. But State Farm still refused to settle the bad-faith lawsuit.[26]

Humphreys was puzzled by State Farm's continued resistance to settling. He reached out to one of the lawyers in his firm, Roger Christensen, for advice. They had been doing insurance defense work for years, and neither of them had seen an insurance company act so belligerently. Something wasn't right. Christensen agreed to help.

Humphreys and Christensen started by reaching out to lawyers around the country. What they found seemed to confirm their worst suspicions: that this wasn't a one-time situation for State Farm; it was a pattern. It appeared that State Farm had a practice of lowballing cases—even when its own clients clearly were liable.[27]

The consensus of this informal network of lawyers was one thing. Proof was another. Humphreys and Christensen next reached out to former State Farm employees. One was Ina DeLong. She had worked for the company for more than twenty-three years, during which she held several positions, including insurance adjuster.[28] She told Christensen and Humphreys that State Farm habitually avoided paying the fair value of a claim. What they heard next shocked them even more. Everyone knows State Farm's advertising slogan: "Like a Good Neighbor." Internally, however, State Farm's slogan was "State Farm, God, and Country." In no uncertain terms,

"State Farm was number one, and everybody else came after that, including God and country."[29]

According to DeLong, State Farm preyed on claimants by exploiting their weakness. She claimed State Farm specifically targeted "minorities," "senior citizens," "females," and people experiencing hardship, such as "a severe injury [from] an automobile accident."[30] She admitted that during her time at State Farm, she had "unfortunately" participated in this practice to keep her job. Indeed, "overpayments" to clients were met with reprimands.[31]

The last straw for DeLong was the Loma Prieta Earthquake, which hit Northern California in 1989. She supervised claims processing for the disaster. When she saw that State Farm was going to try to shortchange the victims, she objected. She convinced her bosses that State Farm needed to audit the processed claims. When they agreed, they found that 1,400 claims had been underpaid to the tune of $175 million.[32] Worse, the audit found claimants had been returned to unsafe homes. When she insisted State Farm "make it right," the company refused. DeLong quit and took evidence of State Farm's misdeeds to the news media.[33]

After she quit, DeLong regularly testified as an expert in cases where State Farm was accused of acting in bad faith.[34] State Farm was so concerned about what she knew that it had assigned a lawyer to be an "Ina DeLong specialist," appearing in court each time she testified as an expert.[35] All across the country, this lawyer would depose her for hours on end, asking the same questions. At one point, the company even had a hotel maid spy on her.[36]

This type of intimidation, when they learned about it, offended and angered Humphreys and Christensen and gave them even more resolve. In all their years of insurance defense, they had never seen an insurance company behave this badly. It seemed like something out of the movies. Apparently, the Campbells' mistreatment was part of State Farm's culture, but they were going to bring the bully down. In Christensen's words, "The reason I went to law school was to fight this sort of thing."[37]

The next piece of the puzzle was Wendell Bennett, the lawyer who had unsuccessfully "represented" the Campbells for State Farm. His files looked like no others they had seen. It is standard practice in the industry for lawyers to issue a "CYA" letter, a sort of disclaimer of the risks involved in litigation. That way, if a lawyer loses at trial, the client cannot claim it has not been warned about the downside of refusing a settlement and going forward with the litigation. But the letters from Bennett to State Farm consistently expressed uncharacteristic and unjustified confidence in success.[38]

Soon Humphreys and Christensen had a hunch why Bennett had sent these letters. Based on evidence they had reviewed, they believed that State Farm must have instructed him to overstate his clients' odds of winning. While they couldn't be 100 percent sure, it was their working theory. And it made sense to them because, that way, when a client lost and accused the insurance company of acting in bad faith—for failing to settle with the other side for an amount within the limits of the policy, for example—State Farm could point to the lawyer's letters to say it had simply acted on the advice of counsel. Indeed, in a bad-faith lawsuit, anything less than a letter assuring victory could be used as evidence that the insurer should have settled. Christensen thought State Farm was making sure that this type of evidence did not exist.[39]

As the case sped toward trial, the parties began "discovery," the process in which they exchange documents. Humphreys and Christensen were amazed when State Farm produced fewer documents than they did—leading them to conclude that the insurance company must be hiding or destroying evidence.[40]

When the case ultimately went to trial, Christensen and Humphreys had an arsenal of evidence at their disposal. During trial, they were able to demonstrate that State Farm had engaged in similar misconduct in previous cases. They argued that taking accident cases such the Campbells' to trial rather than accepting a reasonable settlement was part of a "national scheme to meet corporate fiscal goals by capping payouts on claims company wide."[41] They had experts, including DeLong, testify about the "fraudulent practices by State Farm in its nation-wide operations."[42] From this evidence, they showed that State Farm would decide how much it was willing to pay for an accident and then build a record supporting that number, regardless of any contrary evidence or any responsibility to respect the truth or their duty to their customers.

State Farm's team of lawyers was no match for Christensen and Humphreys. After twenty-nine days of trial and long deliberations, the jury returned with the verdict: $2.6 million in compensatory damages—for things like medical bills and emotional harm—and $145 million in punitive damages, to punish State Farm for its egregious conduct.[43] Shocked, Christensen and Humphreys asked the court whether it had counted the correct number of zeros. It had, much to State Farm's chagrin.[44]

Obviously displeased with this result, State Farm filed a motion with the trial court to reduce the award, arguing that an award that high was not allowed under Utah law. Christensen and Humphreys had just tried and won the case of the century, but they needed a big gun to help them defend the verdict. Their research led them to Harvard Law School professor Laurence Tribe. Considered by many to be one of the greatest legal minds in the country, Professor Tribe graduated from high school at age sixteen, studied mathematics at Harvard, and then went on to Harvard Law School. After obtaining his law degree, he clerked for two judges—including Potter Stewart on the United States Supreme Court—and then returned to Harvard Law School as a professor. From there, he gained such respect in the legal community that when President Bill Clinton had a vacancy on the Supreme Court, many lawyers and legal scholars wanted him to pick Professor Tribe (for the seat that ultimately went to Ruth Bader Ginsburg).[45]

So Humphreys and Christensen called Tribe to ask for his help. They told him about their verdict and asked him to join the team and argue the post-trial motions. Tribe thanked them for their interest but said he was too busy.[46]

They had come too far to take no for an answer, so Humphreys and Christensen hopped on a plane to Boston. If Tribe was going to say no, he would have to say it to their faces. They went to his office at the law school and waited. When he arrived, they sat down and explained the importance of curbing State Farm's targeted, malicious behavior. If that wasn't enough, they offered him a percentage of the verdict and said they had come too far to be rejected. Their persistence finally won Tribe over, elevating the case's profile significantly.[47]

Tribe's involvement made the proceedings a must-see event for the Utah legal community. Students, lawyers, and even a few judges showed up to hear Tribe argue the case. But Tribe didn't expect his celebrity to carry them to victory. He prepared meticulously for every argument, and he had a lot of help. Tribe brought a small team with him, and they worked closely with Christensen, Humphreys, and Karra Porter, an appellate specialist at the Utah firm. Porter was an elite appellate lawyer in her own right and contributed significantly to the post-trial motion, and eventually on the appellate briefs. The entire team would meet before argument, discuss strategy, and often stay up nearly all night preparing.[48]

After two years of post-trial proceedings, the trial court issued a 74-page opinion, finding that "State Farm's misconduct was pervasive." According to the court, State Farm had engaged in a "deliberate and wrongful effort to enhance corporate profits, a scheme that was orchestrated by top officials." The company had exerted "unrelenting pressure to keep down payouts to meet arbitrary claim payment goals." Indeed, State Farm paid its claims adjusters based on how much (or, ideally, how little) they paid out each year.[49]

The trial court also found that State Farm had used unethical methods to cover its tracks. For example, State Farm had "launched elaborate efforts to destroy" all records of its misdeeds, "with the explicit purpose" of preventing plaintiffs like the Campbells from obtaining those records. When a customer dared sue State Farm, the company instructed its attorneys to look into his debts, domestic problems, and affairs. The goal was to embarrass the person into dropping the suit.[50]

Even the suits that were successful didn't change anything at State Farm. The company had no mechanism for reporting bad-faith verdicts up the chain. In fact, just a few years before the Campbells' case, State Farm had lost a $100 million case in Texas, but the company's management claimed never to have heard anything about it.[51]

It's hard to send a message to a company that keeps its head buried in the sand. But the jury did its best, and the trial court believed the evidence supported the jury's conclusion. The court summarized State Farm's practices as "callous, clandestine, fraudulent, and dishonest." However, it concluded that Utah law compelled it to reduce the punitive damages award from $145 million to $25 million, which was only .05% of State Farm's net worth. The court also reduced the compensatory damages from $2.6 million to $1 million.[52]

At this point, both sides appealed to the Utah Supreme Court. There, State Farm argued that since its conduct did not "involve murder, torture, or deliberate poisoning of the environment," punitive damages were not warranted. The Utah Supreme Court disagreed. It seconded the trial court's findings that State Farm "repeatedly and deliberately deceived and cheated its customers" and targeted "poor racial or ethnic minorities, women, and elderly individuals." Basically, anyone "who State Farm believed would be less likely to object or take legal action" was a potential target for exploitation.

Like the trial court before it, the Utah Supreme Court also noted that State Farm "engaged in deliberate concealment and destruction of documents related to this profit scheme." The destruction had occurred even when the litigation was ongoing. State Farm had also "systemically harassed and intimidated opposing claimants, witnesses, and attorneys."

Finally, the Utah Supreme Court found that State Farm's actions had led the Campbells to live "under constant threat of losing everything they had worked for their whole lives." "This threat led to sleeplessness, heartache, and stress in the Campbells' marriage and family relationships." Considering that State Farm routinely engaged in this type of behavior, its conduct could fairly be considered "egregious." The punitive damage reward was therefore justified to deter State Farm from taking advantage of its customers in the future. That was especially true because people like the Campbells trust their insurance company to look out for their best interests. For all these reasons, the Utah Supreme Court reinstated the $145 million punitive damage award.[53]

But State Farm was not done. The company asked the United States Supreme Court to review the case, claiming that the punitive damage award violated State Farm's due process rights. State Farm further claimed that the Utah courts were not allowed to consider State Farm's conduct beyond Utah's borders. The United States Supreme Court granted review and scheduled argument for December 11, 2002—twenty-one years after the original accident. Ospital would have been almost forty.

For its part, State Farm hired a large law firm to handle the case, and Sheila Birnbaum, a partner at the firm, to argue it. Representing the party challenging the lower court's ruling, Birnbaum went first.

Out of the gate, Birnbaum argued that the Utah courts were not allowed to consider State Farm's nationwide conduct, just its conduct in Utah. Justice Scalia asked several pointed questions. First, he asked what provision of the Bill of Rights protected corporations from judgments like this. Due process, Birnbaum answered. Later in the argument, Birnbaum argued that the Court should impose a limit on punitive damages: they must be less than ten times larger than compensatory damages. Still skeptical, Justice Scalia interjected, "10 times is what the Constitution says?" Of course, the number is not in the Constitution—something Birnbaum conceded to a laughing courtroom.

On the other side, Professor Tribe pointed out that the nationwide fraudulent practices were relevant to the question whether State Farm was truly being "a good neighbor." And since most of its customers did not have sufficient resources to battle State Farm, a large verdict was necessary to deter future predatory practices.[54]

As always, when argument finished, the waiting game began. Then, on April 7, 2003, the Supreme Court announced its opinion. Justice Kennedy wrote the majority for six justices, including Chief Justice Rehnquist and Justices Stevens, O'Connor, Souter, and Breyer.

The majority found that the $145 million punitive damage award violated the Constitution's Due Process Clause. While the majority recognized that states have broad discretion over punitive damages, it found the award was "grossly excessive," and thus, furthered "no legitimate purpose" and constituted "an arbitrary deprivation of property."

The majority noted that in a 1996 case, *BMW v. Gore*, it had instructed courts to consider three guideposts: (1) the reprehensibility of the defendant's misconduct; (2) the difference between the actual harm suffered and the punitive damages award; and (3) "the difference between the punitive damages awarded by the jury and the civil penalties authorized or imposed in comparable cases."

As to the first factor, the majority stated, "State Farm's handling of the claims against the Campbells merits no praise." Nonetheless, the majority believed that "a more modest punishment for this reprehensible conduct could have satisfied the State's legitimate objectives, and the Utah courts should have gone no further." The majority said that the Utah courts had gone beyond protecting those "legitimate objectives" when they considered State Farm's conduct in other states. According to the majority, Utah did not have a legitimate interest in punishing out-of-state conduct.

Turning to the second guidepost, the Court noted that it had been hesitant to impose a "bright-line ratio" between harm to the plaintiff and punitive damages, but it averred that "few awards exceeding a single-digit ratio between punitive and compensatory damages . . . will satisfy due process." In the end, the majority asserted, the punishment must be "both reasonable and proportionate." And, according to the Court majority, the punitive damages award in the Campbells' case was not.

Finally, the sanction in Utah for each act of fraud was $10,000, and that amount was "dwarfed by the $145 million punitive damages award."

Since none of the three guideposts were met, the majority sent the case back to the Utah Supreme Court to try again.[55]

Justices Ginsburg, Scalia, and Thomas dissented.

According to Justice Ginsburg, the Supreme Court had no business substituting its judgment for that of "Utah's competent decision makers." And "there [was] a good deal more to the story than the Court's abbreviated account tells." Justice Ginsburg then cataloged the "ample evidence" she believed the majority had ignored. State Farm had personally attacked claimants, questioning their honesty and character. The company had also forced employees to commit dishonest acts to deny or lessen the value of claims. And State Farm intentionally preyed on the weakest and most vulnerable. Justice Ginsburg's opinion echoed the Utah courts' opinions, with a heavy dose of facts showing just how badly State Farm had behaved.

Next, Justice Ginsburg noted that the Campbells' case was representative, not unique. Further, she pointed out that the out-of-state context was relevant to document both how reprehensible State Farm's conduct was and to "rebut State Farm's assertion that its actions towards the Campbells were inadvertent errors or mistakes in judgment."

She concluded by noting that when the Supreme Court first got involved in punitive damages, "it did so moderately" out of respect for the states. "Today's decision exhibits no such respect and restraint." What were once flexible guidelines for states in assessing punitive damages awards had now become "instructions that begin to resemble marching orders."[56]

Justices Scalia and Thomas both wrote short dissents, asserting that the Constitution does not regulate punitive damages.[57] In their dissents, they both relied upon a dissent from the earlier punitive damages due process case, *BMW v. Gore,* which Justice Scalia had written and Justice Thomas had joined.

In the *Gore* dissent, Justice Scalia had explained that "At the time of the adoption of the Fourteenth Amendment, it was well understood that punitive damages represent the assessment by the jury, as the voice of the community, of the measure of punishment the defendant deserved." When the Court displaces these awards, it "is really no more than a disagreement with the community's sense of indignation or outrage expressed in the punitive award." Finally, when the Court creates guideposts, it is doing so not because the Constitution compels it, but rather "to establish federal standards governing hitherto exclusively state law of damages." By requiring state courts to go through these narrow guideposts in assessing jury verdicts, the Court is not according the jury "the respect it deserves." In the end, the "Court has constructed a framework that does not genuinely constrain, that does not inform state legislatures and lower courts—that does nothing at all except confer an artificial air of doctrinal analysis upon its essentially ad hoc determination that this particular award of punitive damages was not fair."

The dissent concluded this way: "By today's logic, *every* dispute as to evidentiary sufficiency in a state civil suit poses a question of constitutional moment, subject to review in this Court. This is a stupefying proposition."[58]

● ● ●

When the Utah Supreme Court received the case back, it reduced the Campbells' punitive damages to just over $9 million, which was nine times the amount of the reduced compensatory damages. The court still held that the company's conduct was reprehensible, but it was constrained by the Supreme Court's cap on punitive damages.[59]

This outcome, Humphreys and Christensen knew, would hardly deter the next State Farm from preying on its clients.[60] If big companies know there is a cap on punitive damages, occasional bad-faith losses become just part of the cost of doing business.

Life-consuming litigation like this often causes lawyers to take significant time away from their family. Christensen thought it would be a good learning experience for his young boys to go to the Supreme Court and see the arguments. While he did not ultimately win the case, his boys, Paul and Kent, fell in love with the law and decided to attend law school. Years later, during law school, Paul met Justice Thomas and was able to discuss the *State Farm* decision with him. He was amazed at Justice Thomas's ability to recall the details of the case his father had worked so hard on, even decades later.[61]

CHAPTER 12

Three Men and a Cross

Virginia v. Black

T he Constitution protects the worst among us: the murderers, the child molesters, and even the Ku Klux Klan. This presents a difficult quandary for many lawyers. And the dilemma is not a new one. For John Adams, upholding the principles of Anglo-American law meant representing the redcoats after the Boston Massacre. For many other lawyers since his day, it has meant representing notorious criminals. The more appalling the crime, the tougher the choice.

Even though the choice to defend a bad person is never easy, some lawyers make it look that way. David Baugh is one such lawyer. He never blinks or backs down. Though the choice often brings public ridicule, Baugh always chooses the same side: he picks the Constitution. Like John Adams, Baugh believes that model citizens and notorious criminals alike deserve the best representation possible. Even the most hated and despised deserve a vigorous defense.

As Baugh puts it, "The responsibility of freedom is tolerating it in others." That responsibility, however, comes with a cost—one that Baugh, as a fighter, has been willing to pay since he was a young man. Indeed, some would say that that fighting spirit is in his blood. His

father was one of the famed Tuskegee Airmen during World War II
and received the Congressional Medal of Freedom. And Baugh's
mother was a dedicated schoolteacher who always reminded him:
"A principle isn't really yours until it's tested."[1]

There seems little doubt that Baugh has lived up to his parents'
principles. During high school, he became active in the Civil Rights
Movement and was arrested during a protest outside of a jail. He was
only sixteen years old. Then, when Baugh attended college, the governor directed his school, historically black Virginia State University,
to give up one third of its programs—in order to meet federal racial
integration guidelines. Baugh led an on-campus protest. He didn't
want Virginia breaking up historically black colleges just to satisfy
government bureaucrats.[2]

Baugh received no medals for his bravery. In fact, his decision to
lead the protest earned him a suspension.

Ever the fighter, Baugh fought his suspension in court and won.
That experience taught him that the law was a place he could make
a real difference. So he went to law school. Shortly after graduating
from Texas Southern University School of Law in 1975, he became a
federal prosecutor in Texas, and then Virginia. But that job only
lasted two years. After he objected to a federal judge's giving harsher
sentences to black defendants than white defendants, he was asked
to resign.

But Baugh wasn't done with the law. He became a defense attorney, and, in so doing, he found his calling. He even insists that before
he became a defense attorney, he succeeded as a prosecutor because
he "was always thinking like the defense."

Baugh immediately started winning victories for his clients,
including for several notorious criminals. But Baugh doesn't only
take cases he can win. In his words, "You don't fight to win—you fight
because it's wrong not to."[3]

So when Barry Black came knocking, Baugh was ready. Before approaching Baugh, Black had been turned down by twelve attorneys.[4] The reason was simple. Black wasn't just any defendant; he was the Imperial Wizard and founder of the Keystone Knights faction of the Ku Klux Klan.[5]

The Klan was originally founded in Pulaski, Tennessee, in 1865. It chose Confederate general Nathan Bedford Forrest as its first leader ("Grand Wizard"). The Klan's goal was an ambitious one: to oppose the Republican Party's Reconstruction Era policies through any means necessary.

The Klan instituted a "reign of terror": its members would threaten, beat, torture, and murder black people, and any white people who supported Reconstruction.[6] It targeted black Americans who voted or exercised their civil rights, white men and women who taught the recently emancipated black Americans, and white and black Republican voters and politicians (the party that backed Reconstruction). The Klan wreaked havoc on a country trying to heal the deep wounds of slavery.

The federal government understood that for Reconstruction to be successful, it could not tolerate this sort of violence. So Congress passed the Ku Klux Klan Act in 1871, and President Ulysses S. Grant signed it into law. President Grant then used his power to target and jail members of the Klan and to disrupt their rallies. This aggressiveness seemed to work; by the late 1870s, the federal government had all but eradicated the Klan.

Yet the government's victory was short-lived. In the early 1900s, popular authors, artists, and filmmakers began romanticizing the Klan's atrocities. These works generated significant sympathetic interest in Klan lore. President Woodrow Wilson even played *The Birth of a Nation*—the most influential of these pro-Klan depictions—at a special film screening in the White House.[7]

This renewed interest in the Klan emboldened William J. Simmons and fifteen others to reestablish the KKK in 1915—holding a rally on Stone Mountain outside of Atlanta, Georgia, on Thanksgiving night. During the rally, they burned a 16-foot cross. For the first time in its history, the Klan adopted official regalia, and also the symbol of the burning cross, which it used to threaten and harass any group it didn't like. Five years later, the Klan had expanded nationwide.[8]

By 1921, a New York newspaper documented 152 acts of Klan violence. The list of groups the Klan disliked had grown to include all racial minorities, as well as Catholics, Jews, and communists. The essential message, however, remained the same: "We shall be true to the faithful maintenance of White Supremacy and will strenuously oppose any compromise thereof in any and all things."[9]

During the Great Depression, however, people changed their focus from political hatred to getting food on the table. Therefore, the Klan's numbers started to dwindle again. But the Civil Rights Movement of the 1950s sparked renewed interest in the Klan. The proposed "mixing" of races infuriated Klan members, and they used this fear to prey on people's fears and grow their ranks.

The Klan also changed its tactics during the Civil Rights Movement. The Klan once again became very violent, as it had been during Reconstruction. In fact, the Klan was responsible for most of the racial violence that occurred in the South during the Civil Rights Era. Virginia was no exception. For example, in 1949, when a black family moved into a white neighborhood in Richmond, they were greeted with a burning cross. Unfortunately for Virginians, this was one of many cross burnings throughout the state. The Virginia governor's condemnation of the cross burnings did nothing to stop or dissuade the Klan. As cross burning increased throughout the Commonwealth, concerned Virginians recognized that they needed to do something more than threaten the Klan. In 1953, Virginia passed a law that banned burning crosses and wearing masks in public. But the calm produced by that law didn't last long.[10]

In 1954, the Supreme Court announced its decision in *Brown v. Board of Education*, which ordered that schools be desegregated.[11] That was all the Klan needed. In response, the Klan not only burned crosses in front of homes and other places associated with the Civil Rights Movement, but it also engaged in other terroristic acts, including "bombings, beatings, shootings, stabbings, and mutilations."[12] The Klan also viewed the burning cross as a critical feature of its gatherings.

By March of 1960, the Klan was hosting rallies throughout the South. Hoping to grow to ten million members, the Klan decided to soften its image by cutting back on violence.[13]

But that attempted softening came to a crashing end in 1966, when an African American church in Richmond, Virginia, was bombed. Though the identity of the bomber was unknown, the act of terrorism bore all the marks of the Klan.

Following this atrocity, the Virginia government initially remained quiet. Only when civil rights groups amped up the pressure did the governor issue a statement condemning the bombing as a "reprehensible" act "long associated with the record of bigotry compiled by the Ku Klux Klan."[14]

The Klan did not back down. In response to the governor's speech, it held even more rallies and burned even more crosses.

So the Commonwealth of Virginia decided to fight back. In 1968, the Virginia legislature further broadened the anti-cross-burning law by prohibiting cross burning on "the property of another, a highway or other public place," and added that jurors could presume that those who burned crosses did so with the intent to intimidate.[15]

This law remained on the books for the next three decades. On August 22, 1998, Barry Black led a Ku Klux Klan rally of about

twenty-five people in Carroll County, Virginia. With the participants having donned white robes and white, pointy hats, the rally
looked like a traditional Klan rally. And with a 30-foot burning
cross in the middle of the group, no one would mistake it for anything else.

Though it was erected on private property, the burning cross was
visible from the roadway. Indeed, when a black family happened
upon the rally, they saw the cross and quickly sped away. And they
weren't the only ones. In total, an estimated forty to fifty cars passed
the assembly.[16]

At the rally, Klan members explicitly touted their racist beliefs.
One Klansman said that he wanted "to take a .30/.30 and just ran-
domly shoot blacks." Another talked about the problems with "blacks
and the Mexicans." One speaker expressed disgust with tax money
going "to black people." Many used the "N-word."[17]

A neighbor who witnessed the gathering was terrified. She wondered if these hooded and cloaked people would harm her, her two
children, and members of her community.[18]

At the conclusion of the rally, the Klan circled around the cross
and played "Amazing Grace" over the loudspeakers. Never mind that
John Newton authored the hymn after becoming an abolitionist, in
an effort to atone for his years captaining slave ships and delivering
humans into bondage.

As Black and his fellow Klansmen were giving speeches, Deputy
Sheriff Richard Clark drove by. The first thing that caught his eye was
two Klansmen decked head to toe in Klan gear. They were standing
on the side of the road with a four-by-eight-foot plyboard sign that
read, "KKK Rally." After reporting what he had seen to the sheriff,
Clark observed the rally for about an hour. When the cross was lit
on fire, the sheriff ordered Clark to arrest the person responsible.
Clark exited his police cruiser and confronted Black, who admitted

he was the leader. Clark then arrested Black for burning a cross with the intent to intimidate others.

On his way to jail, Black asked Clark, "When is the white man going to stand up to the blacks and Mexicans in this area?" Clark asked him what he meant, and Black answered that "blacks and Mexicans were walking up and down the sidewalk with white women, holding hands and taking all the jobs."[19]

Black faced criminal charges under Virginia's anti-cross-burning law. So after his release, he began looking for an attorney. But Black had trouble finding one. No one wanted to represent a member of the Klan for fear of being "ostracized." Black recounted these attorneys as saying things like: "We won't even be able to be a dog catcher around here if we represent you."[20]

That's how Black, a Klansman, met Baugh.

And it must have surprised Black when Baugh—a black man—not only agreed to be his lawyer but did so without insisting that Black abandon his beliefs. Rather, Baugh explained to Black that he had "a right to be a bigot."[21] He also told Black that his job was to protect Black, not to be his friend.

Black was naturally puzzled. He expressed his concern about being represented by a person of color. Baugh's response set the tone for the representation:

"I'm not going to change your views. And my views about you aren't the greatest in the world either," he said, but "I'll defend you 'till the end."

"Good enough," responded Black.[22]

Baugh's decision to represent Black came with consequences. People immediately accused him of being disloyal to his own race. Even the local chapter of the NAACP objected. Of course, Baugh, like John Adams before him, saw things differently. "The Constitution is a set of principles" that protect all Americans, said Baugh. "To protect my right to say what I want to say, I have to defend Mr. Black. It's easy to defend a friend, but when an enemy is having principles you believe in violated, that's a chance to do the right thing." In short, Baugh believed the First Amendment right to free speech protected even detestable acts like cross burning.[23]

Baugh then pointed out the irony of the criticism. If Black's life had been saved by a black doctor, "no one would care."[24] But when Black's rights were protected by a black *attorney*, people saw things differently. Baugh understood that white attorneys would not have had it any better—they would have been accused of being "closet Klansmen" if they were representing him.[25] After weighing all of this in his mind, Baugh had decided he was "the perfect person" to represent Black because he would not shirk his responsibilities under the criticism that was sure to come his way.[26]

Of course, Baugh didn't condone Black's conduct. Far from it. Yet he believed that the First Amendment protected Black's right to burn the cross, no matter how reprehensible that action was. In defending Black, Baugh believed he was defending every American's right to say what they believe. This was a fundamental principle for Baugh, dating back to his high school days participating in the Civil Rights Movement. As the trial approached, he prepared with vigor.

Baugh understood that the First Amendment does not protect true threats—meaning threats of imminent harm. So he built his trial defense around whether Black had actually meant to intimidate others with his actions. He intended to show that when Black burnt the cross, he did so on private property as part of a routine Klan ceremony and that he had no intent to intimidate. Or, at the very least, that the government could not prove otherwise.

Baugh knew that the elephant in the room was Black's membership in the Klan. So in his opening statement at trial, Baugh made clear that it was the jury's responsibility to set aside their personal dislike of Black and instead stand with the Constitution. Baugh understood that speech can hurt someone's feelings or make them feel scared. But, he told the jury, speech does not lose its protection just because it makes someone feel uncomfortable. And because a burning cross was a type of speech, Baugh argued, the jury had to acquit. Respecting speech, however ugly, is the cost of living in this great democracy.

The testimony at trial consisted of two police officers and the neighbor testifying about the burning cross. Before closing arguments, the lawyers had an opportunity to speak with the judge about his instructions to the jury. After the parties are done presenting evidence, the judge typically instructs the jury about what the law is and what they must find to convict or acquit. Making sure that the jury instructions accurately describe the law is very important, and the parties' lawyers object if they believe instructions are wrong.

Baugh did just that. At a conference with the judge, he argued that because the law presumed Black had burned the cross with the intent to intimidate, that law violated Black's First Amendment rights. The intention to intimidate must, rather, be demonstrated from the facts of the case. The trial judge disagreed, noting that the presumption came directly from the Virginia legislature. Thus, he told the jury that "the burning of the cross by itself is sufficient evidence from which you may infer the required intent."

In his closing argument, Baugh immediately returned to the elephant in the room. "I love this case. I love this case because it gives me an opportunity to test my principles. I recognize, based upon my knowledge, that the Ku Klux Klan is a hate group and I view it as a hate group . . . but we have a principle in our case, in our nation that no idea is so reprehensible that it cannot be discussed in the free marketplace of ideas." Then he addressed what must have been puzzling the jury. "The Klan hates African Americans. I'm an African

American. Duh. I know what's going on here." Nevertheless, he, a black man, was representing a Klansman for a good reason: "If you can punish him for thinking something, you can punish me for thinking something." Baugh concluded by arguing that the government had failed to demonstrate an intent to intimidate. Whether they liked or disliked Black or the Klan, the jury had a duty to acquit.[27]

Despite Baugh's powerful closing argument, it took the jury only thirty minutes to convict Black. The government asked for jail time, but the jury imposed a fine of $2500 instead.

Even though he had dodged prison, Black believed he had to appeal. "I can't just say hey, no, here's $2500. Forget it. If I did that, I'm letting my race down. I have to make people know that America is still a land of opportunity, that America is still a land of democracy, and that the Constitution of the United States of America still means something."

The next stop was the Virginia Supreme Court. For the appeal, Baugh teamed up with the dean of Richmond Law School, Rodney Smolla. Smolla specialized in the study of the First Amendment and had graduated first in his class from Duke University Law School.

When Black's case reached the Virginia Supreme Court, it was consolidated with another case of cross burning. In that case, Richard Elliot and Jonathan O'Mara had been upset that Elliot's new neighbor, James Jubilee, had called Elliot's mother about Elliot shooting guns behind the house. Jubilee was black and had just moved his family from California to Virginia four months earlier. When he discovered a burnt cross twenty feet from his house, he was understandably nervous. As he testified, "[A] cross burned in your yard . . . tells you that it's just the first round." The trial court in that case did not give the presumption instruction to the jury even though it was part of the law. Both Elliot and O'Mara were nonetheless convicted and sentenced to ninety days in jail and a $2500 fine.[28]

At the Virginia Supreme Court, the defendants in both cases argued that while true threats could be banned, the law barring cross burning was unconstitutional because it banned speech communicating a particular message. Baugh also argued that the presumption of intent to intimidate was unconstitutional because it deterred people from engaging in protected speech—which included, according to Baugh, cross burning. By a 4–3 vote, the Virginia Supreme Court agreed and threw out the men's convictions.[29]

The Commonwealth was not letting its law die without a fight. Virginia sought and obtained review before the United States Supreme Court. After securing review, Virginia received another piece of good news: the U.S. Department of Justice weighed in on Virginia's side. Like Virginia, the United States uses civil rights laws to prosecute cross burning.[30] Virginia and the United States had a common purpose: to stop the Klan and other hate groups from terrorizing people.

The support of the United States was good news for Virginia, because the United States Supreme Court often pays special deference to the federal government's views. This case was no exception. The Court even allocated some time to the United States to argue on behalf of the State of Virginia.

Oral argument was held on December 11, 2002, and it was eventful. Justice Scalia asked Dean Smolla whether brandishing a weapon was protected by the First Amendment. Smolla argued that the physical properties of a gun added "potency to the threat." Then, in an interesting back and forth, Justice Scalia got Smolla to concede that "a black man at night [would] rather see a man with a rifle than see a burning cross on [his] front lawn."

Surprising everyone, Justice Thomas broke his customary silence to ask the United States' lawyer some questions. In doing so, he characterized cross burnings as "unlike any symbol in our society" because they have "no communication of a particular message" beyond the intent "to cause fear." For this reason, Justice Thomas referred to the burning cross as the very symbol of the Klan's "reign of terror." When argument was over, Justice Thomas's powerful intervention stood out in many attendees' memory.[31]

On April 7, 2003, Justice O'Connor announced the decision for the majority. She found that while Virginia could ban cross burnings done with the intent to intimidate, it could not presume that all cross burnings were done with such intention. She noted that, historically, not all cross burnings were done with an intent to intimidate. Rather, some had burned crosses as a "statement of ideology." For this reason, presuming intent "would create an unacceptable risk of the suppression of ideas" because it could capture cross burnings that were done without an intention to intimidate.

The majority opinion then gave some examples of permissible cross burnings: (1) in a group of like-minded people (for example, at a rally); (2) on one's own private property; or (3) on another's property with permission. According to the majority, all of these would be protected. Six justices joined her opinion.

Justice Scalia had a different view. He believed that Black's conviction was unlawful because the judge's instructions did not require the jury to consider evidence that could rebut the presumption of intent to intimidate. According to Justice Scalia, the jury should have been instructed both that burning a cross is evidence of intent to intimidate and that the jury must consider contrary evidence in determining whether to accept the presumption. Because the jury was not so instructed, he agreed that Black's conviction had to be vacated. Unlike the majority, however, he did not believe that the indictment should be thrown out. Instead, he wanted to send the case back to Virginia so a court could retry Black with a proper jury instruction.

Only Justice Thomas dissented in full. He believed burning a cross was conduct, not speech, and certainly not protected speech. "In every culture, certain things acquire meaning well beyond what outsiders can comprehend," he said. The burning cross is one of those things. Justice Thomas explained that "whatever expressive value cross burning has, the legislature simply wrote it out by banning only intimidating conduct undertaken by a particular means." And since conduct is not speech, it is well established that legislatures may ban intimidating conduct without running afoul of the First Amendment.

According to Justice Thomas, by holding the cross-burning law unconstitutional, the majority "ignore[d] Justice Holmes' familiar aphorism that 'a page of history is worth a volume of logic.'" Quoting a book on the Klan, Justice Thomas pointed out that the Klan was the world's oldest terrorist organization: "Fifty years before the Irish Republican Army was organized, a century before Al Fatah declared its holy war on Israel, the Ku Klux Klan was actively harassing, torturing, and murdering in the United States. Today its members remain fanatically committed to a course of violent opposition to social progress and racial equity in the United States."[32]

He then recounted how the Klan used cross burning solely to intimidate minorities and other groups it did not like. And he pointed out that "for those not easily frightened, cross burning has been followed by more extreme measures, such as beatings and murder."

But Justice Thomas didn't only march through American history. He also showed how cross burnings had ruined people's lives. In one such example, Justice Thomas shared the story of "a black American" who described the burning cross as "the worst thing that can happen to a person." Indeed, after discovering a burning cross on her property, she began "crying on her knees . . . [and] felt feelings of frustration and intimidation." In fact, even "seven months after the incident, the family still lived in fear." Justice Thomas finished the section by

pointing out that "[i]n our culture, cross burning has almost invariably meant lawlessness and understandably instills in its victims
well-grounded fear of physical violence."

Adding further context, Justice Thomas walked through the history of cross burnings in Virginia. In particular, he quoted a newspaper article noting that crosses were historically burned in Virginia
"to intimidate Negroes from seeking their rights as citizens."

This history was so unacceptable to the Virginia legislature that
it prohibited cross burnings in the 1950s and '60s—and this legislature was anything but sympathetic to black people. In fact, the legislature was filled with racial segregationists. But even they couldn't
abide the Klan's "violent and terroristic conduct"—conduct that
invariably began with burning crosses. Thus, according to Justice
Thomas, "even segregationists understood the difference between
intimidating and terroristic conduct and racist expression."

He then concluded by noting that "just as one cannot burn down
someone's house to make a political point, and then seek refuge in
the First Amendment, those who hate cannot terrorize and intimidate to make their point." Thus, since he believed the Virginia statute
banned only conduct—burning the cross with the intent to
intimidate—the First Amendment was not implicated.[33]

Justice Thomas's words were consistent with his originalist philosophy, and also powerful. Their power came in part from personal
experience. Indeed, as a child of the segregated South, this decision
must have rankled Justice Thomas, to say the least.

For his part, Baugh could not say that his representation of Black
was a joyful occasion, either. He did his job and protected the
Constitution, as he was called upon to do. And he did it well. But he
didn't enjoy it.[34]

And while Black, as a white supremacist, may not have truly
respected Baugh, he was grateful to his lawyer for winning his case.

But Black had a very different opinion of Justice Thomas:

> You talk about Mr. Thomas, Clarence Thomas. Where does
> anyone get off calling me a bigot? . . . [I]f that guy wasn't
> racist, wasn't a bigot, I ain't never seen one in my life. I'm
> glad [he asked questions at argument] because he showed
> just how racist and how hateful the black race is to the
> white race, and that's what he did by doing that. You take
> Martin Luther King. He was a communist . . . put down
> there to cause trouble. He caused so much trouble for the
> Kennedys, it wasn't funny. Yet they made a martyr out of
> him because he did what he thought was right for his race.
> I'm only doing what I think is right for my race.[35]

● ● ●

In the end, the burning cross represented three very different
things to these three different men. To Black, it was a symbol of white
supremacy. To Baugh, the burning cross marked the outer limit of
speech protected by the Constitution. To Justice Thomas, it was, and
in American society always necessarily would be, a hateful act of
intimidation and terror.

Conclusion

Every summer, Justice Thomas and his wife, Ginni, travel across America in their motor home. They visit friends, spend their evenings parked in Walmart parking lots, and often stay at RV camp sites. Along the way, they talk and joke with the people they meet without ever disclosing who they are. That's how Justice Thomas likes to spend his free time—on the road, just one of the American people.

It makes sense that a justice who would rather spend his time in Walmart parking lots than at cocktail parties is an originalist. He has seen firsthand the American people's wisdom, their decency, and their dignity. And he knows, like all originalists, that you cannot fully respect a people unless you respect their choices, too.

For that reason, Justice Thomas enforces the Constitution as the American people created it. He understands that ours isn't just a Constitution for the people. It's a Constitution *by* the people. So Justice Thomas sees his job as a humble one: to try his best to figure out what the American people understood the Constitution to mean when they ratified it.

Because of his commitment to the Constitution as the people's law, Justice Thomas doesn't "update" the Constitution according to his own inclinations or the culture's current values. That's too much power for an unelected judge. Instead, the people have the power to change their Constitution through the amendment process. And when they use that process, Justice Thomas applies the same methodology: figure out what the people understood the amendment to mean at the time it was ratified.

The results are plain. Justice Thomas recognizes that the Fourteenth Amendment was meant to realize the full promise of Emancipation. So when some tried to use the Establishment Clause, as applied through the Fourteenth Amendment, to keep poor kids in failing schools in Cleveland, Justice Thomas said no. And when the federal government sought to regulate Angel Raich's medical marijuana, Justice Thomas explained why, according to the Constitution as ratified by the American people, it couldn't. When Chicago tried to stop Otis McDonald from protecting his family with a gun, Justice Thomas presented the history behind the Fourteenth Amendment, which was on McDonald's side. And when the people of Utah rendered judgment for the Campbells against State Farm, Justice Thomas explained why the federal courts should not have intervened.

Sometimes his is a lonely road, as Justice Thomas's solo opinions show. The results of originalism may be inconvenient, unpopular, or not what the "cognoscenti" want. But Justice Thomas's opinions make clear he is not trying to score invitations to cocktail parties; he is trying to apply the law as it was originally understood. Take Susette Kelo's case, where Justice Thomas would have squarely blocked the development (and gentrification) plans of a state in cahoots with a major drug company. Or Barbara Grutter's case, where she was denied admission to a law school almost exclusively because of her skin color.

Sometimes, originalism leads in a direction Justice Thomas might not go if he were in Congress or the Executive Branch. No one would call Justice Thomas pro-drugs or soft on crime. But Angel Raich had his vote, and he eloquently explained why he believed the Constitution required it. And in cases not discussed in this book, such as *Kyollo v. United States*, *Alleyne v. United States*, and *Ramos v. Louisiana*, he regularly sides with criminal defendants when the original meaning of the Constitution compels him to do so.[1]

As these chapters have demonstrated, originalist methodology takes discipline and rigor to apply. Sometimes, the original meaning of the Constitution is clear. But sometimes it is not.

When the original meaning is more difficult to figure out, originalists may even disagree. For example, Justice Scalia was Justice Thomas's most consistent originalist companion on the Court. But that did not mean that the two justices always voted in unison. Both men took their craft very seriously and laid out their work for all to see. Occasionally, they reached different conclusions. Their differences are evidence of the seriousness and care with which faithful originalists approach cases and the Constitution. And it's a sign of the evolving methodology and rigor of originalism that new scholarship has since resolved some of these disagreements.

These cases also show Justice Thomas's compassion and his deep understanding of the challenges Americans have faced throughout our nation's history. Justice Thomas is committed to applying the law's meaning, but he is not blind to the struggles of the people before him. He listens to people like Otis McDonald and the other citizens of Chicago who desperately want to protect their families from gangs. He speaks out for rape survivors like Jane Doe and Kathy McKee. And when victims like Betty Smothers can no longer speak for themselves, he doesn't forget them; he uses his platform to enshrine their story in America's law books.

Since his appointment to the Court, Justice Thomas has participated in a transformation in American law. In the years following
1991, other originalists have joined both the Supreme Court and the
lower federal courts. And that has meant the voice of the American
people has been heard more clearly.

Sometimes, originalism means vindicating the rights that are in
the Constitution—as in *Bruen*, where Justice Thomas wrote the opinion for the majority holding that the Second Amendment extends
beyond the home. Sometimes, it means handing control over the law
back to America's elected representatives, as in *Dobbs*, where the
Court held that the Constitution does not address the question of
abortion. These decisions are not universally popular, but that's the
point—originalism is not about popularity. It's about enforcing our
laws as written and allowing the American people to change those
laws if they decide that is best for the country. In other words, it's
about respecting the American people's choices, rather than enacting
what the "cognoscenti" or vocal interest groups might prefer.

In fact, that's what Justice Thomas writes whenever a student asks
him to sign a copy of the Constitution: "This is *your* Constitution." And
that's the point. The Constitution is the *people's* law. Not anybody else's.

Acknowledgments

T his book would not have been possible without the patience of my amazing family. My kids, Zach, Carmen, and Nick, and especially my wonderful wife, Kim, put up with my distracted weekends, late evenings, and early mornings. They not only supported me throughout the project but read many of the chapters and provided critical feedback. To the four of you, thank you.

At the outset of this endeavor, I was told that writing a book is never a solo project. That turned out to be truer than I ever realized. When you become a judge, you are blessed with a second family: your law clerks. As one of my former clerks, Joe Masterman, is fond of saying, a clerkship for me is one for life.

I could not have written this book without my five amazing current law clerks. Ben Daus showed up at just the right time. Having helped many others write books, he knew what a project like this took, and he encouraged me not to go it alone. Throughout the process, he provided me with critical feedback and research and great editorial suggestions. Three other clerks—Rachel Daley, Josh Hanley, and James Lee—also volunteered their time and provided me with essential help in researching, editing, and, perhaps most important, thinking about the cases. Their remarkable enthusiasm, insight, and dedication speeded this work across the finish line. Finally, Katie Mahoney provided me with very helpful editorial advice and was always willing to do more. When emergencies arose or I just needed some advice, all five would volunteer to help, day or night. As always, the assistance of all five of my clerks was top notch. I can't thank them enough.

Of course, the clerk family is a big one, and many former clerks assisted, too. Once in the family, always in the family. The list of those who contributed to this endeavor include Blake Brickman, Matthew Downer, Joe Masterman, Catherine Padhi, Sam Rudman, Jonathan Urick, Jasmine Stein, Matthew Pociask, Sam Adkisson, David Goldman, Emily Hall, Rishabh Bhandari, DJ Sandoval, Emily Snoddon, Annie McClellan, and David Wenthold.

Three good friends also helped me with thinking about ways to get the message of the book out. Two are like brothers to me—my college roommate, Mark Sexton, and my law school roommate, Alex Fitzpatrick. The other, Garrett Ventry, is a wizard at thinking about messaging and is genuinely unselfish with his time.

Two Sixth Circuit colleagues also provided me with important assistance. Judge Alice Batchelder helped me set up several critical interviews that really brought the second chapter to life, and Judge Danny Boggs provided me with some essential background and historical information.

I am also blessed with many good friends and mentors who read the chapters, lent advice, and talked about the book with me. Lillian BeVier, Mark Paoletta, and Dean Reuter stand foremost among them.

Two other friends deserve special notice: Nicole Garnett and Philip Munoz. I have the privilege of teaching with them at Notre Dame. They are two of the best professors and people I have ever met. Nicole and Philip would often brainstorm with me and look at chapters for me. Each provided critical feedback throughout.

In addition, I had the privilege of teaching with Philip as part of the Center for Citizenship and Constitutional Government at Notre Dame. Through the Center, I met Stephen Wrinn and numerous others who offered great advice. One of our students, Ella Cain, provided helpful research assistance. And Philip put me in touch with the best wordsmith I know, Rebecca Devine. Becca provided incredible feedback throughout the entire process, and I was lucky to have her expert assistance. The book would not be where it is without Becca and the Center.

Throughout this project, several young people volunteered to help me. Two stand out: First, Niklas Vakhil provided research and feedback when the project was just getting off the ground. Second, Abigail Anthony offered helpful thoughts about my writing.

When I began working on this book, I never anticipated all the people I would encounter along the way. As part of the process, I had the privilege of interviewing many remarkable people whose stories these chapters tell. Each was generous with his or her time. I came away from these interviews admiring their decency, their determination, and their willingness to share their stories with me. In many cases, these stories are a critical part of their life. I reference the interviews throughout the endnotes in this book. I could not have written the book without these people; they really make the stories come to life.

I also read many great books and articles in addition to the fascinating cases and pleadings. They are cited throughout, but four in particular deserve to be highlighted: Jeff Benedict's *Little Pink House*, *Running for My Life* by Warrick Dunn and Don Yaeger, David Brennan and Malcolm Baroway's *Victory for Kids*, and Fred Jones and Sue Bowron's *Act of Bravery*. If you've enjoyed this book, I hope you will give those a read. They are well done and provided me with critical background and facts.

Also, Duke Law School has put together a website that includes stories of some of these cases and many more. Professor Tomas Metzloff is the director of the *Voices of American Law Project*. He has compiled a fantastic group of videos. I highly encourage anyone who enjoyed this book to check out the website.

Finally, this book would not have gone to print without the dedication of the Regnery team. Tom Spence encouraged me to finish writing the book and publish it. And when I agreed to do so, Tom assigned a fantastic editor and copy editor to this project, Elizabeth Kantor and Michael Baker, respectively. During the editorial process, it seemed like they never slept. And their feedback was always helpful.

I never thought I would write a book. It became a labor of love that got me (and my dog, Buster) up in the wee morning hours. Of course, Buster was not up by choice. But even he put up with me during this process and patiently waited for his morning walk as I typed away.

There are many more people who listened to me talk about the book and gave me insight and wisdom. I wish I could thank them all by name, but that would require another whole book. I hope you have enjoyed the read.

Bibliography

"2021 Ends as Chicago's Deadliest Year in a Quarter Century." NBC5 Chicago, January 1, 2022. https://www.nbcchicago. com/news/local/2021-ends-as-chicagos-deadliest-year-in-a-quarter-century/2719307.

"2021 Gang Boundaries." City of Chicago Office of Public Safety Administration, January 5, 2022. https://gis.chicagopolice.org/datasets/ChicagoPD::2021-gang-boundaries/about.

"About Kathy McKee." Kathy McKee Casting, n.d. http://www.kathymckeecasting.com/about-kathy.html.

"About West Point." United States Military Academy at West Point, n.d. https://www.westpoint.edu/about.

"A Brief History of West Point." United States Military Academy at West Point, n.d. https://www.westpoint.edu/about/history-of-west-point.

Am. Amusement Mach. Ass'n v. Kendrick, 244 F.3d 572 (7th Cir. 2001).

Amended Complaint, *Doe v. Hagenbeck*, 98 F. Supp. 3d 672 (S.D.N.Y. 2015), ECF No. 14.

Anderson, Craig A., et al. "The Influence of Media Violence on Youth." *Psychological Science in the Public Interest* 4, no. 3 (December 2003): 113–22.

Anderson, Craig A., and Karen E. Dill. "Video Games and Aggressive Thoughts, Feelings, and Behavior in the Laboratory and in Life." *Journal of Personality and Social Psychology* 78, no. 4 (2000): 772–90. https://www.apa.org/pubs/journals/releases/psp784772.pdf.

Appendix to Petition for a Writ of Certiorari, *Hanna Perkins School v. Simmons-Harris*, U.S. No. 00-1777.

Atkins v. Virginia, 536 U.S. 304 (2002).

Author interview with Alan Gura by telephone, September 2, 2002.

Author interview with Alice Batchelder by telephone, November 13, 2022.

Author interview with Bill Patmon by telephone, November 17, 2022.

Author interview with David Baugh by telephone, October 5, 2022.

Author interview with Fred Jones by Zoom, September 15, 2022.

Author interview with Kathrine McKee by telephone, December 20, 2022.

Author interview with Nicole Garnett by telephone, October 21, 2022.

Author interview with Roger Christensen by telephone, December 9, 2022.

Author interview with Scott Bullock by telephone, September 20, 2022.

Author interview with Terry Pell by telephone, December 22, 2022.

Author interview with Zackery Morazzini by telephone, December 6, 2022.

Bailey, Jim. "Ethnic and Racial Minorities, the Indigent, the Elderly, and Eminent Domain: Assessing the Virginia Model of Reform." *Washington and Lee Journal of Civil Rights and Social Justice* 19, no. 1 (September 2012): 91. https://scholarlycommons.law.wlu.edu/cgi/viewcontent.cgi?article=1344&context=crsj.

Barbara Grutter's comments at news conference hosted by Center for Individual Rights. April 1, 2003. Available at https://www.c-span. org/video/?c4678928/user-clip-barbara-grutter.

Barr, William. "Crime, Poverty, and the Family." The Heritage Foundation, July 29, 1992. https://www.heritage.org/crime-and-justice/report/crime-poverty-and-the-familiy.

"Beam, C. Arlen." United States District Court, District of Nebraska, n.d. https://www.ned.uscourts.gov/public/judicial-archive/beam-c-a.

Benedict, Jeff. *Little Pink House: A True Story of Defiance and Courage.* New York: Grand Central Publishing, 2009.

Benzkofer, Stephan. "1974 Was a Deadly Year in Chicago." *Chicago Tribune,* July 8, 2012. https://www.chicagotribune.com/news/ct-pe r-flash-1974-murders-0708-20120708-story.html.

Berisha v. Lawson, 141 S. Ct. 2424 (2021).

Block, Carolyn Rebecca, and Antigone Christakos. *Major Trends in Chicago Homicide: 1965–1994.* Chicago, Illinois: Illinois Criminal Justice Information Authority, September 1995.

Block, Carolyn Rebecca, and Richard Block. *Street Gang Crime in Chicago.* Washington, D.C.: National Institute of Justice, December 1993, 3. https://citeseerx.ist.psu.edu/document?repid=rep1&type= pdf&doi=17bf40fc952dc172cf9b0a008675bdf827c3773d.

BMW of N. Am., Inc. v. Gore, 517 U.S. 559, 607 (1996).

Brief of Amici Curiae National Association for the Advancement of Colored People, *Kelo v. City of New London,* 545 U.S. 469 (2005), 2004 WL 2811057. https://ij.org/wp-content/uploads/2000/12/naacp02.pdf.

Br. of Amicus Curiae of California State Senator Leland Y. Yee, PhD *et al.* at 6, *Brown v. Entertainment Merchants Ass'n,* 564 U.S. 786 (2011) (No. 08-1448).

Brennan, David, and Malcolm Baroway. *Victory for Kids: The Cleveland School Voucher Case.* Beverly Hills, California: New Millennium, 2002.

Brown v. Board of Education, 347 U.S. 483 (1954).

Brown v. Entertainment Merchants Ass'n, 564 U.S. 786 (2011) (No. 08-1448).

Brumfield v. Cain, 576 U.S. 305 (2015).

Brumfield v. Cain, 740 F.3d 946 (5th Cir. 2014).

California Civil Code § 1746.1-.2 (West 2006).

Campbell v. State Farm Mut. Auto. Ins. Co., 65 P.3d 1134 (Utah 2001).

Campbell v. State Farm Mut. Auto. Ins. Co., 98 P.3d 409, 410–11 (Utah 2004).

Campbell v. State Farm Mut. Auto. Ins. Co., No. 890905231 (Utah D. Ct. Aug. 3, 1998).

Chappell v. Wallace, 462 U.S. 296 (1983).

Chiang, Harriet. "Wal-Mart Judge Praised for Compassion, Diligence / Colleagues, Friends Say He Is Well-Suited for Sex-Bias Case." SFGATE, June 23, 2004. https://www.sfgate.com/news/article/Wal-Mart-judge-praised-for-compassion-diligence-2711737.php.

"Chicago Homicide Rates per 100,000 Residents, 1870–2000." Encyclopedia of Chicago, n.d. http://www.encyclopedia.chicagohistory.org/pages/2156.html.

City of Chicago Brief in Supreme Court, *City of Chicago v. Morales,* 527 U. S. 41 (1999) (97–1121).

City of Chicago v. Morales, 527 U. S. 41 (1999).

City of Chicago v. Morales, 687 N. E. 3d 53 (Ill. 1997).

City of Chicago v. Youkhana, 660 NE. 2d 34 (Ill. 1995).

Cleveland City Schools District Performance Audit. March 15, 1996. Cited in State Petitioner's Brief to the Supreme Court, at 2 in *Zelman v. Simmons Harris,* 536 U.S. 639 (2002).

"Cleveland Schools Reopen amid Worries over Vouchers." *Baltimore Sun,* August 26, 1999, 3A. https://www.newspapers.com/image/173284769.

Commandant of the Marine Corps. *Marine Corps Ord. 1500.55.* Washington, D.C.: United States Marine Corps Headquarters, April 12, 1997, 1. https://www.marines.mil/Portals/1/Publications/MCO%201500.55.pdf.

Commonwealth v. Virginia, 553 S.E. 2d 738 (Va. 2001).

Complaint for Declaratory and Injunctive Relief, Joint Appendix at 5, *Brown v. Entertainment Merchants Ass'n,* 564 U.S. 786 (2011) (No. 08-1448).

Coral Ridge Ministries Media, Inc. v. S. Poverty L. Ctr., 142 S. Ct. 2453 (2022).

Curran, John. "Elderly Widow Wins Fight with Trump." Associated Press, July 20, 1998. https://apnews.com/article/ed32d4191419a0a42 8a3d6bdc6d17e12.

Dillon, Nancy. "Bill Cosby Accused of Raping Ex-Girlfriend of Sammy Davis Jr." *New York Daily News,* December 22, 2014. https://www.nydailynews.com/news/national/bill-cosby-accused-raping-ex-girlfriend-sammy-davis-jr-article-1.2052890.

District of Columbia v. Heller, 554 U.S. 570 (2008).

Doe v. Hagenbeck, 870 F. 3d 36 (2d Cir. 2017).

Doe v. United States, 141 S. Ct. 1498 (2021).

Doe v. United States, 815 F. App'x 592 (2d Cir. 2020). Summary order.

Drug Enforcement Administration Chicago Field Division, Federal Bureau of Investigation, and the City Police Department. *Cartels and Gangs in Chicago: Joint Intelligence Report.* Chicago, Illinois: DEA Chicago Field Division, May 2017, 6. https://www. dea. gov/sites/default/files/2018-07/DIR-013-17%20Cartel%20and%20 Gangs%20in%20Chicago%20-%20Unclassified. pdf.

Dunn, Warrick, and Don Yaeger, *Running for My Life: My Journey in the Game of Football and Beyond*. New York: HarperCollins, 2009.

"Eric Harris' Writing—Journals, Diaries and School Papers." A Columbine Site, n.d. https://www.acolumbinesite.com/eric/writing/journal/journal.php.

Fair, Lesley. "$245 Million FTC Settlement Alleges Fortnite Owner Epic Games Used Digital Dark Patterns to Charge Players for Unwanted In-Game Purchases." Federal Trade Commission, December 19, 2022. https://www.ftc.gov/business-guidance/blog/2022/12/245-million-ftc-settlement-alleges-fortnite-owner-epic-games-used-digital-dark-patterns-charge.

Feres v. United States, 340 U.S. 135 (1950).

Forman, James Jr. *Locking Up Our Own: Crime and Punishment in Black America*. New York: Farrar, Straus and Giroux, 2017.

Fox, James Alex. *Trends in Juvenile Violence*. Washington, D.C.: Bureau of Justice Statistics, March 1996, 2.

Fraga, Kaleena. "The Harrowing Story of the 1969 Cuyahoga Fire—and How It Changed America." All That's Interesting, May 24, 2021. https://allthatsinteresting.com/the-cuyahoga-river-fire.

Gabbatt, Adam. "Connecticut Town to Burn Violent Video Games as Sandy Hook Returns to School." *The Guardian*, January 3, 2013. https://www.theguardian.com/world/2013/jan/03/newtown-shooting-video-game-buyback.

Gaffney, Dylan. "Loot Boxes: Virtual Kinder Eggs or Casinos for Kids?" *Columbia Journal of Law & the Arts*, October 8, 2022. https://journals.library.columbia.edu/index.php/lawandarts/announcement/view/545.

Gendreau, Leanne, and Ari Mason. "Former Governor John Rowland Sentenced to 30 Months in Prison." NBC Connecticut, March 18,

2015. https://www.nbcconnecticut.com/news/local/john-rowlands-sentencing-set-for-wednesday/1965046.

Gertz v. Robert Welch, Inc., 418 U.S. 323 (1974).

Gibbs, Nancy, and Timothy Roche. "The Columbine Tapes." *Time*, December 20, 1999. https://content.time.com/time/magazine/article/0,9171,992873,00.html.

Gibson, Ellie. "Schwarzenegger Signs Violent Videogames Bill." GamesIndustry.biz, October 10, 2005. https://www.gamesindustry.biz/schwarzenegger-signs-violent-videogames-bill.

Ginsberg v. New York, 390 U.S. 629 (1968).

Glanton, Dahleen. "Otis McDonald, 1933–2014: Fought Chicago's Gun Ban." *Chicago Tribune*. April 6, 2014. https://www.chicago-tribune.com/news/ct-xpm-2014-04-06-ct-otis-mcdonald-obituary-met-20140406-story.html.

Glose, Bill. "The Loudest: David Baugh Fights to Preserve the Constitution— Including the Rights of Klansmen and Al-Qaida terrorists." Super Lawyers, June 25, 2007. https://www.superlawyers.com/articles/virginia/the-loudest.

"Good Morning L.A. Talk Show." IMDb, n.d. https://www.imdb.com/title/tt2135064.

Good, Owen S. "Anti–Loot Box Bill Gathers Bipartison Support in Senate." Polygon, May 23, 2019. https://www.polygon.com/2019/5/23/18637155/loot-box-laws-us-senate-josh-hawley-ed-markey-richard-blumenthal.

Gonzales v. Raich, 545 U.S. 1 (2005).

Gratz v. Bollinger, 122 F. Supp. 811 (E.D. Mich. 2000).

Grutter, Barbara. "Making Progress." *National Review*, August 19, 2003. https://www.nationalreview.com/2003/08/making-progress-barbara-grutter.

Grutter v. Bollinger, 137 F. Supp. 2d 821 (E.D. Mich 2001). https://law.justia.com/cases/federal/district-courts/FSupp2/137/821/2472469.

Grutter v. Bollinger, 288 F.3d 732 (6th Cir. 2002) (en banc).

Grutter v. Bollinger, 539 U.S. 306 (2003) (No. 02-241).

Gyan, Joe Jr. "Longtime Death-Row Inmate Kevan Brumfield Gets Life in 1993 Baton Rouge Cop-Killing." *The Advocate*, July 20, 2016. https://www.theadvocate.com/baton_rouge/news/courts/longtime-death-row-inmate-kevan-brumfield-gets-life-in-1993-baton-rouge-cop-killing/article_8a2c3e6a-4de3-11e6-bbbc-fb01dbc3e29d.html.

———. "Warrick Dunn: Mother's Killers No Longer Have 'Power over Me or My Family.'" *The Advocate*, September 28, 2018. https://www.theadvocate.com/baton_rouge/news/courts/warrick-dunn-mothers-killers-no-longer-have-power-over-me-or-my-family/article_155833fa-c1bd-11e8-9984-a70b05270caa.html.

Hauser, Christine, and Al Baker. "Keeping Wary Eye on Crime as Economy Sinks." *New York Times*, October 9, 2008. https://www.nytimes.com/2008/10/10/nyregion/10crime.html.

"Hon. Richard Paez—U.S. Court of Appeals for the Ninth Court." University of Washington, October 27, 2008. https://www.law.washington.edu/multimedia/2008/paez/transcript.aspx.

Hopwood v. State of Texas, 78 F.3d 932 (5th Cir. 1996).

"Issue Overview: Do Video Games Cause Violence," NEWSELA, November 28, 2016, https://www.rcsdk12.org/cms/lib/NY01001156/Centricity/Domain/10241/video%20games%20violence.pdf.

Joint Appendix at 816–17, *Brown v. Entertainment Merchants Ass'n*, 564 U.S. 786 (2011) (No. 08-1448).

Joint Appendix, *Commonwealth of Virginia, Petitioner, v. Barry Elton Black*, Richard J. Elliott, and Jonathan O'Mara, Respondents., 2002 WL 32102976 (U.S.), 111a.

Joint Appendix, Volume III, *State Farm Mut. Auto. Ins. Co. v. Campbell*, 538 U.S. 408 (2003) (No. 01-1289), 2002 WL 33933820, at 1096–97a.

Joint Appendix, Volume IV, *State Farm Mut. Auto. Ins. Co. v. Campbell*, 538 U.S. 408 (2003) (No. 01-1289), 2002 WL 33933821, at 1586a, 1659a.

Joint Appendix, Volume VII, *State Farm Mut. Auto. Ins. Co. v. Campbell*, 538 U.S. 408 (2003) (No. 01-1289).

Jones, Frederick, and Sue Bowron. *An Act of Bravery: Otis W. McDonald and the Second Amendment.* Alexandria, Louisiana: Father's Voice Publishing, 2012.

Johnson, Steve. "Killing Our Children." *Chicago Tribune*, January 3, 1993. https://www.chicagotribune. com/news/ct-xpm-1993-01-03-9303151958-story.html.

Kaczynski, Andrew. "Democratic Congressman Makes Shocking Racial Comments about Republicans Clarence Thomas, Mitch McConnell." BuzzFeed News, April 29, 2014, https://www. buzzfeednews.com/article/andrewkaczynski/democratic-congressman-makes-shocking-racial-comments-about.

"Kathy McKee Biography." IMDb, n.d. https://www.imdb.com/name/nm0571181/bio?ref_=nm_ov_bio_sm.

Kirby, Joseph A. "The Death of Dantrell Davis." *Chicago Tribune*, March 7, 2015. https://www.chicagotribune. com/nation-world/chi-chicagodays-dantrelldavis-story-story.html.

Klanwatch Project staff. *Ku Klux Klan: A History of Racism and Violence.* Montgomery, Alabama: Southern Poverty Law Center, 2011. https://www.splcenter.org/sites/default/files/Ku-Klux-Klan-A-History-of-Racism.pdf.

Klukowski, Ken. "Reagan Ally Bill Batchelder Laid to Rest in Ohio." Breitbart, February 21, 2022. https://www.breitbart.com/poltics/2022/02/21/reagan-ally-bill-batchelder-rest-ohio.

Knight v. State of Alabama, 900 F. Supp 272 (N.D. Ala. 1995).

"Ku Klux Klan in Virginia." Encyclopedia Virginia, April 20, 2022. https://encyclopediavirginia.org/entries/ku-klux-klan-in-virginia.

Leary, Margaret A., and Barbara J. Snow. "Gabriel Franklin Hargo: Michigan Law School 1870," University of Michigan Law School, 2009. https://repository.law.umich.edu/cgi/viewcontent.cgi?article=1142&context=miscellaneous.

———, "Michigan's First Woman Lawyer: Sarah Killgore Wertman." *Law Quad. Notes* 48, no. 3 (2006): 8. https://repository.law.umich.edu/cgi/viewcontent.cgi?article=2698&context=articles.

Leung, Rebecca. "Can a Video Game Lead to Murder?" CBS News, March 4, 2005. https://www.cbsnews.com/news/can-a-video-game-lead-to-murder-04-03-2005.

Lindsay-Herrera, Flora. "One City for All? The Characteristics of Residential Displacement in SW DC," *Land* 8, no. 2 (February 2019): 34, https://doi.org/10.3390/land8020034.

Lithwick, Dahlia. "Cruel but Not Unusual." Slate, April 1, 2011. https://slate.com/news-and-politics/2011/04/connick-v-thompson-clarence-thomas-writes-one-of-the-cruelest-supreme-court-decisions-ever.html.

Little, Becky. "How Woodrow Wilson Tried to Reverse Black American Progress." History.com, July 14, 2020. https://www.history.com/news/woodrow-wilson-racial-segregation-jim-crow-ku-klux-klan.

Livingston, Debra A. "Gang Loitering, the Court, and Some Realism about Police Patrol." *Supreme Court Review* 1999, no. 141 (2000): 150–51.

Mattox, William. "How DeSantis Helped Turn the House Republican." *Wall Street Journal*, November 16, 2022. https://www.wsj.com/articles/how-desantis-helped-turn-the-house-republican-black-candidates-redistricting-map-11668638516.

McGeehan, Patrick. "Pfizer to Leave City That Won Land-Use Case," *New York Times*, November 12, 2009. https://www.nytimes.com/2009/11/13/nyregion/13pfizer.html.

McKee v. Cosby, 139 S. Ct. 675 (2019).

McKee v. Cosby, 236 F. Supp. 3d 427 (D. Mass. 2017).

McKee v. Cosby, 874 F. 3d 54, 62 (1st Cir. 2017).

McLaughlin, Dan. "Sotomayor on Thomas: 'The One Justice in the Building That Literally Knows Every Employee's Name.'" *National Review*, July 18, 2022. https://www.nationalreview.com/corner/sotomayor-on-thomas-the-one-justice-in-the-building-that-literally-knows-every-employees-name.

Mehren, Elizabeth. "Ex-Governor Gets a Year in Prison: Illegal Gifts Led to Connecticut Leader's Downfall." SFGATE, March 19, 2005. https://www.sfgate.com/news/article/Ex-governor-gets-a-year-in-prison-Illegal-gifts-2722134.php.

Michak, Don. "Rowland's Former Aide Gets 30 Months in Prison in Corruption Case." *Journal Inquirer*, April 25, 2006. https://www.journalinquirer.com/archives/rowlands-former-aide-gets-30-months-in-prison-in-corruption-case/article_4808287b-22c4-5485-9740-8202e1186d9f.html.

Michigan Amicus Brief, *Students for Fair Admission, Inc. v. Harvard*, 142 S. Ct. 895 (2022) (20-1199) (found at 2022 WL 3130736).

Miraldi, Rob. "Video Games Spur Violence. How Can We Keep Ignoring Their Impact on Gun Culture?" *Poughkeepsie Journal*, July 14, 2022. https://www.poughkeepsiejournal.com/story/opinion/2022/07/14/video-games-spur-violence-how-can-we-keep-ignoring-their-impact-on-gun-culture/65373182007.

Missouri v. Jenkins, 515 U.S. 70 (1995).

Morioka, Sharon. "Meet Michigan's Law Class of 2025." University of Michigan, September 27, 2022. https://michigan.law.umich.edu/news/meet-michigan-laws-class-2025.

Morris, Chris. "Hollywood? Who Needs It?" CNN, January 27, 2003. https://money.cnn.com/2003/01/21/commentary/game_over/column_gaming.

New York Times Co. v. Sullivan, 376 U.S. 254 (1964).

"Notable Graduates." United States Military Academy at West Point, n.d. https://www.westpoint.edu/about/history-of-west-point/notable-graduates.

"Nothing Rotten about the Big Plum." *Time*, June 15, 1981. https://content.time.com/time/subscriber/article/0,33009,949179,00.html.

"Ohio: Cleveland Scholarship Program." EdChoice, January 5, 2023. https://www.edchoice.org/school-choice/programs/ohio-cleveland-scholarship-program.

Papajohn, George, and staff writer. "Most Gang Crime Tied to Four Groups," *Chicago Tribune*, November 29, 1993, https://www.chicagotribune.com/news/ct-xpm-1993-11-29-9311290110-story.html.

Pesto, Mark. "Klan Leader from Johnstown Dies." *Tribune-Democrat*, November 26, 2018. https://www.tribdem.com/news/klan-leader-from-johnstown-dies/article_e03fa8fa-f11f-11e8-866d-5f1ad-a0bca40.html.

Perrino, Nico. "So to Speak Transcript: David Baugh." Foundation for Individual Rights and Expression, June 21, 2016. https://www.thefire.org/so-to-speak-transcript-david-baugh.

Petition for Certiorari, *City of Chicago v. Morales*, 527 U.S. 41 (1999) (97–1121).

Petition for Writ of Certiorari, *McKee v. Cosby*, 139 S. Ct. 675 (2019).

Pick, Grant. "Cops 'n' Neighbors: Community Policing in Beverly-Morgan Park." *Chicago Reader*, October 13, 1994. https://chicagoreader.com/news-politics/cops-n-neighbors-community-policing-in-beverly-morgan-park.

Putre, Laura. "Hangin' with Mother Hough." Scene, March 29, 2001. https://www.clevescene.com/news/hangin-with-mother-hough-1476527.

Raich v. Ashcroft, 248 F. Supp. 2d 918 (N.D. Cal. 2003).

Raich v. Ashcroft, 352 F. 3d 1222 (9th Cir. 2003).

Rainey, Richard. "Groups Assail 'Most Violent' Video Games, Industry Rating System." *Los Angeles Times*, November 24, 2004. https://www.latimes.com/archives/la-xpm-2004-nov-24-na-games24-story.html.

Ralston, Shane J. "Samuel L. Jackson Calls Clarence Thomas an 'Uncle Tom.'" Medium, June 28, 2022. https://medium.com/the-controversial-idea/samuel-jackson-calls-clarence-thomas-out-as-an-uncle-tom-217dec798690.

Reed v. Rhodes, 934 F. Supp. 1533 (N.D. Ohio 1996).

Regents of the Univ. of Cal. v. Bakke, 438 U.S. 265 (1978).

Render, Josh. "What Was Grand Theft Auto: San Andreas' Hot Coffee Controversy?" CBR, October 26, 2021. https://www.cbr.com/what-was-grand-theft-auto-san-andreas-hot-coffee-controversy.

Reisinger, Don. "91 Percent of Kids Are Gamers, Research Says." CNET, October 11, 2011. https://www.cnet.com/home/smart-home/91-percent-of-kids-are-gamers-research-says.

Respondent's Brief against Certiorari, *City of Chicago v. Morales*, 527 U. S. 41 (1999) (97–1121).

Roberts, Sam. "Harry Pregerson, Judge Guided by Conscience, Dies at 94." *New York Times*, November 29, 2017. https://www.nytimes.com/2017/11/29/obituaries/harry-pregerson-dead-ninth-circuit-judge-guided-by-conscience.html.

Robin, Corey. "The Self-Fulfilling Prophecies of Clarence Thomas." *New Yorker*, July 9, 2022. https://www.newyorker.com/news/daily-comment/the-self-fulfilling-prophecies-of-clarence-thomas.

Sacks, Deana Pollard, Brad J. Bushman, and Craig A. Anderson. "Do Violent Video Games Harm Children? Comparing the Scientific Amicus Curiae 'Experts' in Brown v. Entertainment Merchants Association." *Northwestern University Law Review Colloquy* 106 (2011): 1–12. https://papers.ssrn.com/sol3/papers.cfm?abstract_ id=1856116.

Santiago, Ellyn. "Eric Harris & Dylan Klebold: The Basement Tapes." Heavy.com, April 19, 2019. https://heavy.com/news/2019/04/ eric-harris-dylan-klebold-the-basement-tapes.

Schmidt, Peter. "Bush Asks Supreme Court to Strike Down U. of Michigan's Affirmative-Action Policy." *The Chronicle of Higher Education*, January 24, 2003. https://www.chronicle.com/article/ bush-asks-supreme-court-to-strike-down-u-of-michigans- affirmative-action-policy.

Sherry, John L., Kristen Lucas, Bradley S. Greenberg, and Ken Lachlan. "Video Game Uses and Gratifications as Predictors of Use and Game Preference." In *Playing Video Games: Motives, Responses, and Consequences*, edited by Peter Vorderer and Jennings Bryant, 213. Lawrence Erlbaum Associates Publishers, 2006.

Simmons-Harris v. Goff, 711 N.E. 2d 203 (Ohio 1999).

Simmons-Harris v. Zelman, 1999 WL 669222 (N.D. Ohio 1999). Order staying injunction.

Simmons-Harris v. Zelman, 54 F. Supp. 2d 725 (N.D. Ohio 1999). Preliminary injunction.

Simmons-Harris v. Zelman, 72 F. Supp. 2d 834 (N.D. Ohio 1999). Preliminary injunction.

Slaughter-House Cases, 16 Wall. 36, 21 L.Ed. 394 (1873).

Slusher v. Ospital ex rel. Ospital, 777 P.2d 437 (Utah 1989).

Smith, Michael David. "Warrick Dunn Opens Up about the Lingering Effects of His Mother's Murder." NBC Sports, June 28, 2019.

https://profootballtalk.nbcsports.com/2019/06/28/warrick-dunn-opens-up-about-the-lingering-effects-of-his-mothers-murder.

Snow, Shawn. "The Corps Authorized Marines to Play a Special Version of Doom in the Late 90s to Help Train for Combat." *Marine Corps Times*, November 6, 2019. https://www.marinecorpstimes.com/news/your-marine-corps/2019/11/06/the-corps-authorized-marines-to-play-a-special-version-of-doom-in-the-late-90s-to-help-train-for-combat.

Somin, Ilya. "The 15th Anniversary of Kelo v. City of New London." Reason.com, June 23, 2020. https://reason.com/volokh/2020/06/23/the-15th-anniversary-of-kelo-v-city-of-new-london.

State Farm Mut. Auto. Ins. Co. v. Campbell, 538 U.S. 408 (2003) (No. 01-1289).

Stern, Scott W. "The Radicalization of Clarence Thomas." *New Republic*, August 17, 2021. https://newrepublic.com/article/163116/radicalization-clarence-thomas.

Strickler, Laura. "2 Years after Newtown School Shooting, No Research on Gun Violence." CBS News, December 12, 2014. https://www.cbsnews.com/news/2-years-after-newtown-school-shooting-no-research-on-gun-violence.

"Supreme Court Affirmative Action News Conference." C-SPAN, April 1, 2003. At 10:04–10:41. https://www.c-span.org/video/?175921-1/supreme-court-affirmative-action-news-conference.

Testimony of Rebecca Sechrist, *Virginia v. Black*, 538 U.S. 343, Joint Appendix at 68–70; *Commonwealth v. Virginia*, 553 S.E. 2d 738 (Va. 2001).

Thomas, Clarence. "Be Not Afraid." Transcript of speech delivered at the American Enterprise Institute on February 13, 2001. https://www.aei.org/research-products/speech/be-not-afraid.

————. "Speech to the National Bar Association." Transcript of speech delivered at the National Bar Association on July 28, 1998. https://www.blackpast.org/african-american-history/1998-clarence-thomas-speech-national-bar-association.

————. *My Grandfather's Son: A Memoir.* New York: Harper Perennial, 2007.

Tobin, Mike. "Outspoken, Revered Councilwoman Fannie Lewis Dies." Cleveland.com, August 11, 2008. https://www.cleveland.com/metro/2008/08/fannie_lewis_dies_at_82.html.

Tompkins v. Alabama State University, 15 F. Supp. 2d 1160 (N.D. Ala. 1998).

Tompkins v. Alabama State University, 174 F. 3d 203 (11th Cir. 1999).

Transcript of Oral Argument. *Kelo v. City of New London,* 545 U.S. 469 (2005). https://www.supremecourt.gov/oral_arguments/argument_transcripts/2004/04-108.pdf.

Transcript of Oral Argument, *Brown v. Entertainment Merchants Ass'n,* 564 U.S. 786 (2011) (No. 08-1448).

Transcript of Oral Argument, *Brumfield v. Cain,* 576 U.S. 305 (2015) (13-1433).

Transcript of Oral Argument, *Gonzales v. Raich,* 545 U.S. 1 (2005) (No. 03-1454).

Transcript of Oral Argument, *Grutter v. Bollinger,* 539 U.S. 306 (2003) (No. 02-241).

Transcript of Oral Argument, *McDonald v. City of Chicago,* 561 U.S. 742 (2010) (08-1521).

Transcript of Oral Argument, *State Farm Mut. Auto. Ins. Co. v. Campbell,* 538 U.S. 408 (2003) (No. 01-1289).

Transcript of Oral Argument, *Video Software Dealers Ass'n v. Schwarzenegger,* 556 F. 3d 950 (9th Cir. 2009) (No. 07-16620).

Transcript of Oral Argument, *Virginia v. Black,* 538 U.S. 343 (2003) (No. 01-1107).

Transcript of Oral Argument, *Zelman v. Simmons-Harris*, 536 U.S. 639 (2002).

United States Amicus Brief, *Virginia v. Black*, 538 U.S. 343 (2003) (No. 01-1107).

United States v. Cruikshank, 92 U.S. 542 (1876).

United States v. Oakland Cannabis Buyers' Cooperative, 532 U.S. 483 (2001).

"University of Michigan Law School Timeline." University of Michigan, n.d. https://libguides.law.umich.edu/law-school-history-timeline.

Video Software Dealers Ass'n. v. Schwarzenegger, 401 F. Supp. 2d 1034 (N.D. Cal. 2005).

Video Software Dealers Ass'n v. Schwarzenegger, 556 F. 3d 950 (9th Cir. 2009) (No. 07-16620).

Video Software Dealers Ass'n. v. Schwarzenegger, No. 05-CV-04188 (RMW), 2007 WL 2261546 (N.D. Cal. Aug. 6, 2007).

Virginia v. Black, 538 U.S. 343 (2003).

Voices of American Law: Virginia v. Black, *Party Narrative II*. Duke University School of Law. https://law.duke.edu/videofiles/voal/narrative/virginia2.mp4.

Wadhams, Nick. "Video Games under the Gun." NBC News, July 4, 2004. https://www.nbcnews.com/id/wbna5351969.

Walters, Brandon. "It's Been a Year of Private Reversals and Public Trials for Richmond's Best-Known Defense." *Style Weekly*, January 1, 1980. https://www.styleweekly.com/richmond/its-been-a-year-of-private-reversals-and-public-trials-for-richmonds-best-known-defense/Content?oid=1388046.

Whitaker, Ron. "8 of the Most Controversial Videogames Ever Made." The Escapist, June 1, 2015. https://www.escapistmagazine.com/8-of-the-most-controversial-videogames-ever-made.

Wickard v. Filburn, 317 U.S. 111 (1942).

Wijman, Tom. "The Games Market and Beyond in 2021: The Year in Numbers." Newzoo, December 22, 2021. https://newzoo.com/insights/articles/the-games-market-in-2021-the-year-in-numbers-esports-cloud-gaming.

Zelman v. Simmons-Harris, 528 U.S. 983 (1999). Order granting stay.

Zelman v. Simmons Harris, 536 U.S. 639 (2002).

Notes

Introduction

1. Author interview with Nicole Garnett by telephone, October 21, 2022.
2. Dan McLaughlin, "Sotomayor on Thomas: 'The One Justice in the Building That Literally Knows Every Employee's Name,'" *National Review*, July 18, 2022, https://www.nationalreview.com/corner /sotomayor-on-thomas-the-one-justice-in-the-building-that-literally -knows-every-employees-name.
3. Shane J. Ralston, "Samuel L. Jackson Calls Clarence Thomas an 'Uncle Tom,'" Medium, June 28, 2022, https://medium.com/the-controversial -idea/samuel-jackson-calls-clarence-thomas-out-as-an-uncle-tom -217dec798690; Dahlia Lithwick, "Cruel but Not Unusual," Slate, April 1, 2011, https://slate.com/news-and-politics/2011/04/connick -v-thompson-clarence-thomas-writes-one-of-the-cruelest-supreme -court-decisions-ever.html; Andrew Kaczynski, "Democratic Congressman Makes Shocking Racial Comments about Republicans Clarence Thomas, Mitch McConnell," BuzzFeed News, April 29, 2014, https://www.buzzfeednews.com/article/andrewkaczynski/democratic -congressman-makes-shocking-racial-comments-about; Corey Robin, "The Self-Fulfilling Prophecies of Clarence Thomas," *New Yorker*, July 9, 2022, https://www.newyorker.com/news/daily-comment/the-self -fulfilling-prophecies-of-clarence-thomas; Scott W. Stern, "The Radicalization of Clarence Thomas," *New Republic*, August 17, 2021,

https://newrepublic.com/article/163116/radicalization-clarence
-thomas.

4. Clarence Thomas, "Be Not Afraid," transcript of speech delivered at
    the American Enterprise Institute on February 13, 2001, https://www
    .aei.org/research-products/speech/be-not-afraid.

5. Clarence Thomas, *My Grandfather's Son: A Memoir* (New York:
    Harper Perennial, 2007), 13.

6. Clarence Thomas, "Speech to the National Bar Association," transcript
    of speech delivered at the National Bar Association, July 28, 1998,
    https://www.blackpast.org/african-american-history/1998-clarence
    -thomas-speech-national-bar-association.

Chapter 1: "The Wolves Are at Our Door": *Kelo v. City of New London*

1. Jeff Benedict, *Little Pink House: A True Story of Defiance and Courage*
    (New York: Grand Central, 2009), 49. I highly recommend Benedict's
    book to readers who would like to learn more about Susette Kelo and
    the facts and circumstances surrounding this case. Professor Ilya
    Somin has also written numerous articles that detail the factual
    circumstances as well as the legal and policy implications. See, for
    example, Ilya Somin, "Kelo: How Politicians Stole Her Home and
    Gave It to Pfizer (Who Destroyed It for Nothing)" FEE Stories, June 2,
    2015, https://fee.org/articles/kelo-how-politicians-stole-her-home-
    and-gave-it-to-pfizer-who-destroyed-it-for-nothing; Ilya Somin, "The
    Story behind Kelo v. City of New London – How an Obscure Takings
    Case Got to the Supreme Court and Shocked the Nation," *Washington
    Post*, May 29, 2015, https://www.washingtonpost.com/news/volokh-
    conspiracy/wp/2015/05/29/the-story-behind-the-kelo-case-how-an-
    obscure-takings-case-came-to-shock-the-conscience-of-the-nation.
    For anyone interested in the broader legal and policy issues
    surrounding Kelo, I recommend Ilya Somin's book *The Grasping
    Hand: Kelo v. City of New London and the Limits of Eminent Domain*
    (University of Chicago Press, 2015).

2. Benedict, *Little Pink House*, 50.

3. Ibid., 46–57.

4. Ibid., 67.

5. Ibid.; Author interview with Scott Bullock by telephone, September 20, 2022.

6. Benedict, *Little Pink House*, 64.

7. Ibid., 67; *Voices of American Law: Kelo v. New London, Party Narrative*, at 5:12–5:18, Duke University School of Law.

8. Benedict, *Little Pink House*, 67.

9. Ibid., 75, 256.

10. John Curran, "Elderly Widow Wins Fight with Trump," Associated Press, July 20, 1998, https://apnews.com/article/ed32d4191419a0a428a3 d6bdc6d17e12; Benedict, *Little Pink House*, 157.

11. Author interview with Scott Bullock by telephone.

12. Ibid.

13. Ibid.; Benedict, *Little Pink House*, 87.

14. Author interview with Scott Bullock by telephone.

15. Ibid.

16. Ibid.

17. Ibid.

18. Ibid.; Benedict, *Little Pink House*, 261.

19. Brief of Amici Curiae National Association for the Advancement of Colored People, *Kelo v. City of New London*, 545 U.S. 469 (2005), 2004 WL 2811057, *8, https://ij.org/wp-content/uploads/2000/12/naacp02 .pdf.

20. Transcript of Oral Argument at 7, 30–31, 55–57, *Kelo v. City of New London*, 545 U.S. 469 (2005), https://www.supremecourt.gov/oral _arguments/argument_transcripts/2004/04-108.pdf.

21. Benedict, *Little Pink House*, 323.

22. Elizabeth Mehren, "Ex-Governor Gets a Year in Prison: Illegal Gifts Led to Connecticut Leader's Downfall," SFGATE, March 19, 2005, https://www.sfgate.com/news/article/Ex-governor-gets-a-year-in -prison-Illegal-gifts-2722134.php; Don Michak, "Rowland's Former Aide Gets 30 Months in Prison in Corruption Case," *Journal Inquirer*, April 25, 2006, https://www.journalinquirer.com/archives/rowlands -former-aide-gets-30-months-in-prison-in-corruption-case/article _4808287b-22c4-5485-9740-8202e1186d9f.html; LeAnne Gendreau and Ari Mason, "Former Governor John Rowland Sentenced to 30

Months in Prison," NBC Connecticut, March 18, 2015, https://www
.nbcconnecticut.com/news/local/john-rowlands-sentencing-set-for
-wednesday/1965046.

23. Patrick McGeehan, "Pfizer to Leave City That Won Land-Use Case,"
New York Times, November 12, 2009, https://www.nytimes.com/2009
/11/13/nyregion/13pfizer.html.

24. Ilya Somin, "The 15th Anniversary of Kelo v. City of New London,"
Reason.com, June 23, 2020, https://reason.com/volokh/2020/06/23/
the-15th-anniversary-of-kelo-v-city-of-new-london.

Chapter 2: "Education Means Emancipation": *Zelman v. Simmons-Harris*

1. Kaleena Fraga, "The Harrowing Story of the 1969 Cuyahoga Fire—and
How It Changed America," All That's Interesting, May 24, 2021,
https://allthatsinteresting.com/the-cuyahoga-river-fire.

2. "Nothing Rotten about the Big Plum," *Time*, June 15, 1981, https://
content.time.com/time/subscriber/article/0,33009,949179,00.html.

3. Ibid.

4. Wikipedia, s.v. "George Voinovich," last modified December 3, 2022,
20:48, https://en.wikipedia.org/wiki/George_Voinovich.

5. David Brennan and Malcolm Baroway, *Victory for Kids: The Cleveland
School Voucher Case* (Beverly Hills, California: New Millennium,
2002), 32.

6. *Reed v. Rhodes*, 934 F. Supp. 1533 (N.D. Ohio 1996), https://law.justia
.com/cases/federal/district-courts/FSupp/934/1533/1955861.

7. Ibid.

8. Cleveland City Schools District Performance Audit, March 15, 1996,
cited in State Petitioner's Brief to the Supreme Court, at 2 in *Zelman v.
Simmons- Harris*, 536 U.S. 639 (2002).

9. Appendix to Petition for a Writ of Certiorari, at 139a, *Hanna Perkins
School v. Simmons-Harris*, U.S. No. 00-1777.

10. Brennan and Baroway, *Victory for Kids*, 32–33.

11. Ken Klukowski, "Reagan Ally Bill Batchelder Laid to Rest in Ohio,"
Breitbart, February 21, 2022, https://www.breitbart.com/politics/2022
/02/21/reagan-ally-bill-batchelder-rest-ohio.

12. Brennan and Baroway, *Victory for Kids*, 31.
13. Laura Putre, "Hangin' with Mother Hough," Scene, March 29, 2001, https://www.clevescene.com/news/hangin-with-mother-hough-1476527; Mike Tobin, "Outspoken, Revered Councilwoman Fannie Lewis Dies," Cleveland.com, August 11, 2008, https://www.cleveland.com/metro/2008/08/fannie_lewis_dies_at_82.html.
14. Tobin, "Outspoken, Revered Councilwoman Fannie Lewis Dies."
15. Author interview with Bill Patmon by telephone, November 17, 2022.
16. Klukowski, "Reagan Ally Bill Batchelder Laid to Rest in Ohio."
17. Brennan and Baroway, *Victory for Kids*, 24.
18. Ibid., 34–35.
19. Ibid., 36.
20. *Simmons-Harris v. Goff*, 711 N.E. 2d 203 (Ohio 1999).
21. *Simmons-Harris v. Zelman*, 54 F. Supp. 2d 725 (N.D. Ohio 1999) (preliminary injunction).
22. "Cleveland Schools Reopen amid Worries over Vouchers," *Baltimore Sun*, August 26, 1999, https://www.newspapers.com/image/173284769.
23. *Simmons-Harris v. Zelman*, 1999 WL 669222 (N.D. Ohio 1999) (order staying injunction).
24. *Zelman v. Simmons-Harris*, 528 U.S. 983 (1999) (order granting stay).
25. *Simmons-Harris v. Zelman*, 72 F. Supp. 2d 834 (N.D. Ohio 1999) (preliminary injunction).
26. Author interview with Alice Batchelder by telephone, November 13, 2022.
27. Transcript of Oral Argument at 71, *Zelman v. Simmons-Harris*, 536 U.S. 639 (2002).
28. *Zelman*, 536 U.S. at 640–41, 657, 659–60, 676, 678, 680–84.
29. William Mattox, "How DeSantis Helped Turn the House Republican," *Wall Street Journal*, November 16, 2022, https://www.wsj.com/articles/how-desantis-helped-turn-the-house-republican-black-candidates-redistricting-map-11668638516.
30. "Ohio: Cleveland Scholarship Program," EdChoice, January 5, 2023, https://www.edchoice.org/school-choice/programs/ohio-cleveland-scholarship-program.

Chapter 3: "Do Nothing with Us!": *Grutter v. Bollinger*

1. Margaret A. Leary and Barbara J. Snow, "Gabriel Franklin Hargo: Michigan Law 1870," University of Michigan Law School, 2009, https:// repository.law.umich.edu/cgi/viewcontent.cgi?article=1142&context= miscellaneous.

2. "University of Michigan Law School HistoryTimeline," University of Michigan, last updated December 8, 2022, https://libguides.law.umich .edu/law-school-history-timeline.

3. Margaret A. Leary, "Michigan's First Woman Lawyer: Sarah Killgore Wertman," *Law Quad. Notes* 48, no. 3 (2006): 8, https://repository.law .umich.edu/cgi/viewcontent.cgi?article=2698&context=articles.

4. "University of Michigan Law School HistoryTimeline."

5. *Grutter v. Bollinger*, 137 F. Supp. 2d 821, 827 (E.D. Mich. 2001).

6. *Regents of the Univ. of Cal. v. Bakke*, 438 U.S. 265 (1978).

7. Author interview with Terry Pell by telephone, December 22, 2022; *Gratz v. Bollinger*, 122 F. Supp. 811, 827 (E.D. Mich. 2000).

8. *Hopwood v. State of Texas*, 78 F. 3d 932 (5th Cir. 1996).

9. *Tompkins v. Alabama State University*, 15 F. Supp. 2d 1160 (N.D. Ala. 1998).

10. Author interview with Terry Pell by telephone.

11. Barbara Grutter's comments at news conference hosted by Center for Individual Rights on April 1, 2003, at 1:27–2:37, https://www.c-span.org /video/?c4678928/user-clip-barbara-grutter.

12. *Grutter*, 137 F. Supp. 2d at 830.

13. Ibid., 831.

14. Ibid., 832.

15. Ibid., 833.

16. Ibid., 836–39.

17. Ibid., 839.

18. Ibid., 871.

19. *Grutter v. Bollinger*, 288 F. 3d 732, 775 (6th Cir. 2002) (en banc) (Boggs, J., dissenting).

20. Ibid., 751 (majority opinion).

21. Ibid., 797 (Boggs, J., dissenting).

22. Peter Schmidt, "Bush Asks Supreme Court to Strike Down U. of Michigan's Affirmative-Action Policy," *Chronicle of Higher Education*, January 24, 2003, https://www.chronicle.com/article/bush-asks -supreme-court-to-strike-down-u-of-michigans-affirmative-action -policy.

23. Ibid.

24. Ibid.

25. Ibid.

26. Transcript of Oral Argument, *Grutter v. Bollinger*, 539 U.S. 306 (2003) (No. 02-241).

27. "Supreme Court Affirmative Action News Conference," C-SPAN, April 1, 2003, at 10:04–10:41, https://www.c-span.org/video/?175921-1/ supreme-court-affirmative-action-news-conference.

28. *Grutter*, 539 U.S. at 343.

29. Ibid., 379.

30. Barbara Grutter, "Making Progress," *National Review*, August 19, 2003, https://www.nationalreview.com/2003/08/making-progress-barbara -grutter.

31. Sharon Morioka, "Meet Michigan Law's Class of 2025," University of Michigan, September 27, 2022, https://michigan.law.umich.edu/news /meet-michigan-laws-class-2025. "The Class of 2025 is 24 percent LGBTQ+ students and 42 percent people of color; both numbers are the highest in the school's history."

32. Michigan Amicus Brief, *Students for Fair Admission, Inc. v. Harvard*, 142 S. Ct. 895 (2022) (20-1199) (found at 2022 WL 3130736).

33. *Zelman v. Simmons-Harris*, 536 U.S. 639, 683–84 (2002) (Thomas, J., dissenting).

34. Ibid.

35. *Tompkins v. Alabama State University*, 15 F. Supp. 2d 1160 (N.D. Ala. 1998); *Tompkins v. Alabama State University*, 174 F. 3d 203 (11th Cir. 1999).

36. *Knight v. State of Alabama*, 900 F. Supp 272 (N.D. Ala. 1995).

37. *Missouri v. Jenkins*, 515 U.S. 70, 114 (1995) (Thomas, J., concurring).

Chapter 4: The Professor and the Patient: *Gonzales v. Raich*

1. *United States v. Oakland Cannabis Buyers' Cooperative*, 532 U.S. 483 (2001).
2. *Raich v. Ashcroft*, 352 F.3d 1222, 1225–26 (9th Cir. 2003); *Raich v. Ashcroft*, 248 F. Supp. 2d 918 (N.D. Cal. 2003); Diane Monson affidavit at page 4, paragraph 10, found at http://angeljustice.org/angel/United _States_District_Court_of_the_North_District_of_California_files /Declaration%20of%20Diane%20Monson%20October%2030,%20 2002.pdf.
3. U.S. Const. art. I § 8.
4. *Wickard v. Filburn*, 317 U.S. 111 (1942).
5. Harriet Chiang, "Wal-Mart Judge Praised for Compassion, Diligence / Colleagues, Friends Say He Is Well-Suited for Sex-Bias Case," SFGATE, June 23, 2004, https://www.sfgate.com/news/article/Wal -Mart-judge-praised-for-compassion-diligence-2711737.php.
6. *Raich*, 248 F. Supp. 2d 918.
7. Sam Roberts, "Harry Pregerson, Judge Guided by Conscience, Dies at 94," *New York Times*, November 29, 2017, https://www.nytimes.com /2017/11/29/obituaries/harry-pregerson-dead-ninth-circuit-judge -guided-by-conscience.html.
8. "Hon. Richard Paez—U.S. Court of Appeals for the Ninth Court," University of Washington, October 27, 2008, https://www.law .washington.edu/multimedia/2008/paez/transcript.aspx.
9. "Beam, C. Arlen," United States District Court, District of Nebraska, n.d., https://www.ned.uscourts.gov/public/judicial-archive/beam-c-a.
10. Transcript of Oral Argument, *Gonzales v. Raich*, 545 U.S. 1 (2005) (No. 03-1454).
11. *Gonzales*, 545 U.S. at 25–26.

Chapter 5: Standing Alone: *Doe v. United States*

1. Amended Complaint at 2, *Doe v. Hagenbeck*, 98 F. Supp. 3d 672 (S.D.N.Y. 2015), ECF No. 14. The details of Jane's experiences at West Point are taken from her complaint in the case she filed against West Point officials and the United States, which was reviewed twice by the U.S. Court of Appeals for the Second Circuit. See *Doe v. Hagenbeck*,

870 F. 3d 36 (2d Cir. 2017); *Doe v. United States*, 815 F. App'x 592 (2d Cir. 2020) (summary order). The U.S. Supreme Court denied certiorari. *Doe v. United States*, 141 S. Ct. 1498 (2021). One quick legal note: When a case is dismissed at the motion to dismiss stage, the court does not decide whether the plaintiff's allegations of fact are true. Instead, it accepts those facts as true and focuses on the legal issues the motion presents. I take the same approach, putting the reader in the shoes of the court.

2. Amended Complaint at 2, *Doe*, 98 F. Supp. 3d 672; "About West Point," United States Military Academy at West Point, n.d., https://www .westpoint.edu/about.

3. Amended Complaint at 2, *Doe*, 98 F. Supp. 3d 672.

4. "A Brief History of West Point," United States Military Academy at West Point, n.d., https://www.westpoint.edu/about/history-of-west -point.

5. Ibid.

6. Ibid.; "Notable Graduates," United States Military Academy at West Point, n.d., https://www.westpoint.edu/about/history-of-west-point/ notable-graduates.

7. Amended Complaint at 2, *Doe*, 98 F. Supp. 3d 672.

8. Ibid., 2–3.

9. Ibid., 3.

10. Ibid., 4.

11. Ibid.

12. Ibid., 5 ("[West Point leadership] created a misogynistic culture at West Point that marginalized Ms. Doe and other female cadets, caused them to be subjected to routine harassment, suffer emotional distress and other harms, and be pressured to conform to male norms. . . . Ms. Doe and other female cadets felt immense pressure to match the men's physical capabilities and to align themselves with their male colleagues socially and psychologically.").

13. Ibid., 11.

14. Ibid.; *Doe*, 98 F. Supp. 3d at 679.

15. Amended Complaint at 11, *Doe*, 98 F. Supp. 3d 672; "Robert Smith" is a pseudonym Doe used for her alleged rapist.

16. Ibid.
17. Ibid.
18. Ibid. 12.
19. Ibid.; see also *Doe*, 98 F. Supp. 3d at 679; *Doe*, 870 F. 3d at 39; *Doe*, 815 F. App'x at 593; *Doe*, 141 S. Ct. at 1498 (Thomas, J., dissenting from denial of cert.).
20. Amended Complaint at 12, *Doe*, 98 F. Supp. 3d 672.
21. Ibid., 12–13.
22. Ibid., 12.
23. Ibid., 13–14.
24. Ibid., 14.
25. "Although she earned a degree [from another college], she struggled emotionally as she continued to process the experience of having been sexually assaulted at West Point." Ibid.
26. Ibid., 25.
27. Ibid., 21.
28. Ibid., 9 (summarizing a 2011 Department of Defense report).
29. Ibid., 8 ("By failing to adequately punish perpetrators of sexual violence, [West Point leadership] sent the message to male cadets that they would tolerate sexual violence at West Point. They created a system in which male cadets understood that they could sexually assault their female colleagues with near impunity, while at the same time teaching female cadets that they risked their own reputations and military careers by reporting assault and that little or no action would be taken against their assailants."); Ibid., 1 ("West Point officials . . . knew that there was a culture condoning sexual harassment, sexual assault, and rape among the cadets at West Point. Had . . . West Point officials adequately supervised the cadets, the United States could have avoided the harm to Ms. Doe.").
30. Federal Tort Claims Act of 1946, 28 U.S.C. § 1346(b)(1).
31. *Feres v. United States*, 340 U.S. 135, 146 (1950).
32. *Chappell v. Wallace*, 462 U.S. 296 (1983).
33. *Doe*, 815 F. App'x at 594–95.
34. Federal Tort Claims Act of 1946, 28 U.S.C. § 2680(j).
35. *Doe*, 141 S. Ct. at 1498–99 (Thomas, J., dissenting from denial of cert.).

36. Ibid., 1499.
37. Ibid.
38. Ibid.

Chapter 6: Beauty and the Beast: *McKee v. Cosby*

1. Author interview with Kathrine McKee by telephone, December 20, 2022; Exhibit D at 2, *McKee v. Cosby*, 236 F. Supp. 3d 427 (D. Mass. 2017) (No. 15-30221-MGM), ECF No. 42-5. Note her name is spelled as Kathrine McKee in the complaint. In many of the articles about the case, it is spelled Katherine McKee. Since Ms. McKee verified the complaint, I use "Kathrine."
2. Author interview with Kathrine McKee by telephone.
3. Ibid.
4. Ibid.
5. Ibid.
6. Ibid.
7. Ibid.
8. Ibid.; see also Exhibit D at 2, *McKee*, 236 F. Supp. 3d 427 (No. 15-30221-MGM), ECF No. 42-5.
9. Ibid.; "About Kathy McKee," Kathy McKee Casting, n.d., http://www.kathymckeecasting.com/about-kathy.html; Author interview with Kathrine McKee by telephone.
10. Exhibit D at 3, *McKee*, 236 F. Supp. 3d 427 (No. 15-30221-MGM), ECF No. 42-5; "About Kathy McKee"; Author interview with Kathrine McKee by telephone.
11. Nancy Dillon, "Bill Cosby Accused of Raping Ex-Girlfriend of Sammy Davis Jr.," *New York Daily News*, December 22, 2014, https://www.nydailynews.com/news/national/bill-cosby-accused-raping-ex-girlfriend-sammy-davis-jr-article-1.2052890; "About Kathy McKee"; "Kathy McKee Biography," IMDb, n.d., https://www.imdb.com/name/nm0571181/bio?ref_=nm_ov_bio_sm.
12. Dillon, "Bill Cosby Accused"; Amended Complaint at 2, *McKee*, 236 F. Supp. 3d 427 (No. 15-30221-MGM), ECF No. 30.
13. Exhibit D at 3, *McKee*, 236 F. Supp. 3d 427, ECF No. 42-5.
14. Ibid.

15. Ibid.
16. Some of the factual details here and below are taken from McKee's amended complaint. Amended Complaint at 3, *McKee*, 236 F. Supp. 3d 427 (No. 15-30221-MGM), ECF No. 30. The original complaint included substantially similar allegations. Complaint at 2–3, *McKee*, 236 F. Supp. 3d 427 (No. 15-30221-MGM), ECF No. 1. So did the *New York Daily News* article. See Dillon, "Bill Cosby Accused." One quick legal note: When a case is dismissed at the motion to dismiss stage, the court does not decide whether the plaintiff's allegations of fact are true. Instead, it accepts those facts as true and focuses on the legal issues the motion presents. I take the same approach, putting the reader in the shoes of the court.
17. Amended Complaint at 3, *McKee*, 236 F. Supp. 3d 427 (No. 15-30221-MGM), ECF No. 30.
18. Dillon, "Bill Cosby Accused."
19. "The rape was shocking, scary and horrible." Amended Complaint at 3, *McKee*, 236 F. Supp. 3d 427 (No. 15-30221-MGM), ECF No. 30.
20. Dillon, "Bill Cosby Accused."
21. Ibid.; Author interview with Kathrine McKee by telephone.
22. Dillon, "Bill Cosby Accused."
23. Author interview with Kathrine McKee by telephone.
24. Dillon, "Bill Cosby Accused."
25. "About Kathy McKee."
26. Ibid.
27. Ibid.; "Good Morning L.A. Talk Show," IMDb, n.d., https://www.imdb.com/title/tt2135064.
28. Exhibit D at 3, *McKee*, 236 F. Supp. 3d 427 (No. 15-30221-MGM), ECF No. 42-5.
29. Author interview with Kathrine McKee by telephone.
30. "About Kathy McKee."
31. Author interview with Kathrine McKee by telephone.
32. Dillon, "Bill Cosby Accused."
33. Amended Complaint at 5, *McKee*, 236 F. Supp. 3d 427 (No. 15-30221-MGM), ECF No. 30.

34. Exhibit A to Amended Complaint at 3, *McKee*, 236 F. Supp. 3d 427 (No. 15-30221-MGM), ECF No. 30-1 [emphasis omitted].
35. Ibid, 4.
36. Ibid., 9; ECF No. 30.
37. Ibid., 8–9.
38. *New York Times Co. v. Sullivan*, 376 U.S. 254, 279–80 (1964).
39. *McKee v. Cosby*, 139 S. Ct. 675, 675 (2019) (Thomas, J., concurring in denial of cert.) (quoting *Dun & Bradstreet, Inc. v. Greenmoss Builders, Inc.*, 472 U.S. 749, 771 (2019) (White, J., concurring in judgment).
40. *Gertz v. Robert Welch, Inc.*, 418 U.S. 323, 351 (1974).
41. *McKee*, 236 F. Supp. 3d at 453 n.25.
42. *McKee v. Cosby*, 874 F. 3d 54, 62 (1st Cir. 2017) (cleaned up).
43. Petition for Writ of Certiorari at 7–10, *McKee*, 139 S. Ct. 675 (2019) (No. 17-1542).
44. *McKee*, 139 S. Ct. 675 (2019).
45. Ibid., 676 (Thomas, J., concurring in denial of cert.).
46. Ibid., 677 (quoting *Gertz*, 418 U.S. at 345).
47. Ibid., 679.
48. Ibid., 682.
49. *Berisha v. Lawson*, 141 S. Ct. 2424, 2425 (2021) (Thomas, J., dissenting from denial of cert.).
50. *Coral Ridge Ministries Media, Inc. v. S. Poverty L. Ctr.*, 142 S.Ct. 2453 (2022) (Thomas, J., dissenting from denial of cert.).
51. *Berisha*, 141 S. Ct. at 2425 (Thomas, J., dissenting from denial of cert.).

Chapter 7: The Picture: *Brumfield v. Cain*

1. Warrick Dunn and Don Yaeger, *Running for My Life: My Journey in the Game of Football and Beyond* (New York: HarperCollins, 2009). I highly recommend Warrick Dunn's autobiography to readers who would like to learn more about Warrick Dunn and his inspiring story.
2. *Brumfield v. Cain*, 576 U.S. 305, 327 (2015) (Thomas, J., dissenting).
3. Ibid., 327 n.2; Dunn and Yaeger, *Running for My Life*, 12.
4. *Brumfield*, 576 U.S. at 327 (Thomas, J., dissenting).
5. Ibid.
6. Ibid., 327–28.

7. Ibid., 325–27.
8. Ibid., 325–26.
9. Ibid., 326.
10. Dunn and Yaeger, *Running for My Life*, 21.
11. Ibid.
12. Ibid., 23.
13. Ibid., 23–24.
14. *Brumfield*, 576 U.S. at 325-26 (Thomas, J., dissenting).
15. Dunn and Yaeger, *Running for My Life*, 23–24.
16. Ibid.
17. Ibid., 28, 34.
18. Ibid., 111–13.
19. Ibid., 88.
20. *Brumfield*, 576 U.S. at 332 (Thomas, J., dissenting).
21. Ibid., 332–33.
22. *Atkins v. Virginia*, 536 U.S. 304 (2002).
23. *Brumfield v. Cain*, 854 F. Supp. 2d 366, 371–72 (M.D. La. 2012).
24. Dunn and Yaeger, *Running for My Life*, 5; Michael David Smith, "Warrick Dunn Opens Up about the Lingering Effects of His Mother's Murder," NBC Sports, June 28, 2019, https://profootballtalk.nbcsports.com/2019/06/28/warrick-dunn-opens-up-about-the-lingering-effects-of-his-mothers-murder.
25. Dunn and Yaeger, *Running for My Life*, 138–39.
26. Ibid., 1–5.
27. Ibid., 7–15.
28. Ibid., 8.
29. Ibid., 12.
30. Ibid., 14.
31. Ibid., 18.
32. Ibid.
33. *Brumfield*, 854 F. Supp. 2d 366.
34. *Brumfield v. Cain*, 740 F.3d 946 (5th Cir. 2014).
35. Transcript of Oral Argument, *Brumfield*, 576 U.S. 305 (2015) (13-1433).
36. Ibid., 307–24.
37. Ibid.

38. Ibid., 350 (Alito, J., dissenting).
39. Ibid., 350 (Thomas, J., dissenting) (Appendix).
40. Joe Gyan Jr., "Longtime Death-Row Inmate Kevan Brumfield Gets Life in 1993 Baton Rouge Cop-Killing," *The Advocate*, July 20, 2016, https://www.theadvocate.com/baton_rouge/news/courts/longtime -death-row-inmate-kevan-brumfield-gets-life-in-1993-baton-rouge -cop-killing/article_8a2c3e6a-4de3-11e6-bbbc-fb01dbc3e29d.html.
41. Ibid.
42. Joe Gyan Jr., "Warrick Dunn: Mother's Killers No Longer Have 'Power over Me or My Family,'" *The Advocate*, September 28, 2018, https:// www.theadvocate.com/baton_rouge/news/courts/warrick-dunn -mothers-killers-no-longer-have-power-over-me-or-my-family /article_155833fa-c1bd-11e8-9984-a70b05270caa.html.

Chapter 8: Streets of Terror: *City of Chicago v. Morales*

1. Joseph A. Kirby, "The Death of Dantrell Davis," *Chicago Tribune*, March 7, 2015, https://www.chicagotribune. com/nation-world/chi- chicagodays-dantrelldavis-story-story.html.
2. Steve Johnson, "Killing Our Children," *Chicago Tribune*, January 3, 1993, https://www.chicagotribune. com/news/ct-xpm-1993-01-03- 9303151958-story.html.
3. Ibid.
4. Ibid.
5. Ibid.
6. Ibid.; *City of Chicago v. Morales*, 527 U. S. 41, 99–101 (1999) (Thomas J., dissenting).
7. Ibid., 100–01.
8. Ibid., 101.
9. Ibid.
10. George Papajohn and staff writer, "Most Gang Crime Tied to Four Groups," *Chicago Tribune*, November 29, 1993, https://www. chicagotribune. com/news/ct-xpm-1993-11-29-9311290110-story. html; Carolyn Rebecca Block and Richard Block, *Street Gang Crime in Chicago* (Washington, D.C.: National Institute of Justice, December

1993), 3, https://citeseerx.ist.psu.edu/document?repid=rep1&type=pdf &doi=17bf40fc952dc172cf9b0a008675bdf827c3773d.

11. Ibid., 4.

12. Debra A. Livingston, "Gang Loitering, the Court, and Some Realism about Police Patrol," *Supreme Court Review* 1999, no. 141 (2000): 150–51.

13. Ibid.

14. Ibid., 153–54.

15. City of Chicago Brief in Supreme Court at 12, *Morales*, 527 U. S. 41 (97–1121).

16. *City of Chicago v. Youkhana*, 660 N.E. 2d 34 (Ill. 1995).

17. *City of Chicago v. Morales*, 687 N.E. 3d 53 (Ill. 1997).

18. Livingston, "Gang Loitering, the Court, and Some Realism about Police Patrol," 155.

19. Petition for Certiorari, *Morales*, 527 U. S. 41 (1999) (97–1121).

20. Respondent's Brief against Certiorari, *Morales*, 527 U. S. 41 (1999) (97–1121).

21. *Morales*, 527 U. S. 41 (1999).

22. Ibid., 73–74 (Scalia, J., dissenting).

23. Ibid., 97–98 (Scalia, J., dissenting).

24. Ibid., 98–115 (Thomas, J., dissenting).

25. "2021 Ends as Chicago's Deadliest Year in a Quarter Century," NBC5 Chicago, January 1, 2022, https://www.nbcchicago.com/news/local /2021-ends-as-chicagos-deadliest-year-in-a-quarter-century/2719307; "2021 Gang Territorial Boundaries," City of Chicago Office of Public Safety Administration, January 5, 2022, https://gis.chicagopolice.org /datasets/ChicagoPD::2021-gang-boundaries/about; Drug Enforcement Administration Chicago Field Division, Federal Bureau of Investigation, and the City Police Department, *Cartels and Gangs in Chicago: Joint Intelligence Report* (Chicago, Illinois: DEA Chicago Field Division, May 2017), 6, https://www.dea.gov/sites/default/files /2018-07/DIR-013-17%20Cartel%20and%20Gangs%20in%20Chicago %20-%20Unclassified.pdf.

Chapter 9: The Sharecropper's Son: *McDonald v. City of Chicago*

1. Dahleen Glanton, "Otis McDonald, 1933–2014: Fought Chicago's Gun
    Ban," *Chicago Tribune*, April 6, 2014, https://www.chicagotribune.com
    /news/ct-xpm-2014-04-06-ct-otis-mcdonald-obituary-met-20140406
    -story.html; Frederick Jones and Sue Bowron, *An Act of Bravery: Otis
    W. McDonald and the Second Amendment* (Alexandria, Louisiana:
    Father's Voice Publishing, 2012). I highly recommend Jones and
    Bowron's book to readers interested in more details about Otis
    McDonald's life and case.
2. Jones and Bowron, *An Act of Bravery*, 42.
3. Ibid., 51.
4. Ibid., 62.
5. Ibid., 58.
6. Ibid., 63.
7. Ibid.
8. Ibid.
9. Carolyn Rebecca Block and Antigone Christakos, *Major Trends in
    Chicago Homicide: 1965–1994* (Chicago, Illinois: Illinois Criminal
    Justice Information Authority, September 1995); "Chicago Homicide
    Rates per 100,000 Residents, 1870–2000," Encyclopedia of Chicago,
    n.d., http://www.encyclopedia.chicagohistory.org/pages/2156.html;
    Stephan Benzkofer, "1974 Was a Deadly Year in Chicago," *Chicago
    Tribune*, July 8, 2012, https://www.chicagotribune.com/news/ct-per
    -flash-1974-murders-0708-20120708-story.html.
10. James Alan Fox, *Trends in Juvenile Violence* (Washington, D.C.:
    Bureau of Justice Statistics, March 1996), 2; Christine Hauser and Al
    Baker, "Keeping Wary Eye on Crime as Economy Sinks," *New York
    Times*, October 9, 2008, https://www.nytimes.com/2008/10/10
    /nyregion/10crime.html; William Barr, "Crime, Poverty, and the
    Family," The Heritage Foundation, July 29, 1992, https://www.heritage
    .org/crime-and-justice/report/crime-poverty-and-the-familiy.
11. Jones and Bowron, *An Act of Bravery*, 64.
12. Ibid., 64-65; Author interview with Fred Jones by Zoom, September
    15, 2022.
13. Jones and Bowron, *An Act of Bravery*, 65.

14. Ibid., 68.
15. Ibid.
16. Ibid., 69–70.
17. Grant Pick, "Cops 'n' Neighbors: Community Policing in Beverly-Morgan Park," *Chicago Reader*, October 13, 1994, https://chicagoreader .com/news-politics/cops-n-neighbors-community-policing-in -beverly-morgan-park.
18. Jones and Bowron, *An Act of Bravery*, 70-71; Author interview with Fred Jones by Zoom.
19. Jones and Bowron, *An Act of Bravery*, 70-71; Author interview with Fred Jones by Zoom.
20. Jones and Bowron, *An Act of Bravery*, 76; Author interview with Fred Jones by Zoom.
21. *District of Columbia v. Heller*, 554 U.S. 570 (2008).
22. Author interview with Fred Jones by Zoom; Author interview with Alan Gura by telephone, September 2, 2022.
23. *Slaughter-House Cases*, 16 Wall. 36, 21 L.Ed. 394 (1873).
24. *United States v. Cruikshank*, 92 U.S. 542 (1876).
25. U.S. Const. amend. XIV.
26. Author interview with Alan Gura by telephone.
27. Ibid.
28. Author interview with Fred Jones by Zoom.
29. Transcript of Oral Argument, *McDonald v. City of Chicago*, 561 U.S. 742 (2010) (08-1521).
30. *McDonald*, 561 U.S. at 748–90.
31. Ibid., 805–858 (Thomas, J., concurring).
32. Jones and Bowron, *An Act of Bravery*, 97.

Chapter 10: Causation or Correlation?: *Brown v. Entertainment Merchants Association*

1. Nancy Gibbs and Timothy Roche, "The Columbine Tapes," *Time*, December 20, 1999, https://content.time.com/time/magazine/article /0,9171,992873,00.html; Ellyn Santiago, "Eric Harris & Dylan Klebold: The Basement Tapes," Heavy.com, April 19, 2019, https://

heavy.com/news/2019/04/eric-harris-dylan-klebold-the-basement
-tapes.

2. "Eric Harris' Writing—Journals, Diaries and School Papers," A
    Columbine Site, n.d., https://www.acolumbinesite.com/eric/writing
    /journal/journal.php.

3. Rob Miraldi, "Video Games Spur Violence. How Can We Keep
    Ignoring Their Impact on Gun Culture?," *Poughkeepsie Journal*, July
    14, 2022, https://www.poughkeepsiejournal.com/story/opinion/2022
    /07/14/video-games-spur-violence-how-can-we-keep-ignoring-their
    -impact-on-gun-culture/65373182007.

4. Ibid.

5. Ron Whitaker, "8 of the Most Controversial Videogames Ever Made,"
    The Escapist, June 1, 2015, https://www.escapistmagazine.com/8-of-the
    -most-controversial-videogames-ever-made.

6. Commandant of the Marine Corps, *Marine Corps Ord. 1500.55*
    (Washington, D.C.: United States Marine Corps Headquarters, April
    12, 1997), 1, https://www.marines.mil/Portals/1/Publications/MCO
    %201500.55.pdf; Shawn Snow, "The Corps Authorized Marines to Play
    a Special Version of Doom in the Late 90s to Help Train for Combat,"
    Marine Corps Times, November 6, 2019, https://www
    .marinecorpstimes.com/news/your-marine-corps/2019/11/06/the
    -corps-authorized-marines-to-play-a-special-version-of-doom-in-the
    -late-90s-to-help-train-for-combat.

7. Richard Rainey, "Groups Assail 'Most Violent' Video Games, Industry
    Rating System," *Los Angeles Times*, November 24, 2004, https://www
    .latimes.com/archives/la-xpm-2004-nov-24-na-games24-story.html;
    Chris Morris, "Hollywood? Who Needs It?," CNN, January 27, 2003,
    https://money.cnn.com/2003/01/21/commentary/game_over/column
    _gaming.

8. Josh Render, "What Was Grand Theft Auto: San Andreas' Hot Coffee
    Controversy?," CBR, October 26, 2021, https://www.cbr.com/what-was
    -grand-theft-auto-san-andreas-hot-coffee-controversy.

9. Rebecca Leung, "Can a Video Game Lead to Murder?," CBS News,
    March 4, 2005, https://www.cbsnews.com/news/can-a-video-game
    -lead-to-murder-04-03-2005.

10. Nick Wadhams, "Video Games under the Gun," NBC News, July 4, 2004, https://www.nbcnews.com/id/wbna5351969.

11. See, for example, Craig A. Anderson and Karen E. Dill, "Video Games and Aggressive Thoughts, Feelings, and Behavior in the Laboratory and in Life," *Journal of Personality and Social Psychology* 78, no. 4 (2000): 772–90, https://www.apa.org/pubs/journals/releases /psp784772.pdf; Craig A. Anderson et al., "The Influence of Media Violence on Youth," *Psychological Science in the Public Interest* 4, no. 3 (December 2003): 113–22.

12. John L. Sherry, Kristen Lucas, Bradley S. Greenberg, and Ken Lachlan, "Video Game Uses and Gratifications as Predictors of Use and Game Preference," in *Playing Video Games: Motives, Responses, and Consequences*, ed. Peter Vorderer and Jennings Bryant (Lawrence Erlbaum Associates Publishers, 2006), 213.

13. Don Reisinger, "91 Percent of Kids Are Gamers, Research Says," CNET, October 11, 2011, https://www.cnet.com/home/smart-home/91 -percent-of-kids-are-gamers-research-says.

14. Miraldi, "Video Games Spur Violence."

15. Br. of Amicus Curiae of California State Senator Leland Y. Yee, PhD *et al.* at 6, *Brown v. Entertainment Merchants Ass'n*, 564 U.S. 786 (2011) (No. 08-1448).

16. Ibid., 5.

17. Joint Appendix at 816–17, *Brown*, 564 U.S. 786 (2011) (No. 08-1448).

18. California Civil Code § 1746.1-.2 (West 2006).

19. Br. of Amicus Curiae of California State Senator Leland Y. Yee, PhD *et al.* at 4, *Brown*, 564 U.S. 786 (2011) (No. 08-1448); Joint Appendix at 968, *Brown*, 564 U.S. 786 (2011) (No. 08-1448).

20. Ellie Gibson, "Schwarzenegger Signs Violent Videogames Bill," GamesIndustry.biz, October 10, 2005, https://www.gamesindustry.biz/ schwarzenegger-signs-violent-videogames-bill.

21. Complaint for Declaratory and Injunctive Relief, Joint Appendix at 5, *Brown*, 564 U.S. 786 (2011) (No. 08-1448).

22. Author interview with Zackery Morazzini by telephone, December 6, 2022.

23. See *Video Software Dealers Ass'n. v. Schwarzenegger*, 401 F. Supp. 2d 1034 (N.D. Cal. 2005).

24. Ibid., 1043.

25. *Am. Amusement Mach. Ass'n v. Kendrick*, 244 F. 3d 572, 575–77 (7th Cir. 2001).

26. *Video Software Dealers Ass'n.*, 401 F. Supp. 2d 1034 (N.D. Cal. 2005).

27. *Video Software Dealers Ass'n. v. Schwarzenegger*, No. 05-CV-04188 (RMW), 2007 WL 2261546, at 6 (N.D. Cal. Aug. 6, 2007).

28. Transcript of Oral Argument, *Video Software Dealers Ass'n v. Schwarzenegger*, 556 F. 3d 950 (9th Cir. 2009) (No. 07-16620).

29. *Ginsberg v. New York*, 390 U.S. 629 (1968).

30. *Video Software Dealers*, 556 F. 3d 950.

31. Transcript of Oral Argument, *Brown*, 564 U.S. 786 (No. 08-1448).

32. Deana Pollard Sacks, Brad J. Bushman, and Craig A. Anderson, "Do Violent Video Games Harm Children? Comparing the Scientific Amicus Curiae 'Experts' in Brown v. Entertainment Merchants Association," *Northwestern University Law Review Colloquy* 106 (2011): 1–12, https://papers.ssrn.com/sol3/papers.cfm?abstract_id=1856116.

33. Br. of Amicus Curiae of the States, *Brown*, 564 U.S. 786 (2011) (No. 08-1448).

34. Author interview with Zackery Morazzini by telephone.

35. Ibid.

36. Ibid.

37. Transcript of Oral Argument, *Brown*, 564 U.S. 786 (2011) (No. 08-1448).

38. *Brown*, 564 U.S. 786, 788–805 (2011).

39. Ibid., 805–821 (Alito, J., concurring in judgment).

40. Ibid., 840–57 (Breyer, J. dissenting) and 858–72 (appendixes).

41. Ibid. at 821–39 (Thomas, J., dissenting).

42. Author interview with Zackery Morazzini by telephone.

43. Ibid.

44. Tom Wijman, "The Games Market and Beyond in 2021: The Year in Numbers," Newzoo, December 22, 2021, https://newzoo.com/insights/articles/the-games-market-in-2021-the-year-in-numbers-esports-cloud-gaming.

45. "Issue Overview: Do Video Games Cause Violence," NEWSELA, November 28, 2016, https://www.rcsdk12.org/cms/lib/NY01001156 /Centricity/Domain/10241/video%20games%20violence.pdf; Laura Strickler, "2 Years after Newtown School Shooting, No Research on Gun Violence," CBS News, December 12, 2014, https://www.cbsnews .com/news/2-years-after-newtown-school-shooting-no-research-on -gun-violence.

46. Adam Gabbatt, "Connecticut Town to Burn Violent Video Games as Sandy Hook Returns to School," *The Guardian*, January 3, 2013, https://www.theguardian.com/world/2013/jan/03/newtown-shooting -video-game-buyback.

47. Strickler, "2 Years after Newtown School Shooting, No Research on Gun Violence."

48. Ibid.

49. Dylan Gaffney, "Loot Boxes: Virtual Kinder Eggs or Casinos for Kids?," *Columbia Journal of Law & the Arts*, October 8, 2022, https:// journals.library.columbia.edu/index.php/lawandarts/announcement /view/545; Owen S. Good, "Anti–Loot Box Bill Gathers Bipartisan Support in Senate," Polygon, May 23, 2019, https://www.polygon.com /2019/5/23/18637155/loot-box-laws-us-senate-josh-hawley-ed-markey -richard-blumenthal.

50. See Actions Overview, S.1629, 116th Cong. (2019–2020), https://www .congress.gov/bill/116th-congress/senate-bill/1629.

51. Lesley Fair, "$245 Million FTC Settlement Alleges Fortnite Owner Epic Games Used Digital Dark Patterns to Charge Players for Unwanted In-Game Purchases," Federal Trade Commission, December 19, 2022, https://www.ftc.gov/business-guidance/blog/2022 /12/245-million-ftc-settlement-alleges-fortnite-owner-epic-games -used-digital-dark-patterns-charge.

Chapter 11: A Good Neighbor?: *State Farm v. Campbell*

1. Joint Appendix, Volume I at 214a, *State Farm Mut. Auto. Ins. Co. v. Campbell*, 538 U.S. 408 (2003) (No. 01-1289), 2002 WL 33933818; Joint Appendix, Volume II at 794a, *State Farm*, 538 U.S. 408 (No. 01-1289), 2002 WL 33933819.

2. Joint Appendix, Volume II at 820a, 827a, *State Farm*, 538 U.S. 408 (No. 01-1289), 2002 WL 33933819.
3. Joint Appendix, Volume I at 180a, *State Farm*, 538 U.S. 408 (No. 01-1289), 2002 WL 33933818.
4. *Slusher v. Ospital ex rel. Ospital*, 777 P.2d 437, 438–39 (Utah 1989).
5. Ibid.; Joint Appendix, Volume I at 198a, *State Farm*, 538 U.S. 408 (No. 01-1289), 2002 WL 33933818.
6. Ibid., 198a, *State Farm*, 538 U.S. 408 (No. 01-1289), 2002 WL 33933818; Joint Appendix, Volume II at 355a, *State Farm*, 538 U.S. 408 (No. 01-1289), 2002 WL 33933819; Joint Appendix, Volume VII at 2887a, *State Farm*, 538 U.S. 408 (No. 01-1289), 2002 WL 33933824; *Campbell v. State Farm Mut. Auto. Ins. Co.*, 65 P. 3d 1134, 1141 n.2.
7. Joint Appendix, Volume VII at 2890a, *State Farm*, 538 U.S. 408 (No. 01-1289), 2002 WL 33933824 ("Q. What other instructions did [your supervisor] give you, if any, regarding the information in your file which indicated that Mr. Campbell was at fault? A. I objected to the inference of changing, and I was told, 'Summers, do what you're told.'").
8. Ibid., 2894a, *State Farm*, 538 U.S. 408 (No. 01-1289), 2002 WL 33933824 ("Q. All right. Now, did you ever fear that your job would be in jeopardy if you did not follow what [your supervisor] directed you to do? A. Constantly."); *Campbell*, 65 P. 3d at 1141 ("[The] State Farm superintendent [] and divisional superintendent [] rejected a report of State Farm investigator Ray Summers (Summers) that stated there was evidence of fault on Mr. Campbell's part. In particular, [the divisional superintendent] ordered Summers to change the portion of his report describing the facts of the accident and his analysis of liability 'wherein [he] had indicated an exposure [for Mr. Campbell], and that there could be a high settlement value on it.' Additionally, after hearing from [the divisional superintendent], [the superintendent] told Summers that [the superietendent] had 'screwed up' by agreeing with Summers' initial analysis regarding Mr. Campbell's fault and demanded that Summers return to [the superintendent] the letter [the

superintendent] had written indicating his approval. Subsequently, State Farm discontinued Summers' involvement in the case.").

9. Joint Appendix, Volume I at 203a, *State Farm*, 538 U.S. 408 (No. 01-1289), 2002 WL 33933818; *Campbell*, 65 P. 3d at 1141–42.

10. *Campbell*, 65 P. 3d at 1148.

11. Ibid.

12. Ibid., 1141.

13. Joint Appendix, Volume IV at 1977a, *State Farm*, 538 U.S. 408 (No. 01-1289), 2002 WL 33933821; see also Joint Appendix, Volume I at 196a, 341–43a, *State Farm*, 538 U.S. 408 (No. 01-1289), 2002 WL 33933818; Joint Appendix, Volume III at 1257a–60a, *State Farm*, 538 U.S. 408 (No. 01-1289), 2002 WL 33933820; Joint Appendix, Volume VII at 3309a, *State Farm*, 538 U.S. 408 (No. 01-1289), 2002 WL 33933824; Author interview with Roger Christensen by telephone, December 9, 2022.

14. *Campbell*, 65 P. 3d at 1141; Joint Appendix, Volume I at 344–46a, *State Farm*, 538 U.S. 408 (No. 01-1289), 2002 WL 33933818 (noting that Bennett had at least half a dozen opportunities to settle).

15. *Campbell*, 65 P.3d at 1142; Joint Appendix, Volume I at 343–44a, *State Farm*, 538 U.S. 408 (No. 01-1289), 2002 WL 33933818.

16. Joint Appendix, Volume II at 794a, 800–02a, *State Farm*, 538 U.S. 408 (No. 01-1289), 2002 WL 33933819.

17. Ibid., 801a.

18. Joint Appendix, Volume III at 1142a, *State Farm*, 538 U.S. 408 (No. 01-1289), 2002 WL 33933820.

19. Joint Appendix, Volume II at 800–01a, *State Farm*, 538 U.S. 408 (No. 01-1289), 2002 WL 33933819.

20. Joint Appendix, Volume IV at 1586a, 1659a, *State Farm*, 538 U.S. 408 (No. 01-1289), 2002 WL 33933821.

21. Ibid., 1664a.

22. *Campbell*, 65 P. 3d at 1142; Joint Appendix, Volume II at 360–62a, *State Farm*, 538 U.S. 408 (No. 01-1289), 2002 WL 33933819.

23. *Campbell*, 65 P. 3d at 1142; Joint Appendix, Volume II at 750–55a, 771a–73a, *State Farm*, 538 U.S. 408 (No. 01-1289), 2002 WL 33933819.

24. *Campbell*, 65 P. 3d at 1142; Dan B. Dobbs and Caprice L. Roberts, *Law of Remedies: Damages, Equity, Restitution*, 3rd ed. (St. Paul, Minnesota: West Academic Publishing, 2018).

25. *Campbell*, 65 P. 3d at 1142.

26. Ibid.

27. Ibid., 1143 ("[T]he Campbells introduced evidence that State Farm's decision to take the case to trial was a result of a national scheme to meet corporate fiscal goals by capping payouts on claims company wide. This scheme was referred to as State Farm's 'Performance, Planning and Review,' or PP & R, policy. To prove the existence of this scheme, the trial court allowed the Campbells to introduce extensive expert testimony regarding fraudulent practices by State Farm in its nation-wide operations."); Court's Findings, Conclusions and Order Regarding Punitive Damages and Evidentiary Rulings at 20, *Campbell v. State Farm Mut. Auto. Ins. Co.*, No. 890905231 (Utah D. Ct. Aug. 3, 1998) ("'Merit,' in the context of claims adjusting, is explicitly defined by the PP&R program as including the ability to meet preset targets for payouts each year—i.e., targets for payouts that are tied not to the severity and fair value of the claims being handled, but rather to State Farm's goals for making profits, by arbitrarily holding down payouts."); Author interview with Roger Christensen by telephone.

28. Joint Appendix, Volume III at 1082–85a, *State Farm*, 538 U.S. 408 (No. 01-1289), 2002 WL 33933820.

29. Ibid., 1096–97a, *State Farm*, 538 U.S. 408 (No. 01-1289), 2002 WL 33933820.

30. Ibid., 1100–01a.

31. Ibid., 1097a.

32. Ibid., 1166a.

33. Ibid., 1085–86a.

34. Ibid., 1089a.

35. Author interview with Roger Christensen by telephone.

36. *Campbell*, 65 P. 3d at 1148 ("Specifically, the record contains an eighty-page report prepared by State Farm regarding DeLong's personal life, including information obtained by paying a hotel maid to disclose whether DeLong had overnight guests in her room."). Court's

Findings, Conclusions and Order Regarding Punitive Damages and
Evidentiary Rulings at 35, *Campbell*, No. 890905231 (Utah D. Ct. Aug.
3, 1998); Joint Appendix, Volume III at 1163–64a, *State Farm*, 538 U.S.
408 (No. 01-1289), 2002 WL 33933820.

37. Author interview with Roger Christensen by telephone.

38. Ibid.

39. Court's Findings, Conclusions and Order Regarding Punitive
Damages and Evidentiary Rulings at 32–33, *Campbell*, No. 890905231
(Utah D. Ct. Aug. 3, 1998) ("Accordingly, the Handbook has
instructions on padding the file with 'self-serving' documents, as well
as instructions to leave certain critical items out of files, such as
evaluations of the insured's exposure. Such instructions clearly
required manipulation of files to conceal State Farm's misconduct in
excess cases and to make it very difficult for an insured who is
victimized by an excess verdict to ever hold State Farm accountable.");
Author interview with Roger Christensen by telephone.

40. Court's Findings, Conclusions and Order Regarding Punitive
Damages and Evidentiary Rulings at 32–33, *Campbell*, No. 890905231
(Utah D. Ct. Aug. 3, 1998); see also *Campbell*, 65 P. 3d at 1148 ("State
Farm engaged in deliberate concealment and destruction of all
documents related to this profit scheme. State Farm's own witnesses
testified that documents were routinely destroyed so as to avoid their
potential disclosure through discovery requests. Such destruction
even occurred while this litigation was pending. Additionally, State
Farm, as a matter of policy, keeps no corporate records related to
lawsuits against it, thus shielding itself from having to disclose
information related to the number and scope of bad faith actions in
which it has been involved [internal citations omitted]"; Court's
Findings, Conclusions and Order Regarding Punitive Damages and
Evidentiary Rulings at 27–31, *Campbell*, No. 890905231 (Utah D. Ct.
Aug. 3, 1998) (recounting State Farm's "systemic destruction of
documents, requested in litigation, that reveal the profit scheme");
ibid., 28 ("Many documents that were critical to the Campbells' proof
in this case were obtained not through discovery . . . but through the
fortuity that State Farm employees happened to retain them after

leaving the company."); ibid., 29 ("State Farm launched elaborate
efforts to destroy its existing corporate memory on its past claim-
handling practices, with the explicit purpose of keeping them from
discovery in bad-faith cases."). See also *State Farm*, 538 U.S. at 434
(Ginsburg, J., dissenting) (noting that trial evidence indicated that
"State Farm made 'systematic' efforts to destroy internal company
documents that might reveal its scheme.").

41. *Campbell*, 65 P. 3d at 1143.

42. Ibid.

43. Court's Findings, Conclusions and Order Regarding Punitive
   Damages and Evidentiary Rulings at 2, *Campbell*, No. 890905231
   (Utah D. Ct. Aug. 3, 1998).

44. Author interview with Roger Christensen by telephone.

45. "Laurence H. Tribe," Harvard Law School, n.d., https://
   hls.harvard.edu/faculty/laurence-h-tribe.

46. Author interview with Roger Christensen by telephone.

47. Ibid.

48. Ibid.

49. Court's Findings, Conclusions and Order Regarding Punitive Damages
   and Evidentiary Rulings at 13, 23, *Campbell*, No. 890905231 (Utah D. Ct.
   Aug. 3, 1998).

50. Ibid., 29, 34.

51. Ibid., 15.

52. Joint Appendix, Volume VII at 3368–69a, *State Farm*, 538 U.S. 408
   (No. 01-1289), 2002 WL 33933824, at 3368–69a; Court's Findings,
   Conclusions and Order Regarding Punitive Damages and Evidentiary
   Rulings at 73, *Campbell*, No. 890905231 (Utah D. Ct. Aug. 3, 1998).

53. *Campbell*, 65 P. 3d at 1171–72.

54. Transcript of Oral Argument, *State Farm*, 538 U.S. 408 (No. 01-1289).

55. *Campbell*, 538 U.S. at 429.

56. Ibid., 438 (Ginsburg, J., dissenting).

57. Ibid., 429–30 (Scalia, J., and Thomas, J., dissenting).

58. *BMW of N. Am., Inc. v. Gore*, 517 U.S. 559, 607 (1996) (Scalia, J.,
   dissenting).

59. *Campbell v. State Farm Mut. Auto. Ins. Co.*, 98 P. 3d 409, 410–11 (Utah 2004).
60. Author interview with Roger Christensen by telephone.
61. Ibid.

Chapter 12: Three Men and a Cross: *Virginia v. Black*
1. Bill Glose, "The Loudest: David Baugh Fights to Preserve the Constitution—Including the Rights of Klansmen and Al-Qaida Terrorists," Super Lawyers, June 25, 2007, https://www.superlawyers.com/articles/virginia/the-loudest; "About," David P. Baugh, n.d., http://dpbaugh.com/about.html; Author interview with David Baugh by telephone, October 5, 2022.
2. Author interview with David Baugh by telephone.
3. Brandon Walters, "It's Been a Year of Private Reversals and Public Trials for Richmond's Best-Known Defense," *Style Weekly*, January 1, 1980, https://www.styleweekly.com/richmond/its-been-a-year-of-private-reversals-and-public-trials-for-richmonds-best-known-defense/Content?oid=1388046.
4. Glose, "The Loudest."
5. Mark Pesto, "Klan Leader from Johnstown Dies," *Tribune-Democrat*, November 26, 2018, https://www.tribdem.com/news/klan-leader-from-johnstown-dies/article_e03fa8fa-f11f-11e8-866d-5f1adaobca40.html.
6. *Virginia v. Black,* 538 U.S. 343, 353 (2003).
7. Becky Little, "How Woodrow Wilson Tried to Reverse Black American Progress," History.com, July 14, 2020, https://www.history.com/news/woodrow-wilson-racial-segregation-jim-crow-ku-klux-klan.
8. Klanwatch Project staff, *Ku Klux Klan: A History of Racism and Violence* (Montgomery, Alabama: Southern Poverty Law Center, 2011), 28, https://www.splcenter.org/sites/default/files/Ku-Klux-Klan-A-History-of-Racism.pdf.
9. *Virginia*, 538 U.S. at 354.
10. "Ku Klux Klan in Virginia," Encyclopedia Virginia, April 20, 2022, https://encyclopediavirginia.org/entries/ku-klux-klan-in-virginia.

11. *Brown v. Board of Education*, 347 U.S. 483 (1954).
12. *Virginia*, 538 U.S. at 355.
13. Ibid., 356.
14. "Ku Klux Klan in Virginia."
15. *Virginia*, 538 U.S. at 363–64.
16. Ibid., 348–49.
17. Ibid., 349; Testimony of Rebecca Sechrist, *Virginia*, 538 U.S. at 363–64, Joint Appendix at 68–70; *Commonwealth v. Virginia*, 553 S.E. 2d 738, 748 (Va. 2001).
18. Joint Appendix, *Commonwealth of Virginia Petitioner v. Barry Elton Black*, Richard J. Elliott, and Jonathan O'Mara, Respondents., 2002 WL 32102976 (U.S.), 111a.
19. *Virginia*, 538 U.S., Joint Appendix at 57.
20. *Voices of American Law*: Virginia v. Black, *Party Narrative II*, at 8:17–8:27, Duke University School of Law, https://law.duke.edu/videofiles/voal/narrative/virginia2.mp4.
21. Nico Perrino, "So to Speak Transcript: David Baugh," Foundation for Individual Rights and Expression, June 21, 2016, https://www.thefire.org/so-to-speak-transcript-david-baugh; *Voices of American Law* at 5:14–5:31.
22. *Voices of American Law*: Virginia v. Black, *Party Narrative II*, Duke University School of Law, at 9:09–9:27, https://law.duke.edu/videofiles/voal/narrative/virginia2.mp4.
23. Ibid., 2:35–2:52.
24. Ibid.
25. Ibid. 4:29–4:36.
26. Ibid.
27. Joint Appendix, *Commonwealth of Virginia Petitioner v. Barry Elton Black*, Richard J. Elliott, and Jonathan O'Mara, Respondents., 2002 WL 32102976 (U.S.), 149a–160a (closing argument of David Baugh).
28. *Commonwealth*, 553 S.E. 2d at 740–41.
29. Ibid., 740–48.
30. United States Amicus Brief at *1, *Virginia*, 538 U.S. (No. 01-1107).
31. Transcript of Oral Argument, *Virginia*, 538 U.S. (No. 01-1107).
32. *Virginia v. Black*, 538 U.S. at 348 (Thomas, J., dissenting) (quoting M. Newton and J. Newton, *The Ku Klux Klan: An Encyclopedia* vii (1991)).

33. Ibid., 388–400 (Thomas, J., dissenting).
34. Author interview with David Baugh by telephone; *Voices of American Law.*
35. *Voices of American Law* at 11:50–12:31.

Conclusion

1. See, for example, *Kyllo v. United States*, 533 U.S. 27 (2001); *Alleyne v. United States*, 570 U.S. 99 (2013); and *Ramos v. Louisiana*, 140 S. Ct. 1390, 590 U.S. (2020).

Index

Grand Theft Auto (video game
series), 156–57
Great Depression, the, 73, 198
Grutter, Barbara, 46–47, 49–50,
55–57, 59, 65, 212
Grutter v. Bollinger, 45

H
habeas corpus, 113–14, 117–18,
120
Hargo, Gabriel Franklin, 45
Harvard plan, 58, 66
Help Our People's Education
(HOPE), 31
historically black college
(HBC), 49, 63, 66, 196
Homes for the Holidays, 119
Humphreys, Rich, 179, 181–86,
192

I
Illinois State Rifle Association,
145
Illinois Supreme Court, 128–30
interstate commerce, 72–74, 76,
78, 81–83
Institute for Justice (IJ), 8–11, 16,
20, 145–46

J
Jenkins, Martin (judge), 74–75,
77

K
Kennedy, Anthony (justice), 18,
39, 57–58, 81, 130, 168, 189
Kelo, Susette, xvii, xx, 1–3, 6–10,
12–13, 15–18, 20–21, 212
Kelo v. City of New London, 1, 13,
20–21, 212
Killgore, Sarah, 45
Knight v. Alabama, 66
Kolbo, Kirk, 50–51, 57
Ku Klux Klan (KKK), xxi, 148,
195, 197–208

L
Laurence, Tribe (professor),
185–86, 189
Law School Admissions Test
(LSAT), 46–47, 50–53, 55, 64
Law School (UMC), 46–57,
59–66
Lee, Kimon, 109–10, 121
Lewis, Fannie, 27–29, 43, 139
Louisiana Supreme Court, 113

M
McDonald, Laura, 140–45

McDonald, Otis, xviii, 139–54, 212–13

McDonald v. City of Chicago, 139

McKee, Kathrine, 97–106, 213

McKee v. Cosby, 97, 105

medical marijuana, 68–85, 212

Monson, Diane, 70–72, 74–82, 84

Montgomery, Betty (attorney general), 35, 38

Morazzini, Zackery, 160–61, 163–166, 168, 173–74

Morgan Park, 140–42, 144, 146–47

Munzel, Erica, 50–51

N
National Association for the Advancement of Colored People (NAACP), 16, 18, 20, 146, 148, 159, 201

National Football League (NFL), 75, 110, 114–15

National Rifle Association (NRA), 150, 152

New London Development Corporation (NLDC), 3–8, 10–12, 14–15

New York Times v. Sullivan, 103–6

O
Oakland Cannabis Buyers' Cooperative (co-op), 69–72

O'Connor, Sandra Day (justice), 18, 39, 57–59, 82, 85, 131, 189, 206

Ohio Supreme Court, 32

Olson, Theodore (solicitor general), 36, 38, 57

O'Mara, Jonathan, 204

originalism, xviii, xxi, 72, 212–14

Ospital, Todd, 178–79, 188

P
Paez, Richard (judge), 75–76

Patmon, Bill, 27–29, 43

Pfizer Corporation, 4–6, 8, 14–15, 19, 21

Pilla, Anthony M. (bishop), 29–30, 43

Plain Dealer, 26–27, 30

Pregerson, Harry (judge), 75–76

punitive damages, 181, 185, 187, 189–92